US History in
15 Foods

HISTORY IN 15

This pioneering new series offers lively perspectives on regional and global histories. Adopting an innovative thematic approach, each title is structured around fifteen items, concepts, or sources through which the history of a particular region, or the entire world, can be illuminated. From food to films, from cities to songs, this series brings history into focus for students and interested readers.

These approachable books use a consistent set of themes or sources as a lens through which to view the broader history, transforming how the reader understands these items while imparting critical lessons about historical context and analysis. For example, a book on US History in 15 Foods would use fifteen foods to examine the history of the nation, covering key topics and themes in US history.

Series Editors: Laura A. Belmonte (Virginia Tech, USA)

Editorial Board:
Maria Montoya, NYU-Shanghai, China
Kyle Longley, Chapman University, USA
Anne Foster, Indiana State University, USA
Julia Irwin, University of South Florida, USA
Fabian Hilfrich, University of Edinburgh, UK
Justin Hart, Texas Tech, USA
Kelly Shannon, Florida Atlantic University, USA
Holly M. Karibo, Oklahoma State University, USA
Ellen Hartigan O'Connor, UC-Davis, USA
Andrew Rotter, Colgate University, USA

Published:
US History in 15 Foods, Anna Zeide

Forthcoming:
Global History in 15 Epidemics, Andrew Robarts
Queer History in 15 Lives, Laura A. Belmonte

US History in
15 Foods

ANNA ZEIDE

BLOOMSBURY ACADEMIC
LONDON • NEW YORK • OXFORD • NEW DELHI • SYDNEY

BLOOMSBURY ACADEMIC
Bloomsbury Publishing Plc
50 Bedford Square, London, WC1B 3DP, UK
1385 Broadway, New York, NY 10018, USA
29 Earlsfort Terrace, Dublin 2, Ireland

BLOOMSBURY, BLOOMSBURY ACADEMIC and the Diana logo
are trademarks of Bloomsbury Publishing Plc

First published in Great Britain 2023

Cover design: Terry Woodley
Cover image: Adobe Stock

A catalogue record for this book is available from the British Library.

A catalog record for this book is available from the Library of Congress.

ISBN: HB: 978-1-3502-1196-4
         PB: 978-1-3502-1197-1
       ePDF: 978-1-3502-1199-5
      eBook: 978-1-3502-1198-8

Series: History in 15

Typeset by Integra Software Services Pvt. Ltd.
Printed and bound in Great Britain

To find out more about our authors and books visit www.bloomsbury.com
and sign up for our newsletters.

Contents

Illustrations

Acknowledgments

My time writing this book has overlapped almost entirely with the time of the Covid-19 pandemic and concurrent national and global upheavals, during a period when my life—like that of so many of us—has changed dramatically. In some ways, I wrote this book mostly in isolation, with only a cat on my lap and the ideas in my head. But in so many other ways, the writing process has been sustained by the love and support of the many wonderful people in my life, even if I haven't seen them as much in person during this time as I would like. The thanks below are incomplete, but begin the necessary job of giving credit where it's due.

I first began this project when I was a faculty member at Oklahoma State University, where I was lucky enough to have the Venn diagram of my friends and colleagues be almost fully overlapping. I especially want to thank Richard Boles and Sarah Griswold, for their continued support of this project, and of me as a person.

Since arriving at Virginia Tech, my luck has continued, with an enormously supportive new department and community. I'm grateful to Laura Belmonte (along with Susie, Willy, and James) for her confidence in me and all that she's done to help me build my life and work. Jessica Taylor, Danna Agmon, Carmen Gitre, Mindy Quigley, and Helen Schneider, those indomitable "crones," have offered space for shared meals, movie nights, writing retreats and feedback, and much-needed friendship. The Historians' Writing Group (THWG) has been a welcoming space to share research goals and progress, and I particularly thank the group for feedback on Chapters 14 and 15. Thanks to Paul Quigley for his feedback on Chapters 5 and 6. While writing this book, I've also had the fortune to build a Food Studies program, with the able leadership of Danille Christensen, Mark Barrow, Saul Halfon, Letisha Brown, and many others. I'm grateful to librarians Kira Dietz and Bruce Pencek for their food studies and research support. I have appreciated the feedback of my food history students, who have heard versions of some of this book's arguments in course lectures and discussions. Others at VT—Melanie Kiechle, Amanda Demmer, Erin Nuckols, Kim Niewolny, Pete Ziegler, Vivica Kraak, and Jake Lahne, among others—have welcomed me and made space for shared commitments.

Fellow scholars and friends beyond my institution have offered their generous thoughts, support, and feedback. Kendra Smith-Howard has been my buoy through many weekly writing sessions, as we shared the struggles and inspiration of our roles as writers, teachers, and mothers. Ben Cohen and Mookie Kideckel easily made the shift from *Acquired Tastes* co-editors to real friends and much-appreciated readers. Adam Shprintzen, too, has become a friend and has my gratitude for his feedback on Chapter 4. I'm grateful to Kellen Backer for his guidance and comments on Chapter 10, to Helen Veit for suggesting my focus foods for Chapters 7 and 8, and to Andrew Case for his reflections on the Epilogue.

On the editorial side of things, I'd like to thank Maddie Holder and Abigail Lane at Bloomsbury Press for their work on this project, and to Rachel Bridgewater at Macmillan Press for helping the book find a home. I gained much from the helpful and encouraging reviews from Julia Irwin, Jeffrey Pilcher, Ben Siegel, Emily Contois, and from other reviewers who remained anonymous.

Beyond work, I am indebted to friends, near and far, who bring so much light to my days and balance out the demands of work. Lee Vinsel, Abigail Middleton, Henrietta, and Alban have become dear friends through our home-school journey and beyond. Shaila Mehra, Andrew Wadoski, Ishaani, and Naya have shared life's winding pathways with us for nearly the past decade. Phone calls, visits, long walks, and talks with Helen Rubinstein have grounded me and helped me feel whole. Marco Polo messages with Dana Burshell, Abigail Myers, Nazneen Bahrassa, Nancy Rydberg, Ari Eisenberg, and Daniel Crow have been spaces of solace and connection. Rachel Mallinger, Jake Fleming, and Ezekiel and Abel inspire my writing and my hope in the future.

Now for my family. My mama's enduring encouragement and unvarnished love have been true constants in my life. Aaron, Amy, Jeremy, Max, and Abby have shared their interest in this project and their joyful kinship throughout. My papa's memory continues to live on in this work that I do, as I honor all that he gave me, as a scholar, father, and confidante. Jim and Nancy Horn have always been proud and supportive of my accomplishments; we miss Nancy's presence in our lives.

Those who have given the most of themselves to help me write this book, and to make my life deeply rich and meaningful, are my partner and our kids. Every year I spend with Justin Horn, I feel more in awe of how much we energize, challenge, and complement one another, and what a deep sense of comfort and home he offers. Our daughters Nancy and Mira are these glowing, vibrant, affectionate, brilliant people who I marvel at pretty much every day. They have grown up alongside these fifteen foods, even as they have reminded me how to keep my priorities in order.

Thanks to you, too, for reading.

Introduction

Over the past few years, as I worked on this book about understanding US history through fifteen foods, everyone wanted to guess what those fifteen foods were.

"Ooh, apple pie has gotta be one!" "Hotdogs and hamburgers, right?" "Philly cheese steak?" "Twinkies! Ice cream sundaes! Biscuits and gravy? Meatloaf!"

My kids voted for French fries, pizza, and mac and cheese.

All these foods, and many others, could be used to tell this story. American food is as varied as any country's food. It is the product of the diversity that has characterized this land for hundreds of years: the diversity of peoples, customs, environments, landscapes, and resources.

But the foods in this book help us uncover a deeper and broader history for each phase of this nation's past. They may not be definitive, or even particularly iconic, but they clearly evoke major trends, changes, and continuities that characterize US history from pre-colonization to the present. They help us to see well-known stories in new light, from the creation of the thirteen colonies to the American Revolution, the period of enslavement to the Civil War and Reconstruction, Progressive Era reform to the Great Depression and the World Wars, and the civil rights movement to the rise of globalization.

These chapters are about these *foods*, but even more, they are about *history*, and about how that history looks different—clearer, more vibrant, more interconnected—when we use food as a lens.

Food offers key insights into the past, present, and future, making it a particularly rich tool for understanding human society and culture. It is not just another commodity, but has unusual significance in the way it nourishes and becomes part of us when we consume it. As the field of food studies explores so adeptly, food is crucial to how humans make meaning, how we interact with political systems, and how we engage with the material world.

This book shows that food is the critical link among all aspects of American history, among disparate groups of people, among the connections that remind us of our shared humanity. Food is, at once, both fundamentally personal and also embedded in systems far beyond the individual. It thus links the act of eating (consumption) with all the steps that came before (production) to bring food to our tables. It also links many different aspects of history and society that are often studied separately: culture, economics, politics, race and ethnicity, labor, science, technology, inequality, gender, the environment, foreign policy, activism, and so much more. This book is a history of American food, but, really, it's a history of the many forces that shape our daily lives and the broader context in which we all live. This is why food history matters: its ability to unite and illuminate that which we too often artificially divide.

* * *

The fifteen foods and chapters to follow introduce a range of foods, some you may eat regularly, some you may have never heard of. They take us from pre-colonization to the present, with an emphasis on the twentieth and early twenty-first centuries, given this period's rapid and dramatic changes, through which we most clearly see the roots of the contemporary US food system.

Chapter 1 begins with a look at **pemmican**, a preserved food made of animal fat, dried meat, and sometimes berries, from whatever animals and plants were regionally available to Indigenous people across North America before European colonization. This food helps us understand the foraging and hunting practices of Native peoples, the critical role of food preservation, the place of animals in pre-colonized ways of life, and the devastation that accompanied colonization, including the later near-extinction of the bison from the Plains. The dramatic ramifications became entrenched as British colonists arrived on the East coast in the 1600s, where they were dependent on Native American agricultural knowledge for survival. **Chapter 2** explores **corn**, the crop that lay at the heart of Indigenous agricultural practices and that helped colonists reap wealth from the soil, as their growing hunger for land led to the dispossession and destruction of many Native communities.

By the mid-eighteenth century, as the thirteen colonies began to push back against British rule, colonists turned away from British products, like rum made from sugar produced by slave labor in the British West Indies. They turned toward products like whiskey that could be made from crops grown on American soil. **Chapter 3** tells the story of **whiskey** in the lead-up to the American Revolution and afterward, when this drink of the frontier came to stand for local control in the face of government decrees, as in the case of the whiskey rebellions of the 1790s. As the new nation developed and began to expand by the early nineteenth century, Americans continued to imbue food and drink with moral value that could safeguard them against disconcerting societal changes. **Chapter 4** explores **Graham bread**, a whole-wheat bread that its namesake Sylvester Graham believed could help Americans push back against commercialization and excessive stimulation. His dietary guidance was part of a larger period of nineteenth-century reform that encompassed temperance, abolition, women's rights, and religious change.

Throughout the periods of colonization and the creation of the United States, and through the middle of the Civil War, enslaved Africans were forcibly brought to American shores, in many cases to work in agriculture. **Chapter 5** introduces **potlikker**, the broth in which greens were cooked, often with a piece of pork. Enslavers considered the potlikker a waste product, but enslaved people reclaimed the nutritious broth for themselves. Enslavers used food and hunger as a tool of oppression and power, while the enslaved people themselves sometimes salvaged what agency they could through finding access to food and leaving a lasting African-inspired influence on American cuisine. Another food that was associated with enslaved people before the Civil War but rose to broader social acceptance by the early twentieth century was the **peanut**, the focus of **Chapter 6**. Food shortages changed the course of the Civil War and exposed soldiers to new Southern and substitute foods, peanuts among them. After the war, Black ingenuity in breeding, farming, and harvesting led to the rise of peanuts, which were sold by immigrants in growing urban areas, and soon became a staple of vegetarian substitutes in the health sanitariums of the North.

The Progressive Era around the turn of the twentieth century saw the rise of food reform, domestic science, and advertising that reshaped ideas of modern American food. **Chapter 7** introduces **Jell-O**, a new industrial product using gelatin from animal cartilage that was a byproduct of the emergent meatpacking industry and which rose to prominence through the era's emphasis on purity, expertise, and branding. This period was also dramatically transformed by the increase in immigration, especially from Southern and Eastern Europe. **Chapter 8** explores the stories of Italian immigrants and their famous **spaghetti**. Immigrant foodways were the target of Americanization schemes by Progressive reformers, played a role in the food conservation efforts of the First World War, and moved toward mainstream acceptance by the 1920s, even amid a broader backdrop of repression.

The consumerism of the 1920s set the nation up for the Great Depression by the 1930s, during which the federal government had to contend with a farm crisis. **Chapter 9** tells the story of **oranges** as a crop that symbolized the New Deal government's efforts to manage agricultural supply, the centrality of California industrial agriculture and its oppressed immigrant workforce, and the discovery of vitamins and rise of non-alcoholic drinks like orange juice in a time of Prohibition. The crisis of the Great Depression only ended with the start of the Second World War, the story of which is told in **Chapter 10** with its focus on **Spam**, the canned pork product that fed American soldiers,

Allied civilians abroad, and domestic Americans in a time of food rationing. The introduction of this and other processed food products shaped the postwar food supply and asserted American dominance through food abundance on the global stage. US leaders emphasized this theme of dominance through food even more forcefully in the postwar years, with the rise of the Cold War with the Soviet Union. **Chapter 11** describes how **green bean casserole** and other "creatively-assembled" processed foods—products of industry home economics kitchens and "cheerful" housewives—became everyday symbols of capitalist ideology amid the suburbanization and conformity of the 1950s.

By the 1960s and early 1970s, many Americans pushed back against this conformity, protesting the long legacy of racism, the Vietnam war, gender and ethnic oppression, and industrialized food. **Chapter 12** tells the story of **tofu** and the centrality of food to the politics of this protest era. The alternative possibilities imagined by the counterculture of the 1960s soon gave way to the disillusionment, deregulation, and conservative policies of the 1970s and 1980s. In **Chapter 13, chicken nuggets** become our focus. They demonstrate how government subsidies for animal feed, reduced environmental and worker protections, consumer desire for cheap convenience food, inequality driven by tax cuts, and a reductive view of nutrition came together to create a taste for the deep-fried highly-processed chicken product.

The 1990 opening of a McDonald's in Moscow signaled not only the end of the Cold War, but the dominance of a set of American values around capitalism, efficiency, and predictability that the chain represented. **Chapter 14**'s focus on the **Big Mac** shows how some of the same forces that brought the chicken nugget to national prominence extended this reach globally, extending American tastes and practices around the world, despite the protests of anti-globalization activists. Lastly, **Chapter 15** takes the example of the immigrant fusion street food, **Korean tacos,** to describe how twenty-first-century democracy became deeply tied to debates around citizenship and social media. As two outsider presidential candidates, Barack Obama and Donald Trump, came to power with opposite visions for what the nation would look like and who would control the dominant narratives, Korean tacos represented the diversity and democratic spirit that characterized viral protest movements of the era.

***

Several big themes flow from these fifteen stories. One of the most overarching is the dramatic decrease in time that Americans devote to their food. At the beginning of our narrative, acquiring, processing, cooking, and eating food was basically a full-time activity for most people, both for Native Americans pre-colonization and for European colonists after their invasion.

This remained largely true even through the end of the 1700s. But as farms became mechanized, as food processing industries grew, and as people moved into the cities and away from places of food production, this amount of time plummeted. By the twenty-first century, with the near-ubiquity of fast food, take-out, delivery, frozen meals, and other grab-and-go options, many Americans spend only mere minutes on food acquisition and preparation and not many more on the actual act of eating. Even for those who still enjoy preparing a home-cooked meal, they rarely spend more than an hour or two per day on these tasks. This would have been utterly unimaginable just a few generations ago.

This revolution of decreasing time spent has been accompanied by the opposite trend of increasing distance between the producer and the consumer, making the food chain that links the two ever longer with more complex steps and many more players involved. Our food today is the product of unbelievably complicated maneuvers, shaped by massive technologies, global transportation systems, enormously powerful institutions (from the federal government to scientific research centers, from factories to restaurants and grocery stores), influential marketing and advertising campaigns, and political lobbying. We see the rise of all of these throughout the fifteen chapters here—with the role of the federal government growing through pure food reform, the Great Depression, and the World Wars; and with powerful marketing campaigns from brands like Jell-O, Spam, and Campbell's Soup. Understanding the complexity of our food system as the result of particular decisions in the past is critical to directing its future.

This distance has grown even more pronounced into the twenty-first century, with the rise of global transportation systems. But we would do well to remember that the United States and its food supply has always been linked to other places, from the discussion of "Indian corn" by British leaders in the 1600s, to whiskey's domestic accessibility in contrast to imported rum in the fight for independence, and from the symbolism of green bean casserole in the Cold War, to McDonald's international spread. Although this book focuses on the United States, many of the points discussed here have universal application. Food matters everywhere.

These phenomena have brought with them a staggering increase in abundance, as the modern food system has provided more food than ever before. Half as many people in developing regions were hungry in 2015 as compared with just twenty-five years prior.[1] Recent food production has reached amazing feats in terms of efficiency and yield. Humans of earlier eras would no doubt have viewed this output as an unbelievable miracle.

But much of this abundance has come with a high price tag. One immeasurable cost is that of rampant environmental destruction, however invisible it remains to many modern American consumers. As colonists settled on Indigenous lands, they ignored the relationships with the land that had characterized thousands of years of Native practice. Instead, a system of extraction and private land ownership dominated, with the environmental externalities of ecosystem degradation, water and air pollution, and carbon emissions from burning fossil fuels removed from the capitalist calculus. As a result, we have a food system that is profoundly dependent on petroleum, from running farm equipment to producing chemical fertilizers and pesticides, from fueling the food processing industry to large-scale transportation of food products. Food and agriculture in the United States are major contributors to the existential crisis of climate change.

Just as climate change and food system activists today call for a food and political revolution to address these crises, so too have there been efforts at reform throughout US food history. To take just a few examples: the whiskey rebels protested what they saw as unfair taxes; Sylvester Graham saw dietary change as central to moral improvement; the Progressive era reformers made food system change central; civil rights activists demanded access to food and a place at the table; anti-Iraq War activists protested McDonald's. All along, though, those in power have used food and hunger as a tool of oppression— as with the near-destruction of the bison by European colonists, the hunger wielded by enslavers against their enslaved workers, or the use of starvation as a tactic in warfare. And exploited people have long been those who actually produced food, whether enslaved people or itinerant farmworkers or immigrant laborers. Food is, and long has been, fundamentally political.

A final theme that carries through is this: food is never just food. It is always something more. Food system transformations at the broad level and food choices at the individual level are always products of their contexts. What we eat is intimately tied to who we are and where we are from. However little thought some modern consumers may give to their food choices, these daily acts are deeply significant. In this way, eating can be a way of living one's values. Throughout the history in these pages is the balance between all the high-level food system changes that shape these stories and the simple act of a single bite. What we find on our forks is the result of all that has come before.

1

Pemmican:

Food in the Not-So-New World

In one traditional Arapaho story, a family becomes separated from their band and then struggles to find anything to eat. One day, the father of the family encounters a buffalo cow who speaks to him, saying, "I took pity on both of you and your children," and directs him to prepare 100 arrows. Sometime later, when the arrows are ready, the man's wife peers out from their tent to see the buffalo, with an immense herd behind it. The man uses each of his hundred arrows to shoot and kill 100 buffalo in total, yielding food and hides beyond their wildest imaginations. The woman takes the buffalo's best tenderloin meat and bone marrow fats and makes a "nice sweet pemmican," before packing it into an intestinal lining. She gives this pemmican to the man, who goes in search of the people of his band who had left his family behind. When he finds them, he gives the pemmican to the chief, who feeds it to the starving people among his tribe. But as they eat it, something miraculous happens: even as they "came in and took off any amount they wanted and ate it with their children ... it retained its original size."[1]

The pemmican and the buffalo—or American bison—from which it came were the ultimate fountain of plenty, offering a life-giving source of sustenance.[2] The food's role in this history—as well as in stories of the Crow, Blackfoot, Hidatsa, and other peoples of the Great Plains—illuminates the intertwined ways that food and animals represented both spiritual and physical nourishment.

Although the English record of these traditional stories was made after European contact, testimonies like this are among the sources we have to illuminate the earliest histories of people who lived for thousands of years in North America. While Europeans of that era referred to North, Central, and South America as the "New World," native peoples had lived on this land for tens of thousands of years before Christopher Columbus inaugurated a permanent European presence. By 1500, this was very much not a "new world" to the Indigenous people of the Americas. These diverse peoples survived and thrived, drawing sustenance from a range of dramatically different environments through cultural and technological adaptations.

The pemmican that nourished the Arapaho people captures several central elements of early Native American foodways. Pemmican was a combination of dried and pounded meat mixed with animal fat and sometimes dried berries, wrapped tightly in animal skin bags. As in the Arapaho case, pemmican was most often made from bison meat and fat, making use of an animal that had long stampeded through the Great Plains, and in smaller numbers elsewhere in North America. It was also the product of a complex method of food preservation, a cultural adaption that was necessary to keep large amounts of meat from spoiling. It was high in fat, which provided a critical energy source on long hunts and helped maintain body temperature during long winters. The berries incorporated to flavor the pemmican indicate the central role of foraging wild foods in many Indigenous diets. While pemmican was made with bison meat and fat on the Plains, in other parts of the continent, other animal sources were used—like deer in New England or fish in the Pacific Northwest.[3]

Over centuries, hundreds of different communities and tribal nations developed in the Americas, speaking different languages, building different structures, and eating different foods. But all were tied together by a reliance on the land, on the plants and animals that fed them. Pemmican is one food that helps narrate this rich history before the revolution of the European encounters dramatically transformed the human and environmental landscapes of North America.

Human Origins in North America

Recreating the human world of North America before 500 years ago requires attention to a wide range of sources that go beyond the written record. North American Indians used pictures to record important events, but did not have alphabets or written languages. Oral accounts like that of the Arapaho's never-ending pemmican give a sense of Indigenous history, which was consistently passed down from one generation to the next. Otherwise, we rely on archaeological investigations to reconstruct the ancient history of North America. Specialists can analyze a wide range of materials to uncover the history of how people lived and what they ate. Archaeologists study dental remains, skeletons, fossilized feces, seeds, fibers, artifacts, cooking implements, and much more. Carbon-14 dating allows scientists to determine how old an object is by measuring the amount of radioactive carbon-14 atoms that are still present, as the material breaks down at a constant rate over time. DNA analysis of genetic material is also increasingly being used to understand the past.

Using these methods, scientists have determined that, from their origins in Africa, humans crossed into North America via the Bering land bridge that once connected present-day Alaska and Siberia. The range of date estimates for this initial crossing is still debated, but most archaeologists believe it was between 13,000 and 60,000 years ago. During that time, global temperatures cooled, pulling more water into glaciers and lowering the sea levels enough that the Bering land bridge emerged. These early peoples were skilled hunters who had mastered the art of fire, which allowed them to survive in the icy north. By about 13,000 years ago, some of these humans, known as Paleoindians, lived on the land of the present-day United States. They hunted the huge animals that roamed the land, along with gathering wild plants and catching smaller animals. Author Charles Mann captures this world evocatively:

> If time travelers from today were to visit North America in the late Pleistocene, they would see in the forests and plains an impossible bestiary of lumbering mastodons, armored rhinos, great dire wolves, sabertooth cats, and ten-foot-long glyptodonts like enormous armadillos. Beavers the size of armchairs; turtles that weighed almost as much as cars; sloths able to reach tree branches twenty feet high; huge, flightless, predatory birds like rapacious ostriches.[4]

But then, about 8,000 years ago, the earth began to warm in response to a slight change in the axis of the Earth. This climatic event, along with the Paleoindians' hunting prowess, led to the extinction of those giant animals. One large animal that remained—if in smaller form—to live on as the closest reminder of that "impossible bestiary" of the late Pleistocene was the buffalo, or American bison.[5] The Archaic peoples (those who lived around 8000–1000 BCE) developed hunting tools and methods to capture their prey, which were now scarcer. On the Great Plains, hunters sometimes hunted bison with atlatls, or spear throwers. One skeleton from a person who lived about 9,000 years ago, known as Kennewick Man, featured an overdeveloped right arm and pinched hand bones, pointing to his frequent atlatl use and his practice of forming spear points from rocks and bones.[6] Even as humans like Kennewick Man and others continued to hunt bison, they also had to adapt to the changed climate by adopting new practices. They spread out across the continent, forming separate cultures, languages, and dietary patterns in response to distinct local environments. Some continued to hunt and eat meat as their primary food source. Others fished or relied on foraged foods, like acorns and wild greens.

Still others turned to a new revolutionary development: agriculture. This practice of cultivating crops intentionally from seed developed concurrently in Asia and in Central and South America, by around 10,000 years ago, alongside the warming of the late Pleistocene. Native Americans adopted agriculture slowly, and only in certain areas. Maize, or corn, was domesticated in Central America about 3500 BCE, and spread to the American Southwest around 1500 BCE. Maize, along with squash and beans, formed the "three sisters" foundation of much native agriculture. The scale of farming practices, however, remained relatively small, without livestock animals to provide plowing power or manure for fertilizer. While agriculture made settled civilizations possible, and added a measure of security to food acquisition, there is also evidence that it led to a decline in human health and nutrition, and led to an over-dependence on a small number of crops. For these reasons, along with the social stratification that emerged with the agricultural civilizations, geographer Jared Diamond has even gone so far as to controversially call agriculture, "the worst mistake in the history of the human race."[7] Mistake or not, agriculture eventually became the dominant way of life for most humans. Until 1500 in North America, however, agriculture was only adopted by some Native American groups, for whom the local environment and other considerations made it worthwhile.

The Vast Diversity of Native Peoples

By the time Europeans came to North America around 1500, native peoples on this land had created highly complex, environmentally adapted cultures, which thrived for centuries. North of Mexico, there were somewhere between seven and eighteen million people, speaking hundreds of different languages across over 600 tribes.[8] Some were nomadic, while others had created tremendous settlements like the Mississippian cities of Cahokia or the urban developments and irrigation works of the Southwest. Though the American Indians did not have the metal tools, gunpowder, or machines that some Europeans did, they had developed technological innovations for farming, hunting, and fishing to survive in a huge range of environments, tremendous artistic traditions and complex religious rituals, and wide-ranging trade networks.

Although there were contrasts and nuances among these many groups, scholars today divide Native Americans groups before the European invasion into regional "culture areas" as a way of drawing broad patterns. Food and patterns of subsistence are the factors that most centrally define these culture areas. Some anthropologists identify upwards of twenty culture areas, but we will discuss six broad ones here, roughly moving west to east: (1) the fisherpeople of the Northwest Coast and Plateau, (2) the gatherer/hunters of California and the Great Basin, (3) the farmers and gatherer/hunters of the Southwest, (4) the bison hunters of the Plains, and the agricultural woodland societies of both (5) the Southeast and (6) the Northeast. In all these areas, people adopted foodways that best suited their environments and societies, sometimes trading with other tribes to acquire foods to complement their local production. For example, the Plains Indians traded bison meat they hunted for the maize and textiles produced by the Hopi and Zuni of the American southwest, especially as much of the southwestern population shifted eastward in the mid-twelfth to fourteenth centuries.[9]

Beginning with the west, the people of the Northwest Coast and Columbia Plateau, across present-day Washington, Oregon, and Idaho, were largely sedentary and reliant on the ocean and Columbia River for their food sources. The foggy climate made maize agriculture difficult, so instead, fishing, hunting sea mammals and caribou, and gathering wild berries were dominant practices. This yielded a diet high in meat and fat. The Chinook peoples fished and processed huge amounts of salmon, drying strips of the fish as a method of food preservation. Pemmican in this region would have been made with this dried salmon and berries. In California and the Great Basin of present-day Utah and Nevada, many tribes like the Nez Perce and Shoshone gathered pine nuts or acorns, dug for oysters and for wild vegetables like camas root, and hunted small game. They used fire and other methods of plant and animal husbandry to control the landscape and developed cultural adaptations to access nutritious foods. For example, the Yokuts people of California cultivated different species of oak trees, used a labor-intensive process of leaching to remove the inedible tannic acid out of acorns, and made dried acorn meal, which they used throughout the year to make porridge.[10]

In the Southwest and Great Plains, native peoples developed societies dependent on agriculture and hunting bison, respectively. Across parts of present-day Nevada, New Mexico, and Arizona, Indigenous peoples before 1500 established highly developed agricultural systems, cultivating corn, beans, and squash. The Hohokam peoples dug irrigation canals, which provided critical water supplies in the desert environment. The Southwest peoples were largely vegetarian, but trapped small animals, like rabbits, rodents, and birds, when it was possible. On the Great Plains, east of the Rocky Mountains, bison was essential. The American bison, also known as "buffalo," was descended from the giant bison of the late Pleistocene era that had gone extinct. This great lumbering animal stampeded through the Plains in huge numbers, providing meat and fat, hides for shelter and clothing, bones for tools, and a sacred religious symbol for Plains tribes.

The wooded eastern part of the continent was home to a wide range of agricultural societies, who also took advantage of the abundant forests, rivers, and streams for food. In the Southeast, the Mississippi River and the rich croplands beyond supported productive agriculture. The most highly developed of these was Cahokia, an urban agricultural settlement that was home to Mississippian peoples between about 600 CE and 1350, with a population of over 10,000 people at its peak.[11] By the time Europeans reached North America, however, this great civilization had declined, due to complex environmental and social factors. This reminds us that the world Europeans encountered was not a static snapshot of what had always been, but a particular moment in a long and evolving history. In the North, woodlands peoples cultivated corn, beans, and squash; hunted deer and turkeys; and fished in the waters of numerous lakes, rivers, and the Atlantic Ocean. Many northern native peoples who lived along the Great Lakes focused their diets on fishing and harvesting *manoomin*, the Ojibwe word for wild rice. In the Northeast, pemmican was also present, taking advantage of venison as a central ingredient. Northeastern tribes divided along the lines of Algonquian speakers (e.g. the Abenaki, Wampanoag, and Narragansett) and Iroquoian speakers (e.g. the Wendat, Oneida, and Seneca). The latter groups banded together to form the Haudenosaunee (meaning "people of the longhouse") or Iroquois Confederacy by 1450.

The many subsistence patterns among these diverse groups led to different kinds of nutritional outcomes. Archaeological findings suggest that the healthiest Native Americans were those who hunted and gathered in small nomadic groups. Their isolation and mobility removed them from much contact with infectious diseases and from an accumulation of waste that developed in more settled communities. The wild foods they foraged had very high nutrient content, relative to domesticated plants. But one fact that is striking is that in both of the major patterns of subsistence—gathering/hunting and farming—native peoples consumed highly nutritious diets, without any conscious knowledge of nutrition science or a "balanced diet." Historian Linda Berzok writes, "somewhat surprisingly, foragers typically acquired from 1.5 to 5 times the RDA [Recommended Daily Allowance] levels of vitamins and minerals each day."[12] That is, the diets that developed over many generations of nutritional behaviors and adaptations led to a highly nutritious diet. Native peoples ate in small communal groups, passing on strategies for identifying toxic and nontoxic plants, where to dig for roots, the best hunting and fishing strategies, and cooking methods that made foods more digestible. Community historians—and women especially when it came to food knowledge—conveyed this folk memory from one generation to the next. This overall nutritional strength, however, does not erase the fact that hunger was a frequent enemy, especially during late winter, when seasonal diets were strained by lack of fresh foods.

When we describe the non-agricultural societies of the past, we tend to use the term "hunter-gatherer," which gives primacy to the "hunting" activities. And indeed, hunting game, both large and small, was important across many tribes. Animals provided crucial fat supplies, along with calories—though hunting also expended far more energy than gathering wild foods. Hunters developed complex methods: driving herds of deer into rivers, lighting controlled fires to corral deer and bison, using bows and arrows or spears, and building traps. But, in fact, the majority of calories in these non-agricultural groups actually came from plant sources. Wild foods offered a plentiful and varied diet: roots and wild greens, bulbs, tubers, shoots, seaweed, honey, tree sap, eggs, wild rice, nuts, berries, agave, fruits, and so much more. One analysis of fossilized feces from 900 CE, from Southwestern Texas, showed a diet that included, "prickly pear cactus (leaf bases, seeds, pads and fruits), onion bulbs and fiber, ... flowers or seeds from mustard family plants, nuts, sagebrush and grass," along with fish, birds, rodents, and rabbits.[13]

One reason for this disparity between reality and representation, in the emphasis on hunting despite the primacy of gathering, is the gender bias in European written records. In many native societies, men hunted while women farmed and gathered. When Europeans—predominantly men who came as traders, explorers, and missionaries—began to record their impressions of Indigenous peoples, they focused on male activities. They devoted much more attention to hunting, fishing, and warfare than to foodways, dominated as they were by women's work of foraging, farming, and food preparation. For this reason, Berzok suggests we refer to non-agricultural societies as "gatherer-hunters," instead of the other way around, restoring the importance of gathering.[14]

Plains Indians and Bison

Despite the great diversity of native peoples (then and now), by the twentieth century, certain stereotypes of "Indians" came to dominate pop culture, through dime-store novels, Western films, and popular books. These imagined Indians lived in tipis, rode horses, and wore feather headdresses. In truth, these characteristics only held true for a small portion of actual native peoples and, in the case of the horse-riding, only after Europeans brought horses to North America after 1500. But the Indigenous peoples who did use tipis and wear feathered warbonnets were the ones who lived on the Plains. The people of this one region came to falsely represent hundreds of different varied communities, many of which were more densely settled, agricultural, and with more complex material goods and trade networks—that is, more like Europeans.[15] The Plains Indians who rose to the forefront in public imagination were the ones who seemed most "exotic" in European minds.

At the risk of reinforcing this false representation, we will also focus here on the Plains Indians, in relationship with bison and pemmican, as one way of highlighting key features of pre-contact Native American foodways. These features include: hunting and foraging practices, food preservation, environmental management, trade networks, and the role of animals in religious ceremony. First, let's step back to get the lay of the land.

The Plains, in the center of the continent, were and are home to many tribal nations and languages: Blackfoot, Comanche, Crow, Oglala, and Lakota Sioux, among others. These people were, for many centuries, defined in relation to the bison. In one story from the Skagit peoples, after a great flood, a creator figure "blew the people back to the place where they had lived before the flood. Some he placed in the buffalo country, some by the salt water, some by fresh water, some in the forests."[16] The "buffalo country" of this story is the Great Plains, defined by its most symbolic animal. The buffalo was the closest descendent of the Pleistocene megafauna, those huge animals that had gone extinct around 8,000 years ago. Historian Al Crosby writes that the present-day buffalo survived those extinctions "perhaps because they were a shade smarter, perhaps a bit less contemptuous of the threat of the new bipeds, perhaps because they reproduced faster."[17] The bison that survived was still a very large animal, with males weighing about a ton, and females about 700 pounds. Beginning around 2500 BCE, these animals ranged across most of the continent, from the Rocky Mountains to the Appalachians, with smaller herds roaming the East Coast from New York to Georgia.[18] Scientists estimate that there were between twenty-four and sixty million bison before European contact.[19] The Plains Indians developed a culture fully enmeshed with this animal: eating its flesh and fat, using its thick hides for clothing and tipi covers and a material on which to record their "winter count" calendars, turning its horns and bones into tools, weaving its wool into fabric, and incorporating the animals' very essence into spiritual practice.

In order to catch and make use of the rich offerings of the bison, Plains Indians developed effective hunting, foraging, and food preservation practices. The bison migrated seasonally, and the tribes followed, disassembling and moving their tipis and belongings as needed. They lived in small groups throughout the year, but joined together into groups of up to 100 people to hunt bison more effectively in summer. Like native peoples in other parts of the continent who hunted animals like deer, elk, or moose, the Plains peoples hunted bison. They often hunted using bow and arrow or spears to kill bison that had been lured into corrals, sometimes by mimicking the sounds of a distressed bison; or they chased herds over cliffs, sometimes with the use of fire, killing hundreds of animals at once.[20] [Figure 1] In Montana today you can visit more than 300 archaeological sites that preserve this history, including First Peoples Buffalo Jump State Park, which features a cliff with eighteen feet of compacted buffalo remains beneath.[21]

Once the animals were killed, men and women would quickly butcher the bison. The organs and innards were often eaten raw, while the flesh and fat were processed for later consumption. Developing methods of food preservation was critical to the success of the hunt and to long-term survival. These preserved foods could be eaten in times of scarcity, could help overcome seasonal limitations, and minimized the frequency of energy-intensive hunting. Bison meat was processed either into jerky or pemmican. Native women made jerky by cutting meat—whether from bison on the Plains or other animals in other regions—into thin strips and drying it over a fire or by sunlight. Making pemmican was a much more time-intensive process, but yielded a highly valuable product. As in our opening Arapaho account, dried meat was pounded into a powder, mixed with fat or tallow, sometimes combined with dried berries that had been foraged for flavor, and then packed into skin bags, where the mixture would harden into energy-dense blocks yielding more than 3,200 calories per pound. Archaeologists trace the first pemmican back to around 6,000 years ago. The name comes from the Cree language meaning "he makes grease," and the Lakota Sioux name for the

FIGURE 1 *Bison stampeding over a precipice to escape an advancing prairie fire. Lithograph, 1864 (Universal History Archive/Getty Images).*

same food is *wasná*, meaning "grease derived from marrow bones." These names emphasize the "life-giving caloric energy" of the fat, which was the key ingredient that made pemmican so important. When sealed away from air and moisture, pemmican could be stored indefinitely, providing food security and huge energy stores, and allowing Plains peoples to travel for long distances for trade or warfare. Pemmican made from other meats in other areas of the continent offered similar strengths.[22]

The Plains Indians' relationship with the bison also illustrates key ecological, trade, and religious practices. The great prairie grasslands where the bison lived were in fact a carefully managed landscape, with tender grasses cultivated by Native American fires. Historian William Cronon writes that when Indians hunted game animals, they "were harvesting a foodstuff which they had consciously been instrumental in creating. Few English observers could have realized this. People accustomed to keeping domesticated animals lacked the conceptual tools to recognize that the Indians were practicing a more distant kind of husbandry of their own."[23] Although Cronon was referring to animals like deer and turkey in New England, a similar argument applies to the Plains peoples and bison. Further, the focus on bison meat and hides on the Plains illustrates the trade networks that Indians established. By the mid-twelfth century, Apaches and Navajos brought bison products to the Southwest for trade with the Taos and Pecos for items like maize, obsidian, ceramics, and cotton blankets.[24] Finally, the bison was intricately interwoven with the spiritual lives of the Plains peoples. In the Arapaho story, the self-replenishing pemmican was nourishing and supernatural. More generally, Native Americans treated the land and its animals and plants with reverence, often tying ceremonies to harvests, first foods, and successful hunts.[25]

The European Invasion

Beginning most notably with Christopher Columbus's arrival in the Caribbean Islands in 1492, Europeans began to come to the Americas in search of land, wealth, and power. This period, around 1500, is sometimes referred to as the moment of "European contact" or as a "colonial encounter." Those terms, however, soften the impact of what was actually an invasion that had genocidal effects, with violence and disease killing over 50 million people, nearly 90 per cent of the Indigenous population of the Americas.[26] Colonizers brought with them diseases like smallpox, influenza, cholera, and malaria, to which Indigenous peoples had no previous exposure and therefore low immunity. As these epidemics killed off adults who were "responsible for food procurement, defense, and procreation," they had reverberating effects.[27] The invasion led to a dramatic transformation in Native Americans' lives, over the next several centuries. With the Europeans came not only disease, but war, relocation, Christianization, imposition of new subsistence patterns and new foodways, and ecological change—including the near eradication of the bison by the nineteenth century.

When the Spanish explorer Francisco Vásquez de Coronado first came to the Plains around 1540 in search of gold, he instead found a "kind of huge cattle [bison] as numerous as fish in the sea," whose strange appearance frightened the Spanish horses.[28] In the Texas panhandle, Coronado encountered the Apache, who, after killing a bison, "dry the flesh in the sun, cutting it thin like a leaf, and when dry they grind it like meal to keep it and make a sort of sea soup of it to eat .... They season it with fat, which they always try to secure when they kill a cow."[29] His observations on their pemmican preparations were among the many records he made about the Plains Indians' way of life, which dramatically changed with the introduction of horses and guns and then later with white settlers. Along with him, Coronado brought 558 horses; later, other explorers brought even more horses to the Southwest and Plains. From these origins, horses became critical to Plains cultures by the 1700s, especially as a way to hunt bison with speed and stamina.[30]

Perhaps counter-intuitively, the Plains of the 1700s initially offered more bison to hunt than ever before. When Hernando De Soto explored the Southeast around 1540, he encountered no bison, in contrast to Coronado's experience on the Plains. But by the time French explorer Robert de La Salle revisited De Soto's former route around 1670, he encountered big herds of bison. The explanation? As many Native Americans died off due to European diseases in the century and a half between De Soto and La Salle's journeys, the bison population grew, without the hunting pressure of native peoples.[31] But, as the Plains Indians adapted the horse to their culture and hunting regimen, the pressures on bison population grew again.

Soon, new, even fiercer pressures emerged, such that the once abundant animal had been driven nearly extinct by the 1890s. As the fur trade expanded, especially in Canada, pemmican became valuable to traders, driving more wasteful and exploitative hunting practices. As the transcontinental railroad crossed the middle of the country by 1869 and the 1873 economic depression made people desperate, market hunters poured in, seeking the valuable bison hides. They indiscriminately killed bison by the herds, skinned them for their hides and tongue, and then left the rest of the animal to rot. One colonel wrote, "where there were myriads of buffalo the year before, there were now myriads of carcasses. The air was foul with a sickening stench, and the vast plain which only a short twelve months before teemed with animal life, was a dead, solitary desert."[32] Most appallingly, the US federal government sponsored a policy of intentional bison slaughter to eradicate the Indian way of life and force them onto reservations. In 1867, one military officer ordered a hunter, "Kill every buffalo you can! Every buffalo dead is an Indian gone."[33]

And thus, the presence of the majestic animal—one that had survived in some form through the Pleistocene extinctions, that had thundered through the Plains in numbers of more than 30 million by the 1500s, that fed and clothed and housed people for centuries, and that offered a fount of life and spiritual strength for the Arapaho and other Plains Indians—came to an end. Although the twentieth century would see a rebound of both Indigenous cultures and of some bison herds, the near extinction of the bison in the early period reflected the devastating changes to a broader way of life, captured by the pemmican that had offered energy to native peoples for millennia.

2

Corn:

Colonization and Settlement, 1500–1750

John Winthrop — gov of
p. gov of
Connecticut

In 1662, John Winthrop, Jr., governor of the Connecticut Colony, wrote a letter to Robert Boyle in England, a leading natural philosopher who is today considered the first modern chemist. The subject of the letter was "Indian Corne," apparently written in response to a series of questions Boyle had asked of Winthrop. In this time, soon after the English Civil War, British leaders were eager to find new agricultural methods. In his letter, Winthrop directly challenged earlier negative views of corn, like those of herbalist John Gerard who had written in 1597 that it was of "hard and [evil] digestion, a more [convenient] food for swine than for man," even though "the barbarous Indians, which know no better … thinke it a good food." Winthrop claimed that Gerard had no "certain proofe or experience" with corn, but that he, himself, by contrast, had "found by much Experience, that it is wholesome and pleasant for Food." He went on for 8.5 pages, waxing poetic about the "Beautifull noble Eare of Corne," which "Nature hath delighted it selfe to beautify … with a great Variety of Coulours." He described different varieties of corn, planting and harvesting practices, regional variations, how Indians used all the parts of the plant, and a variety of preparation techniques for making foods and drinks from the corn. He made clear that the English had learned all of their methods for working with this crop from the Native Americans, from whom the British appropriated land to establish the colonies in North America in the seventeenth century.[1]

Although it may first seem odd that leading political and scientific figures of the day were interested in this humble grain, corn was one of the very foundations on which the British built their colonies. It had nourished Indigenous peoples in North America for centuries before European colonization and, in a short period of time, became the staple food of the European colonists as well. Control of corn production was central to relationships and conflicts among the colonists and the Native peoples on whose land they encroached. As colonists cultivated the institution of slavery after 1619, enslaved Africans also subsisted on meager rations of corn. And as colonists expanded their settlement beyond the original thirteen colonies, they fought for access to land on which to grow corn, which, along with other crops, made expansion possible.

Corn in the Americas before Colonization

Long before it became the agricultural foundation of the American colonies, corn was domesticated in Mexico from a wild grass called *teosinte*, around 7,000 years ago. At first, the grass had just a few starchy kernels with very thick shells. But over millennia, genetic mutations and human selection led to a cob with much sweeter, softer, larger, more plentiful kernels that Native Americans began to adopt as a staple of their agricultural practices. By 3500 BCE, corn had reached the southwestern part of North America, and spread to the Mississippi Valley and the Northeast some centuries later, as Native peoples developed varieties better suited to the climate. By around 1500, it was the center of agricultural people's diets.

The plant, whose scientific name is *Zea mays*, is known as "maize" in most parts of the world, but British colonists called it "Indian corn," "Indian wheat," and sometimes, "Turkey corn." The term "corn" was a generic term for any kind of grain, but over time came to refer to *Zea mays*. In most cultures, grains have come to be the most important foods, because they are rich in calories and can be dried and preserved easily, rather than quickly decaying like most vegetables and fruits. In other parts of the world, wheat, barley, oats, millet, and rye have predominated. But in the Americas, corn was king.

As described in the previous chapter, only some of the Indigenous peoples of North America relied on agriculture for subsistence; others primarily hunted, fished, foraged, and/or managed woodland. But of those who did adopt agriculture—Southwestern groups like the Hohokam, Mississippian groups in Cahokia, and groups along the woodlands east of the Mississippi River—corn was the centerpiece. It grew easily and was very productive, could be grown along with beans and squash without having to till the soil, came in different varieties and colors, and was incorporated into hundreds of recipes and other uses. Native peoples most often boiled the kernels, then dried and crushed them into a meal, which could be made into cakes baked in the fire, or boiled into a porridge. When traveling, the dried meal could be kept in a leather bag and mixed with water to eat in small portions as needed. Native Americans discovered that cooking corn with wood ash helped remove the kernel's tough skin and made it more digestible. Later nutritional discoveries revealed that this method, known as nixtamalization or alkali processing, also increased corn's nutritional content by making niacin (a form of vitamin B3) more available and thus helped to prevent the nutritional deficiency disease of pellagra.

Due to this centrality of corn to Indigenous diets and cultures, the plant also became deeply interwoven with origin stories and ceremonies. The Iroquois Creation Story tells of the Sky Woman who created the Earth. She later had a daughter who died in childbirth, and from whose grave grew corn, beans, and squash—the storied "three sisters" of Iroquois culture. The Cherokee Creation Story similarly describes how the first man and woman in the world planted corn as their first act. When they died, their children dragged the mother's body around and wherever she was dragged, corn would come up, from which they made bread. The Anishinabe peoples have the story of Mandaamin, the spirit of the corn, who sacrifices himself to bring corn to the people. Further, in many Native agricultural communities, especially those in the Southwest, the time of early corn harvest was celebrated with "green corn ceremonies," in mid to late summer, and a range of brightly colored red, blue, and purple varieties were used for specific tribal ceremonies.

Maize in the Sixteenth Century

After Christopher Columbus's arrival in the islands of the Caribbean at the end of the fifteenth century, many other Spanish, French, and Dutch colonizers followed his lead in the sixteenth century. Like Columbus, they came carrying diseases, Christianizing impulses, and frequent brutality toward Native populations. And also like Columbus, many of them remarked on the towering cornfields throughout the Americas. Columbus wrote about the eighteen miles of cornfields he found in the Americas during his 1498 journey. Hernando de Soto, during his 1540–2 expeditions of the Mississippi River Valley, wrote of the abundant fields of corn, beans, and pumpkins he found there, and the quantity of stored grain in the Mississippians' storehouses. He and his men quickly demanded that the Mississippians share their food, and often took local chiefs hostage "to extort a ransom of maize, women, porters, and guides."[2] Another Spanish explorer, Francisco Vásquez de Coronado, charged into the American Southwest in search of gold. Instead, he found Pueblo people subsisting on maize. He wrote, "The food which they eat in this country is corn, of which they have a great abundance … They make the best corn cakes I have ever seen anywhere, and this is what everybody ordinarily eats. They have the very best arrangement and machinery for grinding that was ever seen." Coronado later dismissed the Plains Indians for their relative lack of maize agriculture compared to the Pueblo, writing, "they do not plant anything and do not have any houses except of skins and sticks, and they wander around with the cows [bison]."[3]

A Spanish viceroy Don Juan de Onate in 1598 embodied the widespread cruelty toward Native Americans and their subsistence agriculture. After Spanish cattle damaged the crops of the Rio Grande Valley, his soldiers extorted the little remaining maize from the Pueblos. When one Pueblo man complained, Onate threw him off a roof, sending him to his death below. And when his soldiers took maize from the Pueblos, it was noted that the Native people reacted "with much feeling and weeping" as if "they and all their descendants were being killed."[4] The corn was the lifeline and center of these communities, which were ravaged by Spanish invasion.

Corn was also a key player in the Columbian Exchange, the centuries-long transfer of plants, animals, bacteria, and viruses that began to travel across the Atlantic Ocean between the Americas (the so-called "New World") and Europe, Asia, and Africa ("Old World"), with European colonization after Columbus's voyages beginning in 1492. Organisms that had evolved separately on distant continents now began to intermingle, as American crops like corn, tomatoes, potatoes, tobacco, and cotton traveled east to Eurasia and Africa, while Old World items like wheat, rice, sugar, horses, cattle, and, notably, germs traveled west to the Americas. Those new germs brought massive devastation, with a large majority of the Native American population dying in the first 150 years after European contact, from a combination of disease, warfare, and enslavement.

In contrast, the Columbian Exchange led to population growth in Europe after 1492, in part because of the new food crops from the Americas. New World crops like corn, but also cassava and potatoes, had higher caloric density per unit of land, as compared with European crops like wheat, barley, and oats. Already by 1498, Columbus wrote of maize, "There is now a lot of it in Castile [Spain]."[5] As corn and potatoes spread throughout Europe in the years after, famines became less frequent, and Europe's population grew dramatically. That which brought destruction for one side of the globe also brought growth for the other.

Settling Virginia and Battling Hunger

At the beginning of the seventeenth century, Spain was the unrivaled leader in the New World, as early French and British settlements on the Atlantic Coast had failed. But as the new century began, English colonies gained foothold, and grew to dominate by 1700. This new strength was due in part to the British colonists' embrace of corn. When English settlers established Jamestown in

Virginia in 1607—the first permanent English settlement in North America—they initially made the same mistakes that their predecessors had made in the failed Virginia colony of Roanoke. They sought gold and wealth instead of cultivating crops, and became dependent on Native Americans for food. But as they shifted their attention to gaining wealth from the soil, and displacing the Native peoples from that soil, the incredibly productive corn plant offered the stability that made permanent British settlement possible.

When the British first established Jamestown, they encroached on the land of the agricultural Powhatan chiefdom, numbering around 20,000, led by the chief Wahunsonacock. For the first two years of the colony, the two groups managed to live mostly in peace, as the Virginia Company that sponsored the settlement urged the colonists to avoid the cruelty that had made the Spanish conquistadores infamous. The two groups established a profitable exchange in the early days, with Wahunsonacock in their first meeting promising to give the colony leader Captain John Smith "'Corn [and] Venison' in return for 'Hatchets and Copper'."[6] Soon, however, drought limited food supplies throughout the region and the Powhatan cut off the colonists' access to corn and foraging opportunities. The colonists struggled to establish a food supply and experienced the "starving time" in the winter of 1609–10, during which most of the 500 Jamestown colonists died, leaving only sixty alive, even after some resorted to cannibalism.

The problem was that the Powhatans could only feed the English for so long, and the early colonists resisted the work required to raise their own corn. Wahunsonacock told John Smith that, though his people appreciated copper, corn was more valuable, as "he could eate his corne, but not his copper."[7] He pleaded with the English to "come in friendly manner to us, and not thus with your guns and swords, as to invade your foes," so that instead "every yeare our friendly trade shall furnish you with Corne."[8] Still, these food shortages led to increased conflicts between the Powhatans and the English.

The relationship between the colonists and Native peoples grew worse, often with corn at the center of the conflict. When seventeen colonists came to one village in search of food, the Indians had had enough; they killed the colonists and "stuffed their dead mouths with maize as a sign of contempt." In retaliation, in August 1610, the British attacked a town of the Paspahegh people, part of the Powhatan chiefdom, killing over sixty people and taking many others as prisoners. The colonists set fires and burned down the homes and the cornfields. Burning the still-growing corn destined the Paspahegh to a destitute winter. And even though the Jamestown colonists were themselves still suffering from hunger, they burned down the abundant cornfields anyway, as an act of terror. They sought to make an example of the Paspahegh, as a dreadful warning to any other Indians who refused to obey the English in providing corn and ceding land.[9]

New England Cornfields

At first, it seemed that the British colonies of New England, established thirteen years after Jamestown, would differ from the Virginia colonies in their overall motivations and their relationships with local Native populations. But, as it turned out, hunger and the desire for corn would also drive them to warfare within a few decades.

The British colonists who arrived at Plymouth Rock in present-day Massachusetts in 1620, commonly known as the Pilgrims, were a group of radical Puritans looking for religious autonomy, in contrast to the profit motive in Virginia. They landed on the shores of the Wampanoag homelands, amid a larger New England area that was home to some 100,000 Native people. The site where they made their new home was an abandoned Indian village whose population had been wiped out by disease brought by earlier European contact, but who had left cleared fields ready for planting corn and a cache of stored corn that helped carry the colony through the dark winter ahead. They also bought "eight hogshead of corn and beans" from local Indians. Still, half the colonists died in that first freezing winter. In the spring, they found hope in a friendly relationship with the English-speaking Tisquantum, or Squanto, who taught the colonists how to plant corn, how to fertilize it with dead fish, and how to pound the kernels into meal. Tisquantum's own international story reminds us that the Massachusetts colony was established more than a century into the extensive contact between the Americas and Europe. Tisquantum had been kidnapped from his home in 1614 and shipped across the Atlantic to Spain, where he had managed to escape to London, learn English, and then return to Massachusetts, only to find that his people, the Patuxet, had been wiped out by disease.

Thanks to Tisquantum, by the end of the colonists' first harvest season, leader Edward Winslow would write that "Our corn did prove well, and God be praised, we had a good increase of Indian corn" after planting "according to the manner of the Indians."[10] This successful harvest of 1621 and the feast that the Plymouth colonists and the Wampanoag Indians shared afterward have been memorialized as the first Thanksgiving. Over several days, the two groups feasted on Indian corn, fish, venison, and fowl—the documented foods that were present on that historic occasion.

As more British colonists came to New England, a new society formed. In contrast to the Virginia colonies, which were dominated by single men, New Englanders came with their families, establishing a patriarchal family structure and stable population. Religious devotion drove them, and also shaped their relationships with Native Americans. Missionaries proselytized to the Native communities, but often found little traction, especially among the largest groups like the Narragansett, Mohegan, and Wampanoag. One Indian wondered why he would convert when "our corn is as good as yours, and we take more pleasure than you." Others rejected the idea of the Christian heaven when learning that "there are no fields and no corn there."[11] In fact, colonists in New England even feared that some among them would find Indian society more attractive, with its plentiful corn. These allusions to corn convey its ongoing centrality. It became the primary means of subsistence for the colonists, as well as a kind of currency, used to pay taxes, rent, and other debts.

Unfortunately, as in Virginia, the relatively friendly relations between the Pilgrims and Native peoples in the first year of colonization did not last. As more English settlers arrived and took over Indian territories, introducing livestock that trampled cornfields and driving away the animals that Indians hunted, relationships understandably soured. These tensions in New England exploded in the Pequot War of 1636–8, in which the Pequot people battled against British colonists from Massachusetts and Connecticut, along with their Narragansett and Mohegan allies. Standard narratives point to trade conflict or the murder of English traders as the causes of the war. But, as historian Katherine Grandjean has argued, at the heart of the conflict was food scarcity, and in particular, access to Indian corn. Hunger drove brutality. Corn is a recurring theme in the records of the war—colonists stole it, dug up reserves of it, and burned fields of it. As Grandjean writes, "war narratives show almost a bald obsession with" corn.[12] When the colonists finally vanquished the Pequots in 1637, killing or selling into Caribbean slavery the members of this once-powerful group, corn was among the central spoils of war. Then, with one of the most powerful Native groups of the region destroyed, the Connecticut River valley was opened further to European settlement, with lots of space to plant more corn.

Entrenched British Colonization

Having looked at the particular cases of Virginia and New England, let's step back a bit to consider the overall picture of corn and colonization in the first half of the seventeenth century. When the British arrived in North America, they were already familiar with corn as something Spanish traders had brought to England in the sixteenth century. But, as herbalist John Gerard's comments in our opening vignette suggest, they were most familiar with corn as a feed for pigs. As the colonists discovered its central role in Indian subsistence, and came to see its great productivity, they quickly adopted it into their own diet. Remarking on the amazing crop, Puritan minister Francis Higginson wrote, "the abundant increase of corn proves this country to be a wonderment. ... It is almost incredible what great gain some of our English planters have had by our Indian corn."[13] American soil nurtured corn tremendously, in contrast to wheat and other traditional British crops, which were not yet adapted to this part of the world. Even after settlers bred new varieties of their traditional crops, corn remained "the most common grain to appear in New England inventories for the first two hundred years of the colonies' existence."[14]

Colonists ate corn in a variety of preparations, often following the lead of their Native American neighbors. British traveler John Josselyn observed of "Indian wheat" that

> the *English* make a kind of Loblolly [porridge] of it to eat with Milk, which they call *Sampe*; they beat it in a Morter, and lift the flower out of it; the remainer they call *Homminey* so boiled, and mix their Flower with it, cast it into a deed Bason in which they form the Loaf ... the Flower makes excellent Puddens.[15]

Porridge, hominy, bread, puddings—all of these and more came from the bounty of the corn plant. The Dutch in New York, especially those of the middle and lower classes, similarly ate a great deal of corn porridge, which they called *sappan*. Other colonists brewed the corn into a beer and distilled it into a liquor. Despite the importance of corn in the colonists' diet, the foodways of at least the New England (Massachusetts, New Hampshire, Connecticut, Rhode Island) and Middle Colonies (New York, Pennsylvania, New Jersey, Delaware) remained otherwise largely European in nature. In addition to corn, their diet included Old World vegetables from the garden; pork, beef, milk, butter, and cheese from European livestock, and they began to grow traditional crops like wheat, barley, and rye.

Still, even though corn was the most common food in the early colonies, the British sought ways to distance themselves from its Indian origins and to deny the presence of Indian agriculture in justifying land dispossession. A British minister raised the obvious question in the early phase of colonization: "by what right or warrant can we enter into the land of these Savages, take away their rightful inheritance from them, and plant ourselves in their places?"[16] Although there was no real right or warrant, one of the answers the British came up with was to claim that the Indians did not "use" or "improve" the land. Captain John Smith observed that Virginia was "overgrown with trees and weedes, being a plaine wilderness as God first made it," ignoring the Native villages and extensive cornfields that helped him and the Jamestown colonists survive through their first years.[17]

Even when the British did acknowledge Indian agriculture, they largely resisted its methods. Native Americans tended to inter-plant corn with beans

FIGURE 2 *Engraving by James Smillie from a drawing by Captain Seth Eastman, showing Native American women scaring birds away from their maize, in an act of care for this crop that sustained many Indigenous communities. British colonists, while also dependent on Indian corn, looked down on women's central role in tending to the crop. (SSPL/Getty Images).*

and squash on mounded earth, amid trees or in a roughly cleared field. The English, instead, separated their crops in segregated fields, which had been tediously cleared of all trees. Although the colonists did, at first, adopt some methods like using dead fish as fertilizer, they otherwise rejected Indigenous agricultural practices. Finally, the British were critical of the fact that Native women were responsible for corn cultivation, while men took up hunting and fishing—activities that were considered only fit for leisure in Europe, in contrast to the expected keeping of livestock (Figure 2).

Corn and Enslavement

Even before the Puritans landed at Plymouth Rock, another group of people were forced onto North American shores. In 1619, a group of around thirty enslaved Africans landed in Virginia, carried by a Dutch ship. Although they weren't the first enslaved people on this land, this marked the beginning of an increasing reliance on the transatlantic slave trade in the British colonies. These enslaved people, like those that came after them, were seized and sold into slavery in West Africa, and then shipped across the Atlantic in horrific conditions, in the part of the journey known as the Middle Passage. They had little power to resist the conditions set by the enslavers, not least when it came to the question of food. One surgeon who worked on slave ships, Alexander Falconbridge, described the diets aboard the ships, and the methods of terror used to force enslaved people to eat if they tried to fast as a form of resistance. He describes the boiled horse-beans, yams, and rice that were given to the enslaved Africans in small portions, mentioning that "in their own country, the negroes in general live on animal food and fish, with roots, yams, and Indian corn."[18] Corn spread across West Africa beginning around 1500 after its introduction by Portuguese traders, rapidly becoming a popular crop. In enslavement, however, Africans had no choice about what to eat.

Most of the enslaved peoples forced to the New World ended up in Brazil or the West Indies, where treacherous sugar plantations demanded labor. But traders brought about 5 percent to North America. There, the enslaved Africans slowly began to replace the indentured servants who had offered term-limited free labor in the early years of the colonies, in exchange for transportation to the colonies from England. In Carolina, once a servant had served his term, he was granted land, clothes, basic tools, and—as the key to his subsistence until he grew his own crops—"a barrel of maize."[19] Enslaved people, in contrast, never got their freedom. As tobacco agriculture spread in Virginia and Maryland in the second half of the seventeenth century, the status of Black and white laborers grew more divergent. Although "race" as a socially constructed ideology had not yet developed as it would in later years, color lines became more entrenched. And as access to freedom came to be tied to color, more restrictions were placed on those with dark skin. In 1705, the Virginia House of Burgesses passed restrictive slave codes that fostered white supremacy and severely limited Black freedom, making slavery the economic foundation of the colony.

By the middle of the eighteenth century, slavery reigned throughout the British colonies—from the Virginia area tobacco plantations, to the South Carolina and Georgia rice plantations, to the non-plantation slavery of the Middle Colonies and New England. Whichever crop was under production, this cruel system of forced labor in the Americas subordinated workers based on skin color. Then, to keep the concentration of labor from leading to rebellion—as with the Stono Rebellion in South Carolina in 1739—the colonies policed the enslaved people ever-more heavily by the mid-eighteenth century, tightening restrictive slave codes and demanding harder labor with brutal punishment.

Corn was among the main foods that were fed to enslaved people on American plantations. Virginian John Mitchell described large plantations "where they maintain their negroes entirely on Indian Corn."[20] The nutritional value of this Native American crop became evident in the 1730s, when more wheat began to be grown in Virginia. Leading planter William Byrd wrote that after giving wheat to his enslaved workers, they "found themselves so weak that they begged to allow them Indian Corn again."[21] Abolitionist Frederick Douglass, who escaped from slavery in Maryland, later described the demeaning conditions in which they were fed: "Our food was coarse corn meal boiled. ... It was put into a large wooden tray or trough, and set down upon the ground. The children were then called, like so many pigs, and like so many pigs they would come and devour the mush ... few left the trough satisfied."[22] Some enslaved people did reclaim agency around food by tending subsistence gardens or hunting small animals in nearby woods, but many relied on the cheap corn provided by their enslavers.

Maturing Colonies' Corn Dependence

With the establishment of Georgia as a settlement for debtors in 1732, the original thirteen colonies were complete. In rough order of settlement, they were: Virginia, Massachusetts, New Hampshire, Maryland, Connecticut, Rhode Island, Delaware, North and South Carolina, New York, New Jersey, Pennsylvania, and Georgia. Throughout the colonies, land use and farming practices shaped regional cultures. Before 1700, most colonists were frontierspeople who lived in primitive conditions and relied on the country's abundant natural resources for food. Their homes were very sparsely furnished and they ate simple porridges of corn, legumes, and pork from common bowls, without utensils. Historian James McWilliams describes the daily labor of one Maryland woman. In order to have the evening meal ready,

> Rebecca had started soaking corn kernels at the crack of down to soften them for pounding, an exhausting task made necessary by the lack of a local gristmill. She knew that she needed about six cups of cornmeal to feed her husband, five children, and herself. So for the next couple of hours, Rebecca and her two daughters dutifully hunched over a large mortar, took wooden pestles in hand, and reduced a tub of white corn kernels into a gritty heap of meal.[23]

With the exception of wealthy plantation owners, this laborious connection to food was commonplace.

The end of the seventeenth century brought a series of crises, many of which were centered around colonists' growing need for land to plant corn and other crops—land that was to be taken from Native Americans. The years 1675–6 saw King Philip's War, also known as Metacom's War, with clashes between the Wampanoag Indians and New Englanders. Massachusetts colonist Mary Rowlandson described the cruel colonial strategy: "It was thought, if [Indians'] corn were cut down, they would starve and die with hunger."[24] Though both groups committed brutalities, the result was expanded access to land and the freedom it brought for the white settlers, and dispossession for the Wampanoag. It also left a lasting impression of Native peoples as murderous savages. In Virginia, meanwhile, the same years brought Bacon's Rebellion, in which Nathaniel Bacon led a group of frontiersmen, including many freed indentured servants, against Colonial Governor William Berkeley, in part to pressure him to open up Indian lands on Virginia's western frontier for settlement. The result, once again, was not only the displacement of Native peoples, but also a further shift toward African slavery, since enslaved peoples would not become free to demand more land as many indentured servants did.

These and other conflicts gave way to the relatively peaceful early eighteenth century, during which British North America expanded, alongside French settlement in Louisiana, the large center part of the continent. In 1700, a significant portion of British North America lay in the backcountry, the uncolonized lands beyond the Appalachian Mountains, along the colonies' western borders. White settlers and newcomers moved into this land, taking over what had once been Indian country. English settlers would clear some ground, build a house, and then plant a field of corn as a first course of action, laying the foundation for subsistence. French settlers meanwhile did the same throughout French Louisiana, taking over the land of Native peoples like the Natchez. One chief in 1725 asked, "Why did the French come into our country? Before they came, did we not live better than we do [now], seeing we deprive ourselves of a part of our corn, our game, and fish, to give a part to them?"[25] The eighteenth century saw ongoing conflicts between the British and French, culminating in the French and Indian War of 1754–63. One result of this war and its lead-up was colonists' increasing identification with Great Britain.

This British identity was further reinforced by the eighteenth-century consumer revolution and the convergence of regional dietary habits by 1750. As the British overtook the Dutch in the production of consumer goods, more of these items flowed to the American colonies—linens, pots and pans, utensils, cookbooks, glassware, clothing, and more. This changed the way colonists ate, dressed, and thought of themselves as part of the British Empire. In parallel, the colonists adopted British legal, economic, and social values. But all the while, they championed the great freedoms that set them apart from Europe: voting rights for those who didn't own land (as long as you were a white male), access to land and independent farming, and freedom of religion. All of this, of course, came at the cost of Indian land dispossession and the Atlantic slave trade, but it produced for most white Americans an unprecedented set of liberties. And all throughout, this liberty was fed and fueled by that most Native American of crops, the "Beautifull noble Eare[s] of Corne."

3

Whiskey:

Eating and Drinking in a New Nation, 1750–1800

[handwritten: Tax of Whiskey]

[handwritten margin: Pennsylvanians didn't want tax]

[handwritten: Side 1 calling for a tax on distilled spirits]

[handwritten: Side 2 no tax]

[handwritten: author of Tully letters Alex. Ham.]

On August 26, 1794, a letter was published in one of America's leading daily newspapers, authored under the pseudonym "Tully." It presented two sides in an ongoing dispute. On the one side was the new nation's federal government calling for a tax on distilled spirits: "Your Representatives have said, and four times repeated it, 'an excise on distilled spirits *shall* be collected.'" On the other side was "four western counties of Pennsylvania," who said the tax on distilled spirits "*shall not* be collected .... [They say] The sovereignty shall not reside with you, but with us. If you presume to dispute the point by force—we are ready to measure swords with you."[1]

The true author of this Tully letter, along with three other letters published around the same time, was none other than Alexander Hamilton, the United States' first Secretary of the Treasury. It was he who had led Congress to pass an "excise on distilled spirits"—a tax on whiskey—in 1791 and it was he who now rallied militiamen to subdue the western backcountry Pennsylvanians who were protesting against that whiskey tax and were "ready to measure swords."

This conflict emerged in the heated context of the late eighteenth century, just on the heels of the American Revolution. The brand-new United States was struggling to figure out if its democratic experiment could work, if the tensions between federal authority and individual freedoms could be resolved, and what exactly its newly won independence meant. While Hamilton may have dismissed the Pennsylvania protest as a "Whiskey Rebellion"—just some backwoods frontiersmen clinging to their drink of choice—there was in fact much more at stake. Whiskey represented the heart of American identity in this period, embodying the fruits of farmers' labor and of the rich American soils, the centrality of land and agricultural production, the promise of the frontier and the rejection of British elitism, and the desire for equality and economic justice.

The conflicts over the whiskey tax followed a half-century of changing drinking habits and ideologies in what would become the United States. Americans adjusted their consumption and agricultural practices to reflect their changing relationships with England, as they moved toward independence.

Colonial Drinking and Rum

Before whiskey emerged as the most popular drink by the early nineteenth century, other kinds of alcohol predominated in the American colonies: beer, wine, cider, brandy, and especially rum. Drinking alcohol in general was much more common in the seventeenth and eighteenth centuries than it is in the United States today. One estimate suggests that, on average, each American in 1770 drank the equivalent of seven shots of liquor every day.[2] People drank to escape boredom, to engage in social life, to help fuel hard labor, to complement meals and provide calories, to stay warm and aid digestion, and to slake their thirst without exposing themselves to contaminated water or spoiled milk. The fermentation and distillation processes used to produce alcohol preserved the grain and fruit ingredients, delaying spoilage or bacterial contamination. Beer, in particular, was made from a wide variety of ingredients, depending on regional availability; one source offers this list of options for beer ingredients: "Indian Corn Malted with drying in a Stove; with Persimmons dried in Cakes and baked; with potatoes and with the green stalks of Indian Corn cut small and bruised; with Pom-pions [pumpkins], with the Jerusalem artichoke ..."[3]

These diverse beers and ciders were first produced largely at home by women, as part of their extensive and laborious food preparation practices. But by the end of the seventeenth century, as farms began to specialize, taverns emerged as a more centralized space for alcohol consumption, especially for men. These widespread taverns imported drinks from different parts of the colonies and from abroad, serving as important nodes in the economy. Even more notably, they created a new and distinct social space that brought people and travelers into conversation. Men especially gathered in taverns to read newspapers, carry out business transactions, discuss politics, and—as colonial discontent grew—to plan revolutionary activities.

By the 1720s, the most important drink available in these taverns was rum. This distilled liquor was produced from molasses, a byproduct of sugar production in the West Indies—the Caribbean islands colonized by European powers. The sugar plantations there were almost entirely dependent on sugar = slave labor

West Indies Sugar → Europe → colonies rum

Africa

slave labor, with wealthy plantation owners forcing enslaved Africans into the unforgiving work of planting and harvesting sugar cane, extracting sugary liquid by crushing the cane with large rollers, boiling the liquid until it crystallized, processing the sugar, and distilling the molasses byproduct into rum. These sugar plantations had very high death rates, which led to ongoing demand for more enslavement. The eighteenth century was the peak of the Atlantic slave trade, forcing around 4 million enslaved Africans to the Americas. The majority of these people were taken to the West Indies or Brazil, with less than 5 percent arriving in North America. And of those people who were forced onto the slave ships to make the harrowing Middle Passage journey across the Atlantic under terrible conditions, 20 percent died before reaching the other side. This destructive and deeply immoral slave trade enriched many European traders and American planters who benefited from the unpaid labor. In the three nodes of the "triangle trade," the sugar and rum from the West Indies were shipped to Europe, then manufactured goods from England and additional rum were shipped to the colonies and to Africa, where people were enslaved and pressed into labor in the American colonies.

very high death rates in sugar plan.

distilled it themselves

As a result of this trade, New Englanders developed a taste for rum by the late 1600s. Around 1700, they began to import molasses directly from Barbados and distill it into rum themselves. The distillation process vaporized the liquid and then cooled it to allow the alcohol within to condense again. This increased the alcohol content, making distilled liquors less perishable and easier to transport. As sugar production boomed in the early eighteenth century, the price of molasses fell, making rum affordable for all classes. By the beginning of the American Revolution, there were 141 distilleries in the colonies, the majority in Massachusetts, Rhode Island, and Connecticut.[4] In addition to the triangle trade that linked the Americas with Europe and Africa, rum was also a critical part of internal trade within the American colonies. The resulting colonial trade routes began to integrate the colonies, across culture, consumption, and taste. Whereas the 1600s had seen very distinct colonial diets, these began to converge by the mid-1700s. According to historian James McWilliams, using the pathways created by the trade in rum, "colonists eager to sample the foods of other regions were soon placing orders for bread and beer from Philadelphia, beef from New England, okra and rice from Carolina, and ham from Virginia."[5] These trade routes lay the foundation for the later trade in whiskey as well.

molasses

combine → native → fermented drinks

Another consequence of liquor consumption was the further weakening of Native American cultures. Although Native peoples had made fermented drinks from crops like corn or agave before colonization, the higher alcohol content of the distilled spirits introduced by the British led to more destructive effects. Colonists used rum and whiskey in their trading with Native Americans, both as a commodity of exchange and as a way of bringing on clouded judgment to take advantage.[6] Alcohol could offer short-term solace in the context of more than a century of corrosive effects from European colonization: epidemic diseases, land dispossession, and ongoing warfare. A number of Native leaders sought to curb drinking, decrying "wicked whiskey-sellers," and in Pennsylvania pleading with colonial authorities: "We beg you would prevent its coming in such quantities. We desire it may be forbidden and none sold in the Indian country."[7] Despite these pleas and other efforts, rum and later whiskey contributed to the undermining of Native American communities.

A Changing Landscape toward Revolution

By the middle of the eighteenth century, whiskey was emerging as an ever more popular drink among American colonists, especially for those who lived on the frontier—the western part of the colonies inland from the Atlantic coast along the Appalachian Mountains. The drink, made from distilled grains, was introduced by immigrants from Scotland and Ireland who settled in the isolated western regions of Pennsylvania, Kentucky, Maryland, Virginia, and the Carolinas. Although, in their home countries, they had distilled whiskey from barley, wheat, and rye, when they reached the American colonies, the grain that was most abundant was corn. Distilling corn and later rye was a way of preserving it and making it easier to transport from isolated locales to trading centers. As Steven Stoll writes, "A horse carried three or four bushels of grain, but it carried the equivalent of twenty bushels converted into liquor."[8] And because whiskey could be made from American-grown grains, it was not reliant on imports from the West Indies, as rum was. Whiskey thus became a crucial part of the economy and lifestyle of the American frontier.

In fact, whiskey came to be associated with the rough and tumble nature of the frontier more broadly, for better or worse. Elite members of society thought of whiskey as a drink for poor people, preferring imported offerings like wine for themselves. They looked down upon the frontiersmen, who were associated with "gambling, fighting, and whoring" to accompany their whiskey drinking.[9] By the end of the 1700s, these views contributed to a broader moral reform movement that sought to reduce alcohol consumption. Philadelphian Dr. Benjamin Rush was a leading crusader against liquor. In his 1784 book, *An Inquiry into the Effects of Ardent Spirits upon the Human Body and Mind,* Rush expressed fears that democracy itself was imperiled by drunkenness and the poor behavior that accompanied it, leaving the country to be "governed by men, chosen by intemperate and corrupted voters."[10] He got his friend and future president John Adams on board, asking him to pass a resolution during the Revolutionary War stating that "If any major or Brigadier General shall drink more than One quart of Whisky, or get drunk more than Once in 24 hours he shall be publickly reprimanded."[11] Adams joined Rush in his outrage, asking "is it not mortifying beyond all expression that we Americans should exceed all other & millions of people in the world in this degrading beastly vise of Intemperance?"[12] And while later temperance movements against alcohol would become tied up with religious views, this entanglement was not characteristic of the eighteenth-century moral reform movement. By contrast, the evangelical Protestant revivals of the Great Awakening in the 1730s and 1740s supported the characteristics of the frontier, without reference to alcohol, in democratizing religion and diminishing the authority of the upper-class ministers and merchants who reigned in the cities of the Atlantic coast.

The frontier was also the site of the French and Indian War, part of the broader Seven Years' War. From 1754 to 1763, the British colonists and their Native American allies on the eastern seaboard fought against New France and its own Native allies for rights to the Ohio Valley. After years of violence on both sides, Great Britain emerged victorious. The Treaty of Paris of 1763 set the terms of the resolution, with England taking possession of nearly all the land east of the Mississippi River. At the end of the war, the American colonists and their British homeland found themselves with complex feelings toward each other. On the one hand, fighting together against the French had created a feeling of unity that made Americans celebrate British foods, consumer goods, and identity. On the other hand, new points of tension had emerged. During the war, some American farmers had resisted supplementing British soldiers' measly rations, leading to the British using force to claim local food supplies. Other colonists had taken advantage of British needs by price-gouging.[13] All of this led to sour feelings after the war, which, combined with the British levying taxes to cover the war's expenses and ongoing territorial disputes, laid the foundation for the American Revolution.

The British needed money to repay their war debts and to help police the borders of its expanded territory in North America. They felt it was only fair that the colonists contribute to these expenses. In 1764, the British prime minister introduced the Sugar Act which, ironically, *lowered* the existing tax on imported molasses. Since 1733, the Molasses Tax had been in place, which charged 6 pence per gallon on molasses and other sugar byproducts imported to the colonies from non-British sources. The goal was to force the colonists to buy their rum directly from the British West Indies, instead of importing cheap French molasses and distilling their own rum. But the 1733 tax had no teeth, with little enforcement. In contrast, when Britain passed the *taxes even/when* [handwritten note in left margin]

1764 Sugar Act, although the tax was reduced to 3 pence per gallon, it was accompanied by real enforcement measures, such as using British warships to police American ports and collect the import tax as needed.[14]

The Sugar Act was part of a broader set of actions that angered colonists and spurred them to revolution a decade later. The Proclamation of 1763 outlawed further settlement beyond the Appalachian Mountains, which particularly frustrated the settlers on the frontier, though it most hurt wealthier landowners and speculators. Then, in 1765, the Stamp Act taxed any printed colonial material, and the Quartering Act stationed British troops throughout colonial villages and required American farmers to feed them. The 1767 Townshend Duties taxed manufactured imports and tea, among others. Although several of these were repealed within a year of passage, they contributed to many colonists' sense that they were powerless and that they were being taxed without being able to vote on the representatives who created those taxes, leading to the infamous complaints of "no taxation without representation."

Historians have largely portrayed the colonists' reaction to these taxes as outrage over infringement on their rights as British subjects. But, as James McWilliams argues, the complaints were perhaps more fundamentally about infringements on the availability of material goods, and especially the food that sustained them and which shored up their identity as Americans. The British policies restricted colonists' access to tea, sugar, and their own farm produce, which they had to feed to British troops under the Quartering Act. All of these food products had, by the 1760s, become "vivid manifestations of several cultural values," representing "concrete aspects of life, such as the colonists' upward mobility, their increasing sense of choice, and even their identity as British Americans."[15] In regulating American food production, the British were challenging a part of the colonial economy that the colonists were most proud of, that they felt embodied their particular strengths and self-sufficiency, at least when it came to farm production.

These challenges pushed the revolutionaries to adopt a coherent radical Whig ideology, connected to the virtue of farming and food production. As they fought for freedom, they fought for their rights to the land and the food it produced, which had provided the American colonies a surprisingly high standard of living. In enacting this ideology, colonists began to boycott British consumer goods, replacing them with products that they saw as more "American" or that could be produced locally. The most famous example of this is the boycott of tea in favor of coffee, with the Boston Tea Party, but colonists also replaced rum with whiskey and beer, and imported textiles with homespun clothing. Whiskey, and its other American counterparts, came to symbolize a home-grown and patriotic spirit, in contrast to the denounced luxuries of Britain.

Revolution, Whiskey, and American Identity

[handwritten margin notes: "rum → whiskey", "war - transition"]

In April 1775, the tensions that had been roiling the colonies for a decade led to the official beginning of the Revolutionary War at Lexington and Concord, in Massachusetts. For the next eight years, under the leadership of George Washington, the Continental Army fought against Great Britain to establish independence. Although the British had the upper hand at the beginning of the war, with far more money, preparation, and military training, the American revolutionaries tenaciously fought on their own soil and successfully recruited new soldiers, despite a high casualty rate and food shortages. The large size of the colonies and later support from France and other European nations turned the tide in favor of the revolutionaries, with the British finally surrendering at Yorktown, Virginia in 1781.

During the war, the transition from rum to whiskey accelerated. The British Royal Navy blockaded American ports, which limited access to molasses and rum imports from the British West Indies. The Continental Army, to boost morale, provided a daily ration of liquor, often whiskey. And Congress sometimes even offered the drink as a reward, as when it shipped an extra thirty casks of whiskey to Continental troops after the October 1777 loss at Germantown.[16] Soldiers fighting near the frontier especially developed a new taste for whiskey, as many sutlers, or civilian merchants, circled the military camps offering cheap libations. The rising demand led to the establishment of new whiskey distilleries. There was even concern that too much grain would be consumed by the distilleries, with George Washington writing in support of "Acts prohibiting the distilling of unreasonable Quantities of Wheat and other Grain into Whisky."[17] Such restrictions contributed to rye becoming the primary grain used in distilling whiskey in the years after the war.

Territorial expansion in the years following the Revolution accelerated the shift toward American crops and drinks like whiskey. As the United States claimed control of new lands, earlier British restrictions on settling the land west of the Appalachian Mountains no longer applied, expanding frontier settlement and westward movement. Frontier farmers raised livestock and cultivated corn and rye, distilling excess grain into whiskey and thereby boosting a small-scale but vibrant distilling industry. In 1799, an average distillery in Virginia could produce about 650 gallons of whiskey per year.[18] For rural backcountry economies where cash was scarce, whiskey became an important commodity, a crucial tool of exchange. Farmers used whiskey to pay debts, barter for other commodities, pay their rent, or as wages for laborers.

If whiskey's economic value proved important in the post-Revolutionary years, so too did its symbolism. The drink came to be part of a new American culinary identity, which embraced food qualities like "frugality, pragmatism, honesty, and a lack of pretension," all of which contrasted with European cuisine, which was perceived as snobbish.[19] These qualities went hand in hand with the veneration of the frontier and of farmers that emerged in the late eighteenth century, as many Americans began to think of themselves as a united agricultural people. J. Hector St. John de Crèvecœur, a French-American whose 1782 book *Letters from an American Farmer* significantly shaped European perceptions of the new nation, exalted the frontier and the farm as the foundation of the American Dream. He wrote, "The instant I enter on my own land, the bright idea of property, of exclusive right, of independence exalt my mind. Precious soil ... What should we American farmers be without the distinct possession of that soil? It feeds, it clothes us, from it we draw even a great exuberancy, our best meat, our richest drink ..."[20] Of course, the "distinct possession" of the soil that westerners celebrated required the removal of the Native Americans, the original inhabitants. Crèvecœur's view was further developed by Thomas Jefferson, in his idealization of the yeoman farmer as part of an agrarian myth that he saw as foundational to democracy. Whiskey was one embodiment of this agrarian nation.

This conception of whiskey, along with its critical role in the frontier economy, explains why the conflicts over the whiskey taxes and resulting Whiskey Rebellion became so heated. At the heart of the conflict were also broader disagreements between Jefferson and his rival Alexander Hamilton, which laid the foundation for the first political parties in the new United States. Jefferson and his followers favored farmers and ordinary people, a weak federal government, state banks, and free trade. Hamilton and his Federalist party, in contrast, championed an elite manufacturing society, a strong central government, a national bank, and protective tariffs. Thus, when Hamilton led Congress in passing "an excise on distilled spirits" in 1791 in order to raise revenue to pay down the national debt, he was not only taxing whiskey but also enacting his political views in leveraging the power of the federal government to bring the backcountry frontiersmen who produced whiskey in line with a modern manufacturing economy. But the westerners targeted by this tax fought back—again, not only to protect their whiskey, but to protect their own political views and ways of life. This event and the frontier in which it took place were key to early American politics.

The "Whiskey Rebellion" and Its Aftermath

In calling this episode in US history the "Whiskey Rebellion," scholars have followed the lead of Alexander Hamilton himself who was understandably antagonistic toward the rebels. Historian Terry Bouton argues that this term

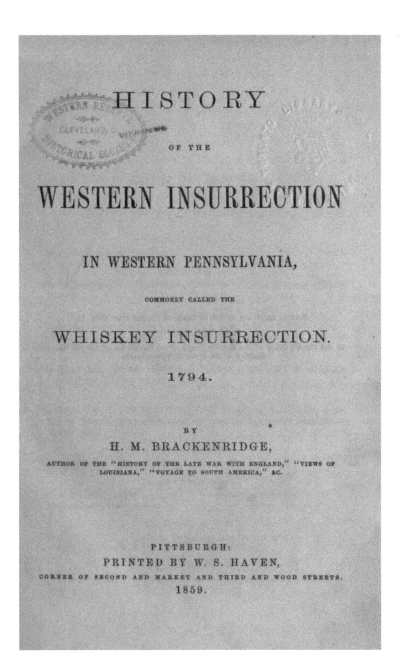

FIGURE 3 *The cover of Henry Brackenridge's* History of the Western Insurrection in Western Pennsylvania *(Pittsburgh: W.S. Haven, 1859). The book's title, by subordinating the "Whiskey Insurrection" subtitle, reframes the event as a principled effort at regulation, rather than a drunken outburst.*

diminishes the frontiersmen's position, making us think of them as "drunken, gun-wielding hillbillies, frightening but too comical to be taken seriously." Instead, he argues that it should more appropriately be called the "Pennsylvania Regulations," to place the events into the context of other "regulations," or prior efforts in the backcountry to regulate the government and influence political leaders.[21] Contemporaries who supported the insurrectionists put forward similar claims, as with Henry Brackenridge, whose 1794 book is titled *History of the Western Insurrection*, with only a reference to the common (but less accurate) name of the "Whiskey Insurrection" in the subtitle (Figure 3). And indeed, the actions of western Pennsylvanians had precedents in earlier agrarian protests and in efforts to combat taxes that Americans saw as unjust. In fact, the entire American Revolution might be seen as one such precedent. In the hit Broadway musical *Hamilton,* Thomas Jefferson's character makes this connection when he raps, "Look, when Britain taxed our tea, we got frisky. Imagine what gon' happen when you try to tax our whisky."[22] In this way, the "Whiskey Rebellion" was akin to the Boston Tea Party itself, only with Hamilton on the other side. Hamilton and the Federalists, for their part, denied this comparison, arguing that, in this case, the taxation followed fair elected representation in Congress—taxation *with* representation.

However, despite these previous movements against government overreach, whiskey itself *did* matter in this instance. Whiskey mattered, but not because the frontiersmen were hillbillies obsessed with getting drunk. As this chapter has illustrated, whiskey mattered because it facilitated trade. It mattered because it allowed for far-flung farm producers to bring their grain to market. It mattered because it was a product that embodied frontier self-sufficiency. It thus makes sense to call this episode the "Whiskey Rebellion" because the material properties of this food product, not simply the regulatory overreach, were what motivated backcountry farmers to rally behind it.

Soon after Congress passed the whiskey tax in January 1791, rebellions began throughout the whole western region, across western Pennsylvania, Kentucky, Virginia, and North Carolina. They were often led by poor farmers or landless workers. Tax collectors faced violence and resistance when trying to enforce the law. By September 1792, President George Washington put forth a proclamation in support of the tax, writing "nor can the Government longer remain a passive spectator of the contempt with which [the Laws] are treated."[23] This had some effect, but by January 1794, acts of resistance escalated again, as westerners destroyed stills and barns of those who complied with the tax. The height of the action came in July 1794, when excise inspector John Neville served a $250 warrant to his western Pennsylvania neighbor William Miller for refusing to comply with the whiskey tax. Miller harbored hatred for Neville, who he saw as a traitor to the cause—Neville had apparently gone from fighting against taxation to being a tax collector when

Hamilton offered him a job, seemingly changing his position overnight. As a result of his disloyalty, he had grown rich, living "in frontier elegance with eighteen slaves who waited on him night and day."[24] Miller ran Neville off, and then organized a militia of 500 armed men to attack Neville's home. When President Washington heard the news, he passed another proclamation in August 1794 in defense of the federal government's right to enforce the laws. Alexander Hamilton, publishing under the pseudonym Tully, as described in our opening vignette, rallied public opinion in favor of federal action. Washington then claimed his role as commander in chief, organizing his own militia, comprised of 12,950 men from New Jersey, Maryland, Virginia, and eastern Pennsylvania. As this intimidating army marched on western Pennsylvania, the rebels voted to submit, ending the multi-year resistance struggle.

Many traditional narratives portray this event as the first time that the new federal government exercised its power in the face of disobedience, representing the rebels as unruly fringe radicals who needed to be suppressed. But a more complicated read allows us to examine the broader commitments of both sides in this conflict. For his part, Alexander Hamilton was not only trying to pay off national debts and reduce whiskey consumption, but also exercising a form of social engineering. As historian Steven Stoll argues, the whiskey tax was a kind of "education tax," pushing the backcountry residents to become part of the broader US economy by using money, paying taxes, and seeing themselves as part of a commercial system.[25]

Those who rebelled against the tax felt that they were being punished for their cash scarcity and that Hamilton was pushing a symptom of regressive taxation. In contrast to the image of the rebels as "spontaneous drunks," they actually published a series of resolutions, in which they argued that the tax was "not in proportion to property"—hurting the poorest people most.[26] They especially resented the fact that, of all the things Hamilton could have chosen to tax, he targeted one of the most important parts of the frontier economy; whiskey was a product of the soil that agrarians were able to convert into a kind of currency. Taxing whiskey was like taxing the land itself. Further, the government's strong enforcement measures also felt brutish and patronizing, worse than anything Britain had imposed. The rebels saw the government's actions as undermining equality and democracy, the very ideals the Revolution fought for and that the Great Awakening had popularized. Stoll puts it this way: "Hamilton assumed that the Revolution had secured the independence of the United States, but he confronted backcountry citizens who believed that they had fought for their own independence."[27]

Still, with George Washington's show of federal force, those backcountry citizens retreated. In the aftermath, few insurgents were punished due to contradictory testimony and a lack of credible witnesses. Ironically, the economy of western Pennsylvania actually got a boost from the soldiers who had come to enforce the whiskey tax and who then spent money on local food, drink, and lodging.[28] Washington and Hamilton felt victorious, as they showcased the power of the federal government. But the frontierspeople also continued to rise up periodically in the late eighteenth century to regulate the government. And their broader movement helped bring Thomas Jefferson and his anti-Federalist party to power in the election of 1800. Once in office, Jefferson repealed the whiskey tax in 1802. The next year, Jefferson oversaw the acquisition of the Louisiana Territory, the entire middle part of the present-day United States, which made the frontier seem limitless.

Throughout all of this, whiskey consumption only grew. The price increase that had accompanied the excise tax in 1791 had not diminished American's enthusiasm for the liquor even before its repeal. Distilleries grew larger and more sophisticated. As rum consumption continued to decline with the ban on the international slave trade in the early 1800s, whiskey became the most popular and cheapest alcoholic drink. The period between the 1790s and the 1820s saw Americans drinking more alcohol overall than ever before or since, stimulating the rise of the temperance movement. But nothing could restrain the centrality of whiskey as a truly American icon in the fledgling democratic nation.

4

Graham Bread:
Early Nineteenth-Century Diet and Reform

In 1837, Sylvester Graham published *A Treatise on Bread and Bread-Making*, considering its publication a service to society as he taught his fellow citizens to bake high-quality bread (Figure 4). He lamented that people "eat the most miserable trash that can be imagined, in the form of bread, and never seem to think that … it is an evil to eat such vile stuff as they do." He argued that "the character of their bread is [intimately and closely] connected with the dearest interests of man."[1] The solution to taking care of these dearest interests was to make bread from unbolted wheat—basically, what we would now call whole-wheat flour—that had been grown in "pure virgin soil" and then, ideally, prepared by "good mothers," who patiently stand "over their bread troughs, kneading and moulding their dough."[2] The result was a heavy, dark brown bread that came to be known as "Graham bread." Some sixty years later, the National Biscuit Company (soon abbreviated Nabisco) would capitalize on Graham's name and memory to market Graham crackers, despite their only very distant resemblance to their namesake bread.[3]

how its made

Sylvester Graham rose to prominence in the first half of the nineteenth century, a time of urban health epidemics, not only for his promotion of Graham bread, but for his larger health reform ideology based on diet and sex. During the 1830s and 1840s, Graham spoke before audiences of thousands of people all throughout the East Coast, he wrote eight books that were studied by tens of thousands of followers, and he ignited debates among medical practitioners, butchers, commercial bakers, and many others. In a time when other reformers were organizing against alcohol, against slavery, for women's

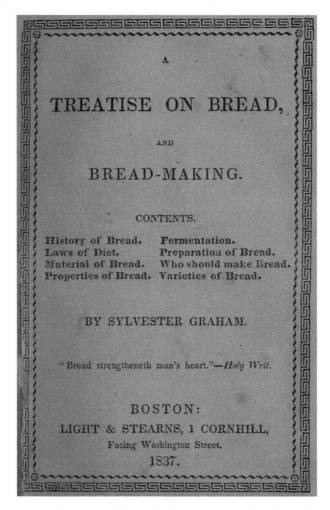

FIGURE 4 *The cover of Sylvester Graham's* A Treatise on Bread and Bread-Making *(Boston: Light & Stearns, 1837). His use of scripture conveys the connection between his dietary and moral guidance.*

rights, and for political and religious reform, Graham focused his attention on food, championing the right diet as central to human and societal flourishing. In addition to dense wheat bread, Graham pushed his audiences to reject meat and alcohol, and to eat fresh fruits and vegetables.

Graham's work embodies the United States of the early nineteenth century. It was a time of widening if still limited democracy, of political upheaval, a time of national expansion and technological innovation, of religious ferment and public health reform, and a time of transformed foodways. Most Americans of the period lived in a society that would have been unrecognizable just a couple of generations before. Many people struggled with those dramatic changes, wrestling with them and trying to mold them in useful directions. The emphasis on self-governance that emerged from the American Revolution applied not only to the new nation, but to its citizens, who turned inward to see possibilities for social reform through a change in their personal behavior, including the food they ate. Eating Graham bread, adopting a vegetarian diet, avoiding alcohol—these all were thought to pave the way for a better world.

Graham and His Bread

Graham bread was the idea to start a better world

temperance movement

Sylvester Graham's personal biography is largely a sad tale. He was born in 1794, the last of seventeen children of his seventy-two-year-old father, Reverend John Graham Jr. Within two years, his father died, and within six years, his mother Ruth lost custody due to mental illness. Sylvester was moved from one home to another, suffering from a range of his own physical and mental illnesses. He failed out of Amherst Academy under difficult circumstances and fell into a deep depression. In 1823, he delivered his first public lecture, on the evils of hard liquor such as whiskey and rum. From there, he found his calling in the growing temperance movement, leaving his post as a minister to become an agent for the Pennsylvania Society for Discouraging the Use of Ardent Spirits by 1830. Soon, Graham's pronouncements on drink and food took on special appeal during the 1832 cholera epidemic that swept North America and Europe. This launched him to fame over the next seven years, as he delivered his lectures on "The Science of Human Life," wrote his books, and inspired a Grahamite movement of boardinghouses and publications and related health reform organizations. By 1839, he retreated from the public circuit to live in Northampton, Massachusetts with his wife and two children. He died at the age of fifty-seven, suffering from health concerns that his own Grahamite diet could not fix.[4]

home life

Despite this biography, Graham's influence spread far and long outlived him. The bread that carried his name was at the heart of his moral and dietary philosophy. Graham argued that the bread of the 1830s was so heavily processed that it overtaxed and overstimulated the body. Other foods and activities—meat, alcohol, tobacco, masturbation, sex out of wedlock— had similarly detrimental effects, in his view. Following the ideas of French physiologists, Graham theorized that the digestive system was linked to the brain and to the sex organs, such that stimulating foods and drinks would affect all these bodily systems in tandem. Thus, when early nineteenth-century Americans consumed their heavy diets, the whole body suffered. One historian writes that ceremonial banquets of the time featured "as many as thirty or more kinds of meat and fish at one occasion. And leisurely antebellum gentlemen sometimes sat at the festive board for as much as seven hours at a stretch."[5] This was a time of dietary excess, to which Graham was reacting.

Bread had not always been this way, however. Graham recalled better times, with nostalgia: "Who that can look back 30 or 40 years to those blessed days of New England's prosperity and happiness, when our good mothers used to make the family bread …"[6] But between about 1800 and 1830 wheat agriculture and bread production had changed, producing a white bread that Graham now condemned. When the British first settled the North American colonies, their European wheat varieties did not flourish, leaving the colonists dependent on Indian corn. But by the beginning of the eighteenth century, New York and Pennsylvania began to grow newly adapted varieties of wheat, which spread south as the soil of the Middle Colonies was depleted. Wheat flour remained expensive until the nineteenth century, however, with most average Americans relying more on corn or rye, or sometimes "thirded bread," a mixture of corn, rye, and wheat.[7] Bread had been a core part of the human diet since time immemorial, the staff of life. But as wheat production expanded westward in the nineteenth century and wheat prices fell, alongside new grain milling practices, bread became no longer a product of "good mothers," but of commercial bakeries.

It was this production practice that Graham railed against. He believed that all food processing "put asunder what God has joined together … by separating the flour from the part commonly called the bran."[8] Refining wheat—producing finer, whiter flour—concentrated the nutritious matter and separated it from the bulk, weakening the digestive tract. The answer? Bread made from unbolted, whole-grain, wheat flour—Graham bread. No food, Graham wrote, "more invigorates the alimentary canal, and restores, and keeps up the regular and healthful functions of the stomach and intestines."[9] Eating Graham bread was a way to push back against the commercialization of food and agricultural production that was transforming early nineteenth-century America. Graham blamed commercially baked bread not only because it used unhealthful white flour, but he also pushed back against chemical leavening agents that bakers used as a shortcut for yeast's long rise—forerunners of baking powder—and against other adulterants like "chalk, pipe clay, and plaster of Paris," which he claimed were widely used.[10]

Graham bread, as one could imagine, had its supporters and its opponents. By 1839, famed cookbook author Sarah Josepha Hale recommended Graham bread for certain demographics. She offered a recipe for it, directing readers to combine "six quarts of this [coarsely-ground] wheat meal, one tea-cup of good yeast, and half a tea-cup of molasses … a pint of milk-warm water and a teaspoonful of pearlash or salaeratus [leavening agents]."[11] Many of Graham's followers who heard his lectures, read his books, or lived in Grahamite boardinghouses, too, were smitten by the bread, testifying in hundreds of pages of published accounts to the miraculous effects of Graham's diet.[12]

Others, however, were less enamored. Ralph Waldo Emerson dismissed Graham as "the prophet of bran bread and pumpkins." Others claimed that bran was indigestible, that the Graham diet was nothing but "sawdust and sand," and that the bread was hard enough to break a window.[13] In 1837, Graham was mobbed in Boston by rioters who disliked his teachings.[14]

But, as this chapter has already argued, Graham's dietary pronouncements were not just about food. They were a response to the dramatic changes that were transforming the nation in the early nineteenth century, in the realms of politics, industrialization and technological change, expansion and racial conflict, and reform.

Ideals of Democracy

At the turn of the nineteenth century, the United States was still a very young nation, reconfiguring itself in response to new ideas and new leaders. These ideas lay the foundation for Graham's appeal by the 1830s. The first half of the nineteenth century was dominated by two American presidents: Thomas Jefferson (in office 1801–09) and Andrew Jackson (1829–37). Even beyond the two terms in office that each of these men held, their ideas extended for longer periods of time, with historians referring to the 1790s–1820s as a period of Jeffersonian democracy, and roughly 1824–54 as the Jacksonian Era. Jefferson's election in 1800 paved the way for the rise of the Democratic-Republican party and the downfall of the opposing Federalist Party, led by Alexander Hamilton. Jefferson's party celebrated the non-elite yeoman farmers and plain folk of the United States, and expanded the vote to more white males, instead of only those who held property. Although all women and non-white people were still denied the right to vote along lines of gender and race, class became a less decisive factor in voting rights.

In the 1824 election, Jefferson's Democratic-Republican Party began to split, forming the modern Democratic Party on the one hand and the National Republican (later, Whig) Party on the other. Taking on the mantle of the Democratic party was Andrew Jackson, who would come to define the political era in which Sylvester Graham rose to popularity. Jackson was known as a military hero in the War of 1812, in which the United States fought against the British over free trade rights and against the practice of impressment, in which the British Navy would force American sailors into service. Some historians have referred to the War of 1812 as a second American Revolution, in that Americans cemented their patriotism and sense of superiority relative to Britain. Andrew Jackson helped defeat a British invasion at the Battle of

New Orleans, bringing the War of 1812 to a decisive end. In later years, he would draw on this broad appeal as the "Hero of New Orleans" and as a tough man of the frontier—he was the US Senator from the western border state of Tennessee—to appeal to ordinary Americans from the South and West and to fight against elite interests. The Election of 1828 brought Jackson to the presidency, where he oversaw westward expansion and the growth of democracy and the market revolution.[15] Sylvester Graham's dietary advice resonated with many Americans in this context, celebrating westward expansion by championing the "virgin soil" in which the best whole-grain wheat grew, and encouraging individual attention to and responsibility for one's own body that aligned with democratizing forces that uplifted the individual contributions to American government.

The expansion of democracy was also aided by the rise of technologies for information dissemination, through traveling lecture circuits and printed publications, both of which Graham's movement used. Graham traveled through New England and the Mid-Atlantic states delivering lectures—first on temperance, and later on dietary and sexual issues—often to huge crowds. His lectures were part of a larger lyceum system that developed in the United States from the 1820s to spread education and moral uplift.[16] In addition to the spoken word, the printed word became ever more accessible by the 1830s, with new printing technologies that made newspapers, pamphlets, journals, and books cheaper and more widespread, expanding the size of the reading public. This made possible, for example, the publication of the *Graham Journal of Health and Longevity* between 1837 and 1839, edited by Graham's disciple, David Cambell.[17] Domestic guidance manuals, too, benefited from this information revolution, with more publications offering household advice, like that of Sarah Josepha Hale described above, which came to guide American cooking practices.

The rise of such domestic guides in the early nineteenth century also illustrates a new role for women within this expanding democracy. Around the American Revolution, middle-class white women were expected to practice republican motherhood, or to use their authority as the head of the home and child-raising to inculcate important republican values that would support the democracy, like hard work and frugality. But as more men entered the urbanizing market economy, the ideology of "separate spheres" pushed women further into the home. This led to what historians have called the "cult of domesticity," in which middle-class urban white women were responsible not only for all the ongoing unpaid labor of the home, including food preparation, but also for embodying "feminine" virtues like beauty, sexual purity, piety, and submissiveness. As Mary Randolph writes in her 1824 *The Virginia House-Wife*, a husband whose wife follows the guidance within her book, "will feel pride and exultation in the possession of a companion, who gives to his home charms that gratify every wish of his soul." Such a woman would raise sons who are "moral men" and daughters who "will each be a treasure to her husband."[18] These views both expanded the role women could play as household authorities and as those who raised future democratic citizens and also, obviously, limited women's own political participation outside the home.

Market and Technological Revolution

Alongside the democratic moves of this period came a market revolution that transformed not only the American economy, but technology, transportation and communication networks, cities, and factories. These processes changed how people moved, lived, dressed, ate, worked, and related to the environment. It was these many changes that Graham's restrictive ideology reacted against, as individuals tried to adapt their lifestyles to the tumult all around them.

The first few decades of the nineteenth century saw a shift from subsistence agriculture and self-sufficiency to an integrated commercial economy. Around 1800, Americans mostly ate food that they or their neighbors grew and used manufactured goods produced in their own homes and communities. By the 1830s, this was changing significantly. In 1832, Lydia Marie Child in *The American Frugal Housewife* had to chide her readers: "Make your own bread and cake. Some people think it is just as cheap to buy of the baker and confectioner; but it is not half as cheap." Her admonition signifies the widespread practice of buying commercially prepared baked goods.[19] By 1836, Graham wrote, "In cities and large towns, most people depend on public bakers for their bread."[20] This shift was the result of many new technologies: the automated grain mill patented by Oliver Evans in 1790, Robert Fulton's invention of steam-powered boats by 1807, the completion of the Erie Canal in 1825, the first long-distance rail line from the Baltimore & Ohio (B&O) Rail Road Company in 1827, Cyrus McCormick's harvesting reaper by 1831, and John Deere's steel plow by 1837, among others.

Evans's grain mill automated the process of moving grain through a series of grinding stones, which lowered the price of flour, and produced a much finer white flour from the more complete separation of the starchy endosperm of a wheat kernel from the fibrous bran and oily germ. Evans filed the third patent with the brand-new Patent Office in 1790, and by the 1840s, there were nearly 24,000 gristmills in the United States, most of them using Evans's design. As historian Andrew Smith argues, Evans's process had effects all down the line, as it reduced operating costs for commercial bakers because the fine flour took less time to bake, led bakers to add sugar and other additives to dough to make up for loss of flavor and texture, contributed to the rise of advertising to help distinguish products made by identical processes, concentrated the milling industry in the hands of large operators, and led to an emphasis on efficiency and automation in the food industry.[21] Graham blamed these commercial bakers under capitalism for working using whatever "expedients" needed "to increase the lucrativeness of their business," since they work "more for the sake of securing their own emolument than for the public good."[22] As historian Stephen Nissenbaum writes, Graham's desire for whole wheat breads produced by mothers in their homes "was a historical vision as well—the sentimentalized memory of a precapitalist order ... where people did not have to rely on the unfeeling exchanges of the marketplace for either their physical or their emotional sustenance. Graham recognized and lamented the fact that such a world had all but disappeared."[23]

The other major factor in the rise of commercial bread along with the automated mill was the transportation revolution, and especially the construction of the Erie Canal. In 1800, in order to reach New York, goods produced in the Midwest had to travel south along the Mississippi River to New Orleans, before being shipped up the Gulf and Atlantic coasts, taking fifty days or more. This made it very hard for farmers on the frontier to market their crops. Shipping difficulties during the War of 1812 further highlighted how limited transportation in early America was. In 1815, President James Madison proposed the American System plan for economic development, which, along with a national bank and import tariffs, offered financing for roads and canals. As part of this plan, construction began in 1817 on the Erie Canal—an engineering marvel, dug by hand at a depth of four feet and width of forty-two feet, stretching for 363 miles between Albany and Lake Erie. The canal, when combined with the new invention of the steamboat, made it efficient to ship wheat and other products grown throughout the Midwest to the East Coast and then over the Atlantic to ports beyond. Aided by new agricultural technologies and the invention of the telegraph by 1843, the US output of wheat nearly tripled between 1840 and 1860.[24]

A related and overlapping phenomenon was the early growth of cities and factories in the first half of the nineteenth century. As British imports slowed after the Embargo Act of 1807 and the War of 1812, the United States established its own textile mills with the loom plans that Francis Cabot Lowell recreated from those he observed in Manchester, England. The town of Lowell, Massachusetts soon became the center of textile milling, bringing in 10,000 workers—young farm girls—to power the mills and lay the foundation for the modern American company. This early industrialization and the market revolution, alongside westward expansion that made eastern farming less profitable, fueled the growth of cities. At the same time, Irish, German, and Jewish immigrants escaped political unrest in Europe by coming to American cities (and sometimes triggering nativist and anti-Catholic backlash, as with the rise of the Know-Nothing movement by the mid-1850s). These combined forces of industrialization and immigration led to urbanization, with the number of cities with populations above 5,000 rising from twelve in 1820 to almost 150 by 1850.[25]

The many newcomers who came to the cities needed places to live, and often found themselves in urban boardinghouses, which rented rooms and provided meals to people coming to the city without their families. One strand of the Grahamite movement was rooted in the rise of Graham boardinghouses by 1833, operated by his disciples. In Boston and New York, Graham's followers could find diets free of meat and white flour, along with others who held similar views on a wide range of contemporary issues. One such boardinghouse resident, referencing famed abolitionist William Garrison, observed, "the Boarders in this establishment are not only Grahamites but Garrisonites—not only reformers in diet, but radicalists in Politics. Such a knot of Abolitionists I never before fell in with."[26] One reform was tied into the other, with abolitionists using boarding houses to further their multi-racial, mixed-sex movement.[27]

A final set of impacts of the market revolution was rising inequality and an unstable economy that led to a series of depressions or "panics," that followed overspeculation in a range of commodities, including land, enslaved laborers, and railroad bonds. Andrew Jackson blamed the Panic of 1819 on the national bank, which became one of his central enemies while he was in office. Sylvester Graham linked the unhealthy boom and bust cycles of the economy to—you guessed it—the unhealthy dietary stimulants of white flour, meat, coffee, and liquor. Both humans and the economy needed the "state of serenity and subsistence" that Graham bread could offer.[28]

Westward Expansion and Racial Conflict

The market and transportation revolutions promoted westward expansion, propelling the idea of Manifest Destiny that ordained and justified western settlement in the nineteenth century. This contested settlement led to further tensions around the ongoing displacement of Native Americans and the issue of slavery in the United States. The "virgin soils" that Graham celebrated as productive of the best wheat were formerly the lands of Indigenous peoples that were taken by seizure or often coercive treaties. As scholar Aaron Bobrow-Strain writes, "For Graham and his followers, building the Kingdom of God on Earth from the stomach out was inseparable from their emerging imperial ambitions of their young Republic."[29] And indeed, the nineteenth century saw the acquisition of more and more land, as with the Louisiana Purchase of 1804, the annexation of Texas in 1845, and the American Southwest at the end of the Mexican-American War in 1848. New modes of transportation made it possible for land-hungry settlers to flood these new areas.

The Native Americans who had been pushed west as British colonists took over the eastern seaboard, and who had in many cases allied with the British against Americans in the War of 1812, now fought to survive in light of further encroachment. Shawnee brothers Tecumseh and Tenskwatawa organized pan-Indian resistance to white settlement, headquartered in a new community called Prophetstown, at the intersection of the Tippecanoe and Wabash Rivers. Future president William Henry Harrison led a siege on the town in 1811, burning it to the ground, earning his nickname "Old Tippecanoe," which was later used as the campaign slogan under "Tippecanoe and Tyler Too," when he and his vice-presidential candidate John Tyler ran in the 1840 presidential election. In 1813, Tecumseh was killed at the Battle of the Thames during the War of 1812, which stifled the resistance movement. By 1830, the fierce pressure for more Southern land in which to grow cotton with enslaved labor led to the passage of the Indian Removal Act, under President Andrew Jackson. The so-called "Five Civilized Tribes"—the Cherokee, Chickasaw, Choctaw, Creek/Muscogee, and Seminole—despite having adopted Western practices of religion, government, and language, were forced off their lands in the Southeast and marched via the Trail of Tears to the less agriculturally-valuable "Indian Territory" in present-day Oklahoma. Thousands of people died in the series of forced relocations between 1830 and 1850, with at least 4,000 dying in just the Cherokee forced march of 1838–9 alone.[30]

The lands vacated by the "Five Civilized Tribes" were quickly replanted with cotton, testifying to the growth of plantation slavery in this period and its link to westward expansion. Even as abolition movements like those in the Graham boardinghouses grew in the North, and as the year 1808 saw the end of the external slave trade, slavery continued to expand in the South. Demand for cotton with the rise of textile mills and the invention of the cotton gin in 1793—which allowed for the more efficient separation of cotton fibers from its sticky seeds—made slavery increasingly profitable. When the cotton gin was first designed, the United States produced 5 million pounds of cotton. Less than thirty years later, that number had grown to almost 170 million pounds.[31] These changes occurred alongside increasing racialized policing and disenfranchisement. The Haitian Revolution between 1791 and 1804, in which enslaved people successfully overthrew the French colonizers in Haiti, along with instances of American resistance like Gabriel's Rebellion in 1800 and efforts by Denmark Vesey in 1822 and Nat Turner by 1831, made American enslavers increasingly nervous. In response, they policed enslaved peoples more heavily, promoted pseudoscience to argue for the racial superiority of the white race, and more heavily limited Black voting rights.

The place of slavery became even more hotly contested as new states sought to enter the Union with territorial expansion, pressing decisions about whether they would be free or slave states. The same canals and new technologies that brought wheat to market and challenged Sylvester Graham's ideals also opened new territories for possible settlement by enslavers. In 1819, when Missouri petitioned to join the United States as a slave state, this threatened to tip the existing balance of free and slave states. After much debate, Congress agreed to the Missouri Compromise, in which Missouri would enter as a slave state, Maine would enter as a new state and would be free, and no more slavery would be allowed north of Missouri's southern border. This period also saw the Nullification Crisis, in which vice president John C. Calhoun argued that individual states, like his home state of South Carolina, could choose to assert their state's rights and choose to nullify federal tariffs, challenging federal power. This set an important precedent for Southern states' protection of slavery in the face of federal opposition, later leading to South Carolina's supposed grounds for secession at the start of the Civil War.

An Age of Reform

These many and varied pressures on American society in the rapidly changing period of the first half of the nineteenth century led many Americans to pursue reform efforts, often led by middle-class women as both an extension of and reaction against the cult of domesticity. Sylvester Graham came to see salvation in dietary change, but he first got his start in ministry and in the temperance movement. His role as a minister was in keeping with the religious revivalism of the period's Second Great Awakening, which spread via traveling preachers and tent revivals to democratize religion and offered a spiritual community and religious purpose for those trying to cope with a changing American society. By 1830, Graham's interest in the ministry shifted toward temperance, the most successful of the era's strands of social reform. In part in response to the dramatic increase in whiskey consumption after the American Revolution, reformers like Graham and his fellow Philadelphian Dr. Benjamin Rush advocated limits on alcohol.

Soon, however, the 1832 cholera epidemic gave Graham the space to shift to a more expansive set of reforms that focused on health and "The Science of Human Life." Graham blamed the epidemic on "dietetic intemperance and lewdness," which only the right diet and lifestyle could fix. Some responses were highly critical: one New York newspaper wrote, "if the cholera comes here, all the Grahamites will certainly die." But others found Graham's arguments against white bread and meat very compelling, especially considering the ineffective and painful mainstream "heroic medicine," which employed techniques like bloodletting and poisonous mercury treatments.[32]

Famed newspaper editor Horace Greeley linked Graham's promotion of a vegetarian diet with the promise of achieving more in the space of other reforms like abolition and women's suffrage, explaining that a meat-free diet would bring strength and energy to tackle the much-needed reforms.[33] Abolitionism as a movement grew in the first half of the nineteenth century, with Black and white anti-slavery activists mobilizing consumer boycotts of slavery-produced sugar, giving lectures, publishing abolitionist pamphlets and newspapers, and pushing for immediate emancipation—in contrast to the gradual emancipation or back-to-Africa colonizationist movements of earlier periods. The movement reached its heights by the 1830s, when anti-abolition aggression after Nat Turner's rebellion in 1831, along with an internal divide over the question of women's rights, halted the momentum. However, organized abolitionism laid the needed groundwork for the rise of Abraham Lincoln's antislavery Republican Party.

The American Anti-Slavery Society made space for women's leadership and supported women's suffrage. Although not all abolitionists were on board with this mission, leading to the splintered movement, women's activism also took on important momentum during this reform era. Sarah Moore Grimké and Angelina Emily Grimké were two sisters who took prominent roles within the antislavery movement, often speaking to mixed audiences of men and women, scandalizing those who wanted to keep such crowds sex-segregated. They came to see fighting the oppression of women as a cause aligned with fighting the oppression of slavery. Lucretia Mott also came to women's activism after being denied the right to vote, because of her sex, at the World Anti-Slavery Convention in London in 1840. Eight years later, she and Elizabeth Cady Stanton organized the 1848 Seneca Falls Convention, which launched the women's suffrage movement, though it would be seventy more years before the passage of the Nineteenth Amendment that gave women the right to vote. These women pushed back against the cult of domesticity to assert their place in the public sphere, especially when it came to moral issues. Many of these women—Angelina Grimké prominently among them—also became followers of Graham and his health reform. Although the presence of women in his audiences, especially when the lectures were focused on taboo topics like masturbation, often led to protest.

Sylvester Graham and his followers came to see diet as the key to changing society for the better along all these axes of reform. While he as an individual came to be remembered as a crackpot—when he has been remembered at all—many of the changes in American health and dietary practices that followed him indeed moved in the direction of his guidance. Americans came to eat more vegetables, consider whole grains healthy, and drink less alcohol. Even as the country accelerated the move toward industrialization and expansion more rapidly than Sylvester Graham could even have imagined, his ideas have lived on.

5

Potlikker:

Food and Slavery in the Antebellum South

In his 1855 book *My Bondage and My Freedom*, Frederick Douglass, who had escaped from slavery, recited one song common among enslaved people, "We raise de wheat,/ Dey gib us de corn; ... We peal de meat,/ Dey gib us de skin, .../We skim de pot,/ Dey gib us the liquor,/ And say dat's good enough for n——r." Douglass, highlighting the cruelty within these feeding practices, continues: "This is not a bad summary of the palpable injustice and fraud of slavery."[1] And indeed, withholding food and wielding hunger were key tools in enslavers' arsenal of dehumanizing tactics in the long history of American slavery. Enslaved peoples, especially on large Southern plantations, ate corn, skin from meat, and the "liquor" from the pot or "potlikker" broth that remained in the pot after greens were boiled long and slow. They ate what they could get their hands on, what remained after the white Southern enslavers filled their groaning tables with an abundance of foods.

But they also ate what they could grow in their own gardens, what they could fish and hunt from the nearby woods they came to know so intimately, and what they developed methods for cooking in the enslavers' kitchens. Enslaved people in the United States found ways to reclaim power through food, even against the backdrop of lives of unceasing toil, cruel punishment, and a constant fear of losing family members through sale. They found sustenance in food however they could. And the potlikker that enslavers may have conceived of as a waste product after the greens were eaten from it turned out to be even more nutritious than the boiled greens themselves, as the vitamins leached into the broth. Although vitamins had not yet been discovered, many enslaved people did consider the potlikker healthy and as a welcome addition to their diets. As Anna Wright of North Carolina recalled, "Cornmeal dumplin's wus oiled in de turnip greens, collards, cabbages, an' so on, even ter snap beans, an' at supper de pot licker wus eat wid de dumplin's. Dat's why de folks wus so healthy."[2] She attested to the core knowledge of potlikker's healthfulness and described the common cooking method, in which a variety of greens—collards, turnips greens, cabbage, mustard greens, or whatever was available—were cooked usually with a piece of salt pork for at least an hour. As the meat flavor and texture permeated the cooking liquid, along with the nutritious essence of the greens, a rich broth resulted. As Wright described, the broth was often soaked up with cornmeal dumplings or other forms of cornbread.

Potlikker embodies many elements of the story of food in enslavement. The practice of dipping a grain-based food into a rich vegetable base and the practice of eating a wide variety of greens both were drawn from the African homelands of the enslaved people who were forced into labor in the United States. Potlikker was a common first food for enslaved children as they weaned from their mother's milk. Tragically, enslavers and traders sometimes rubbed the oily potlikker on enslaved people's skin and mouths to make them look healthy and well-fed when subjecting them to the auction block. And it was among the more common foods referenced in the narratives of formerly enslaved people.[3] As author Michael Twitty writes, "For formerly enslaved people reflecting on their days under the whip, pot likker brought up mixed feelings of nurturance, comfort, near-starvation, and even the indignities of being sold at auction."[4]

While potlikker serves as a symbol, it is important to remember that there was no one singular "slave food." The institution of slavery—and its attendant foodways—changed dramatically over its nearly 250-year existence, varying regionally, across rural and urban divides, across different kinds of plantations, and even across the different positions of enslaved peoples on the same plantation. This chapter focuses most on the antebellum period, in the decades before the Civil War when cotton rose in prominence and reshaped slavery dramatically, but begins with an overview of enslavement in the United States before this period.

The Changing Institution of Slavery

In August 1619, a group of Dutch traders forcibly brought about twenty Africans to the settlement at Jamestown, Virginia, launching African enslavement in the British colonies. In the beginning, however, these Africans were part of a class of "unfree" servants alongside the white indentured servants who came from Europe. In this early phase, until the latter part of the seventeenth century, servitude was less clearly race-based and typically led to eventual freedom. These Black servants often developed economies of their own, grew their own food, and bartered or sold excess to earn enough to purchase their freedom. But by the turn of the eighteenth century, this began to change, with laws codifying slavery on the basis of race. As planters began to build large plantations around profitable cash crops, like tobacco in Virginia by the 1630s and rice in the Carolinas by 1700, they captured and enslaved more and more Africans to provide labor. Enslavers rarely provided sufficient food, which—along with exposure to new disease environments—led to high death rates. With heightened control and labor expectations under the plantation regime, enslaved peoples had less opportunity to supplement their meager rations with their own garden production, especially in Virginia where enslavers restricted food access.[5] Although over 95 percent of Africans forced onto slave ships were taken to sugar plantations in the West Indies and Brazil via the deathly voyage known as the Middle Passage, the North American enslaved population continued to grow by natural increase, in part because of the more plentiful food available in contrast to Central and South America. By the mid-1700s, there were a half-million enslaved people in the US South, with an additional 50,000 in the North, where they served as domestic servants, artisans, and dockworkers, among other professions.[6]

The American Revolution brought the beginning of a wave of emancipations in the North, but a retrenchment of a slave society in the South. Free Blacks and their white allies used the language of liberty and equality to push Congress to end the slave trade and abolish slavery in Northern states. In 1807, both Britain and the United States banned the international slave trade. But the ban did not extend to the domestic trade within the US South, and because enslavement was an inherited condition, new babies meant a growing enslaved population. As tobacco wore out the soil in Virginia and the economies of the upper South diversified, hundreds of thousands of enslaved people were shipped to the lower South, to work on the newly emerging cotton plantations.[7]

A number of developments in the first decades of the nineteenth century led to the dramatic increase in cotton production by the 1830s: Eli Whitney's 1793 invention of a machine for de-seeding cotton called the cotton gin; the acquisition of new lands in the middle of the continent with the Louisiana Purchase of 1803; the invention of the steamboat in 1807, which made it easier to ship cotton to global ports; the 1820 discovery of an especially productive species of cotton known as Petit Gulf; the Indian Removal Act of 1830, which made fertile lands in the Southeast available for cotton agriculture; and the rise of industrial textile production in England and the US North that created a demand for more cotton. Cotton was soon the United States' major export each year until the Civil War. This astronomical growth, the rise of the Cotton Kingdom, relied on the dehumanizing system of slavery, which became more grueling and more tightly controlled. Southern leaders came to vigorously defend slavery in the nineteenth century as a way of vigorously defending their economic and social dependence on cotton. Although only one-quarter of Southerners actually owned enslaved people, everyone who lived in the South—whether in cities or on farms—was shaped by the institution of slavery and the reign of the planter class.[8]

African Origins

When enslaved people drank potlikker, ate greens, or sopped up the liquid with corn pone, they were carrying on a long and storied food tradition that they and their ancestors brought with them from different parts of the African continent. These influences permeated the culture of the American South, extending to food, music, and religion—not only of enslaved Black people, but of white society as well.

As traders chained and forced Africans onto slave ships beginning in the sixteenth century, they also had to find ways to feed these people on the long Middle Passage journey across the Atlantic Ocean. Accompanying the slave trade was a secondary trade in, as historian Jessica Harris writes, "the foodstuffs necessary for the enslaved Africans to endure their arduous and unspeakable journey." Most prominent among these foodstuffs were three common foods of West Africa: corn, rice, and yams.[9] Enslaved people on these ships often used the refusal of food as a tool of resistance, subjecting themselves to starvation or throwing themselves overboard to escape their bondage. Enslavers, however, wanted to protect their "valuable assets," and thus tortured enslaved peoples to force them to eat, or sometimes force fed them with a tool that held their mouths open, called a *speculum oris*.[10] British surgeon Alexander Falconbridge, observing the horrific conditions on a slave ship in the late eighteenth century, wrote, "Upon the negroes refusing to take sustenance, I have seen coals of fire, glowing hot, put on a shovel, and placed so near the lips, as to scorch and burn them."[11]

Upon the slave ships' arrival in the ports of the Americas, the enslaved were prepared for sale. Captain Thomas Phillips described in 1693 how the Africans would be shaved and "sleeked with palm oil" to make them look healthy and young.[12] Later, in the domestic slave trade in the United States, potlikker would be used in a similar way. William J. Anderson who was sold in Natchez, Mississippi, observed that "slaves are made to shave and wash in greasy pot liquor, to make them look sleek and nice."[13] Robert Nealy, born into slavery, later recalled that his enslaver wiped greasy meat skins on children's mouths before slave auctions to make it look like they had eaten meat.[14]

Although enslaved people could not bring any belongings with them, they did bring tastes, cooking methods, rituals, and a vast knowledge about the natural world. The Columbian Exchange had brought many New World crops, especially corn, to Africa by the time that the slave trade to the British colonies began. Thus, Africans who came to Virginia after 1619—and especially those of the Igbo and Mande ethnic groups that were most represented among the early arrivals—were entering an agricultural landscape that was recognizable. They grew familiar crops like cabbages, spinach, black-eyed peas (cowpeas), okra, squash, watermelon, and peanuts, in addition to foraging in the woods for a wide variety of leaves and roots. Greens especially were a testament to the African legacy, with the West and Central African climate supporting a continuous supply of greens in the markets, gardens, and wild lands. Further, the use of cornbread to sop up potlikker mirrors the common Igbo practice of using fufu—starchy dough balls—to scoop up bites of stew.[15]

African tastes influenced not only what enslaved peoples ate, but also what African cooks prepared for their white enslavers, and thus influenced the broader Southern—and indeed American—diet. One of the most influential cookbooks of early America, Mary Randolph's 1823 *The Virginia Housewife*, included dishes made with the African vegetable okra, and West Indian dishes like pepper pot and gumbo. While Randolph was likely unaware that some of her core ingredients came from Africa, there is no doubt that the enslaved cooks who fed her and her politically significant family left their imprint through these foods and dishes.[16]

How the Enslaved Ate

Throughout the antebellum South, many enslaved people went hungry. This of course varied from plantation to plantation, with some enslaved workers likely receiving enough to eat, especially during harvest times. But many accounts refer to stark food deprivation. Frederick Douglass notably wrote of the "close-fisted stinginess that fed the poor slave on coarse corn-meal and tainted meat."[17] George Womble of Georgia recalled times that he was so hungry that he would take part of the food he was supposed to feed the cows—a "mixture of cotton seed, collard stalks, and small ears of corn"—and eat it himself under the cover of night.[18] Harriet Jacobs, who published *Incidents in the Life of a Slave Girl* in 1861 after her escape from slavery, described how one old man, "who had faithfully served the Flint family through three generations ... hobbled up to get his bit of meat," only to be met by the cruel mistress who "said he was too old to have any allowance [and] ... ought to be fed on grass."[19] The hunger and injustice were exacerbated by the abundance of food on the tables of many white enslavers.

In the earlier years, when enslaved people lived communally, they were often fed from a centralized kitchen. But as plantations grew and enslaved populations grew, this system shifted to a distribution of standard scheduled rations. These rations were monotonous and relatively meager, typically consisting of cornmeal and some pork or fish for adults, or broken rice in the Carolina low country. Sometimes they were given vegetables, but more often enslaved people grew vegetables on their own small plots of land, in addition to supplementing through hunting, fishing, and foraging, as described below. A number of accounts recall the lack of meat on some plantations, like that of Israel Jackson of Arkansas who said, "As for meat, we didn't know what dat was," or Eli Smith of Alabama, who described his diet as an enslaved child, as "ash-cake wid milk over hit, den sometime us had pot-licker and giv de grown folks de greens, dey didn't never give us no meat."[20] Children were often fed communally from large wooden troughs without the aid of utensils, with cornbreads crumbled into buttermilk or potlikker.

Adults were also often fed from troughs, reinforcing dehumanizing associations between enslaved people and animals. Author Michael Twitty recalls asking his grandmother in the later twentieth century why she crumbled cornbread in a glass of buttermilk, to which she replied, "At least I didn't have to eat it from a trough," testifying to the embodied memory of those slavery practices, even generations later.[21] The potlikker poured into those troughs was only one of the many "waste product" foods that enslavers cast off. Enslaved people were often given the "less desirable parts of an animal, such as ... the hog's tail, brain, gizzard, and chitterlings," especially during the winter "hog-killing" months.[22] Ruth Hastings, a white Northern tutor who traveled to a large South Carolina cotton plantation in 1852, reflected in a letter home, "They give the [slave] children ... bones half picked and bits of meat or anything they happen to eat at lunch."[23]

Other dimensions of food on plantations further highlight the inhumanity of slavery. Enslaved workers got very little time to eat in the middle of the day, with cooks bringing food—such as corncakes and a "tray wid cabbage an' bucket wid pot liquor"—to the fields, where they had just a few minutes to eat before the overseer called them back to work, often for many more hours of toil before sundown.[24] Many of Frederick Douglass's most poignant observations connect to feeding practices. He recalled how enslaved people who stole food out of desperation or dared ask for more were forced to eat large quantities of that food until they became sick; how one enslaver tarred the top of the fence of his beautiful garden so that any hungry enslaved person who tried to sneak in to take some fruit would be marked by tar and then "severely whipped by the chief gardener"; how the incongruousness of plentiful food and drink during the Christmas holidays was emblematic of "the gross fraud, wrong, and inhumanity of slavery" as the enslavers used this permissive time to prevent insurrection and foment conflict.[25]

-greens
-pork
-cornbread

What the Enslaved Ate

Our organizing food potlikker gives entrée into three important foods that poor Black and white southerners alike ate most often, all of which deserve a closer look. These were the central leafy greens, the pork with which they were cooked, and the cornbreads eaten alongside.

The tradition of eating greens was especially common among enslaved Africans and their descendants, in contrast to many white southerners. Native Americans further exposed enslaved people to a wide variety of wild greens. Eating many greens, like wild dandelions and the tops of beets and turnips, was a way to reduce food waste and take advantage of available nutrition. The warm Southern climate, like that of Western Africa, provided a longer growing season that allowed for several plantings of quick-growing leafy greens, even through the winter. Collard greens, which have come to be symbolic of African-American and Southern food, were brought to the Americas by European colonists, but were sustained and developed by African Americans, who were "likely the leading preservers of collard culture," according to geographers Edward Davis and John Morgan.[26] Enslaved people also ate turnip greens in their potlikker, salvaging the top part of the plant which white Southerners had often tossed aside in favor of the white bulbous root.[27] Cabbages, too, were a widely used vegetable whose tightly bound leaves yielded a rich potlikker.

The pork with which greens were cooked points to another core food of the American South. Pigs were brought to the Americas by the earliest Spanish colonists, but became the cheapest source of meat by the nineteenth century, as wild predators were eradicated and better breeding methods developed. Pigs produced large litters, could forage or be fed on any discarded food, and had muscle fibers that conformed to meat preservation like smoking or salting, in contrast to beef, which had to be eaten fresh in a time before refrigeration or widespread canning. Salt pork was thus the most common addition to potlikker, though ham hock, pigs' feet, bacon grease, or other meats could be used. The greasy meat helped season the iron pots to keep food from sticking to the surface, and the long cooking of potlikker helped break down the connective tissue of the lower-quality meats and the fibrous greens for easier digestion. Pigs and greens were often even raised together, with the muck of the pigpen fertilizing the growing greens seeded on its periphery. Although enslaved people were given the cast-off parts of the pig after hog-killing time, they were rarely allowed to raise hogs or other large animals themselves. And the act of stealing hogs was considered among the most serious crimes. Michael Twitty points out that it is likely no coincidence that Gabriel Prosser and Nat Turner, each of whom organized large slave revolts, are remembered as "devising their plots to overthrow the inequities of slavery while eating a meal of stolen roast hog."[28]

Finally, corn, as we know, was the foundational food of the Americas, introduced to the British colonists by the Native Americans. It came to be the primary food of enslaved Africans as well. The process of nixtamalization, developed thousands of years before in Mexico, made corn into hominy, a more nutritious and digestible form that allowed it to sustain a growing population of enslaved Africans in the North American colonies. The classic enslaved diet was referred to as "hog and hominy." Corn was typically ground into cornmeal and then combined with water to form a thick dough that was cooked in a variety of ways—baked on the griddle (or back of a hoe) for hoecake, in the skillet or oven for corn-pone or corn-dodger, or rolled in cabbage leaves and put directly in hot ashes for ashcake.[29]

Finding Sustenance

Enslaved people found ways—often through food-related practices—to resist and reclaim power where they could. They supplemented their rations through the practices of foraging, fishing, hunting, and gardening, all of which took advantage of their close environmental knowledge. And in some cases, they built their own economies, using their knowledge and labor for personal betterment.

In creating an agricultural landscape in America, colonists displaced native peoples and used the labor of enslaved peoples to cultivate land. As one historian writes, the "landscape was lifted from the forests and swamps literally on the backs of slaves," giving them a knowledge of the natural world that "was both detailed and practical."[30] Scottish-born Jen Schaw traveled through North Carolina in the 1770s, observing that "The Negroes are the only people that seem to pay any attention to the various uses that the wild vegetables may be put to."[31] They put these wild vegetables to use in supplementing their diets, finding medicinal herbs, and sometimes in poisoning their enslavers.[32] They also hunted when possible, learning methods for catching fish and small wild animals from their Native American neighbors. Solomon Northup, who wrote *Twelve Years a Slave* after his escape from slavery, wrote that it was customary to "hunt in the swamps for coon and opossum."[33] Although enslaved people rarely had access to guns, they used a variety of traps and snares. These practices offered a critical measure of independence and autonomy.

Gardens, perhaps most of all, offered diverse tastes and freedoms. On many plantations, enslaved people were given a small plot of land, sometimes called a truck-patch, on which to cultivate vegetables and sometimes raise chickens to supplement their diets. They had to squeeze in the garden work where they could, often turning the soil at night by the light of the moon after a long day in the fields, or on Sundays when they were given some free time. They grew a range of greens, beans, corn, squashes, sweet potatoes, melons, peanuts, and other vegetables—cultivating African gardening traditions and a space of psychological reprieve (Figure 5).

These gardens were also, at times, a space of economic reprieve, when enslaved people found markets for their produce. This produce was sometimes sold to the plantation owners, in exchange for cash, trade goods, or extra privileges. When cities lay nearby, enslaved people would bring their wares to urban markets. One visitor to rice plantation areas of the Carolinas noted enslaved people returning "from the city, whither they had taken their small wares—eggs, fowls, and vegetables—for sale, as they do two or three times a week."[34] By selling their preferred crops to their white neighbors, enslaved

FIGURE 5 *African-American woman tends a garden in front of old slave quarters on a plantation Thomastown, Louisiana. This photo was taken in 1940, but it conveys a sense of what some enslaved people's homes and subsistence gardens may have looked like (Smith Collection/Gado/Getty Images).*

Black people also shaped white diets, which began to incorporate these same crops. The market spaces also became meeting places, providing for human interactions that allowed "the yoke of enslavement [to be] lifted," if only "for a few brief moments."[35] And there were more cities in the South by the 1830s, as the region began to modernize in response to the rise of the Cotton Kingdom and the market and transportation revolutions of the time. Black people, both enslaved and free, also lived in these cities, often working with food—as domestic laborers, cooks, street vendors, and tavern workers. Free Black people flocked to cities and built their own communities, but still had limited rights.

In the Big House

A final space where enslaved Black southerners engaged with food—and shaped US history—was in the plantation owner's home, sometimes known as "the big house." Antebellum Southern kitchens and dining rooms came to be romanticized as part of a glorified Old South, with the abundance of the plantation table often credited to the white mistress. But in fact, it was the Black cooks who typically created this culinary splendor, shaping the creation of American cuisine.

In one scene of the hugely popular novel *Gone with the Wind*—which, along with the 1939 film version, perpetuated racist stereotypes and romanticized slavery—the protagonist Scarlett O'Hara recalls the delicious food on her family's plantation before the Civil War: "biscuits and waffles, dripping butter ... Ham at one end of the table and fried chicken at the other, collards swimming richly in pot liquor iridescent with grease, snap beans in mountains on brightly flowered porcelain ... and three desserts, so everyone might have his choice."[36] The opulence was overwhelming, but the coerced labor behind it was hidden.

Enslaved cooks' skills were highly valued, with slave advertisements referencing these abilities. They brought to the kitchen their knowledge of how to cook traditional African American food, such as hoecakes, potlikker, sweet potatoes, and fried chicken—a taste for which transferred to white plantation owners, even as Black people rarely received credit. Anthropologist Sidney Mintz writes that African influences on Americans have been obscured by the false "assumption that, under conditions of oppression, acculturation is a one-way street."[37] In fact, as Michael Twitty argues, "The Old South is a forgotten Little Africa but nobody speaks of it that way."[38] One of the most famous enslaved cooks, whose legacy in American food is evident, was James Hemings, who was enslaved by Thomas Jefferson and his wife Martha (who was also Hemings's half-sister). Hemings traveled with Jefferson

privilage &
challenge
in house cooking

to Paris, where he was trained alongside leading French chefs. He brought this training and taste for particular foods—"ice cream, spaghetti, cornbread stuffing, waffles, and vanilla" among them—back to Virginia, where he cooked for domestic and foreign leaders.[39] Although he earned his freedom from Jefferson, his life came to a tragic end, with death by suicide at the age of thirty-six, worn down by a lifetime of enslavement.[40]

Hemings's life points to both the privileges and tragedies of working in the kitchen. Working in the big house gave cooks—along with other enslaved domestic workers—some measure of power. They often were able to bring their children to work with them and live together above the kitchens. They had access to white conversations about politics and about plans for selling or punishing other enslaved people, which they could relay. They sometimes learned basic reading and arithmetic as was needed to read and interpret recipes. And at times they could eat better foods. But kitchen work also brought challenges. Black cooks were often under the watchful eye of white mistresses, who kept the keys to locked pantries and wielded their power, sometimes punishing cooks who made kitchen mistakes. In a time when their counterparts in the North were organizing reform societies, well-to-do women in the South were especially constrained by domestic duties, which they took seriously, often at the expense of enslaved laborers. And because most enslaved cooks were women, the kitchen could also be a dangerous place in a world filled with sexual violence. White plantation owners routinely raped and assaulted enslaved women, with the kitchen serving as one integrated space that was often the site of this exploitation.[41]

While the kitchen was part of the big house system, it was often physically located in a detached building, both to separate the fire hazards of the open hearth and to remove the enslaved people to a more segregated space as racial codes hardened. Food was cooked in iron pots, skillets, roasting spits, and Dutch ovens known as "spiders" inside the huge fireplace, which could be ten feet across. Other kitchen activities took place in external spaces like the garden, workyard, smokehouse, icehouse, and root cellar.[42] By the nineteenth century, as conflicts over the system of slavery intensified, these kitchen spaces were policed and surveilled more harshly as white enslavers feared that kitchen knives could be used as weapons and that food could be poisoned.[43]

The Civil War Looms

Such concerns about rebellion indicated the rising conflicts between the North and the South by the middle of the nineteenth century that help us to understand the wider backdrop against which the foodways of enslaved peoples developed. Although the 1820 Missouri Compromise had settled for the time being the question of whether new states would allow slavery, these problems took on new form with continued territorial expansion. Indian removal, the 1837 depression and its aftermath, the takeover of Southwestern lands from Mexico at the end of the Mexican-American War in 1848, and the beginning of the California gold rush that same year were all factors that drove expansion. The failure of the Wilmot Proviso in 1846, which would have banned slavery from territories taken from Mexico, revealed how deeply the country was divided along geographic lines, rather than party lines, with all northerners from both the Democrat and Whig parties voting for it, and most southerners voting against. Senator Henry Clay then negotiated the Compromise of 1850, a series of five laws, which brought California into the union as a free state, let Utah and New Mexico decide for themselves whether to allow slavery, banned the slave trade in Washington D.C., redefined the boundary between Texas and New Mexico, and passed the Fugitive Slave Act of 1850. The last was the most controversial, in that it gave federal agents the power to capture freedom seekers and return them to slavery without the right to a jury trial. It exposed the hypocrisy of white southerners who claimed they wanted states' rights, but who supported the federal government overriding local power in the case of returning runaways to their enslavers. This Act strengthened and made increasingly vital the Underground Railroad, a series of safe houses and hideaways that had allowed some 30,000 freedom seekers to escape from slavery since the 1830s.[44]

The abolition movement and sometimes-violent resistance also accelerated. Free Black communities continued to agitate for the antislavery struggle, along with white allies. The popular first-hand testimonies of people like Frederick Douglass who had escaped from enslavement—many of which relied on vivid illustrations of food deprivation and hunger to emphasize the injustices of slavery—brought abolitionist sentiment to wider audiences. Harriet Beecher Stowe's 1852 novel *Uncle Tom's Cabin* also became a key tool in the antislavery fight. The years 1855–9 saw violent fighting in Kansas over whether it would be a free or slave state, the savage attack of anti-slavery Senator Charles Sumner by the pro-slavery Congressman Preston Brooks on the Senate floor, the Dred Scott decision which denied American citizenship to Black people, and John Brown's raid on a federal armory at Harpers Ferry, Virginia in hopes of inspiring a slave revolt.

Southern enslavers, meanwhile, consolidated their commitment to this corrosive system. The growing population of enslaved people—reaching nearly 4 million by the beginning of the Civil War—made white Southerners especially fear rebellion and push for a strong pro-slavery government. Even as the North had begun to urbanize and industrialize (partly through textile factories that depended on cotton produced by enslaved labor), the South had put most of its stock in agriculture, making it wholly dependent on cotton production and the slavery that fueled it. An observer noted in 1857: "[slaves] and cotton—cotton and [slaves]; these are the law and the prophets to the men of the South."[45] Many Southern churches had come to preach a pro-slavery theology, which was used as one pillar of justification—along with deep-seated racism—for the system.

These rising conflicts were reflected in national politics, with the emergence of a number of anti-slavery political movements, including the Liberty Party and Free Soil Movement, and finally the Republican Party. The latter emerged by 1856 as a clear alternative to the southern pro-slavery Democratic party. In the 1860 election, the Republican party ran Abraham Lincoln as its candidate and he rose to victory, on the foundation abolitionists had been laying for many decades. In response to Lincoln's election, South Carolina seceded from the Union on December 21, 1860, due to the "increasing hostility on the part of the non-slaveholding States to the Institution of Slavery."[46] In the following months before Lincoln's inauguration in March 1861, Mississippi, Florida, Alabama, Georgia, Louisiana, and Texas followed South Carolina's lead, forming the Confederate States of America. By April 12, 1861, the confederate rebels opened fire on the Union's Fort Sumter in South Carolina, and the American Civil War had officially begun. The war would finally bring emancipation to millions of Black people in the United States, who would continue to turn to foods like potlikker for sustenance through the coming upheavals, as they had for centuries.

6

Peanuts:

The Civil War, Reconstruction, and After

In 1918, *The Peanut Promoter* journal printed a poem from Mrs. Jessie Bradford Bond, in which she reflected on the peanut's transformation: "... It used to be when circus-day came/You'd carry away a sackful in shame./ But now you eat 'em right on the street/ And so does every one else that you meet."[1] These rhyming lines pointed to a significant shift in how Americans consumed and viewed peanuts in the late nineteenth century and into the early twentieth. A 1908 article wrote that peanut used to be a "low caste nut," sold "mostly by dagos"—an ethnic slur that referred to Italian- or Spanish-speaking people. But this was no more. The article continued: "The peanut vendor is no longer an 'undesirable citizen,' to be 'moved on' by a policeman," and instead the peanut now "goes to pink teas" and is used to make "near-meat" products for vegetarian audiences, is made into peanut butter and candies, and is the focus of agricultural bulletins.[2] Even earlier, in 1903, Etta Morse Hudders speculated on why "the patrician palate has generally tabooed the peanut" and concluded that it was "possibly because this little plebeian has shown a marked preference for the sawdust of the circus" or because it grows low to the ground instead of from a "stately tree."[3]

In this moment when Hudders wrote, forty years after the end of slavery, in the middle of the repressive Jim Crow era, Hudders may have been too polite or evasive to point to a central reason that peanuts had so long been disparaged. But a 1913 *McClure's* article had no such reluctance: the author relayed how peanuts in the years after the Civil War were known as "n—r trash" in Virginia, and how New York merchants rejected the idea of buying Virginia peanuts to sell up North: "Peanuts! Who wanted peanuts? They might be all right for n——rs down South, but they were poor trash for white folks anywhere!"[4]

Since slavery's origin in the British colonies in 1619, enslaved Africans and their descendants had been the main group of people to cultivate and eat the peanut—or ground nut, pindar, or goober pea, as it was also known. It was also used as a food for hogs, further creating a negative association among white "patricians." Although the peanut's botanical origin is in Brazil, it traveled to Africa with Spanish and Portuguese traders by the seventeenth century, where it was widely adopted. When enslaved Africans were forced to North America, Bantu-speakers brought their knowledge and taste for *nguba* or *mpinda*—which evolved into "goober" and "pindar"—with them, growing them in their small gardens. The peanut is actually a legume, related to beans and peas, rather than a nut, despite its rich oil content and nutty taste.[5]

The peanut rose in status by the turn of the twentieth century, after coming to be more widely accepted over the course of the Civil War. After the war, during Reconstruction, it seemed that something similar might be possible for the Black people who had first recognized the peanut's value in the United States. But despite emancipation, the unfinished revolution of Reconstruction and the rise of Jim Crow only further subjugated Black Americans during this period. Immigrant laborers like the peanut vendors were also oppressed during the late nineteenth century, as they were subject to racist and nativist attacks, even as a coalescing notion of "whiteness" would alter their ethnic identities. Nevertheless, along with immigrant labor, it was Black agricultural and intellectual work that would help launch the peanut. Black men, women, and children—many of them sharecroppers—picked, sorted, and cleaned the peanuts that were sold onward. And Black geniuses like Ben Hicks, who invented a mechanical peanut picker, and George Washington Carver, who promoted the peanut as a tool of Black economic uplift and came to be known as "Peanut Man," are central to this story. Through their work, peanuts rose from food of the enslaved, to food vended by immigrants in burgeoning cities, to food served at vegetarian sanitariums and suffragist tea parties.

Hunger in the Civil War

The Civil War was a turning point for many aspects of American history, including food. The war launched the beginning of a wider acceptance of peanuts, as soldiers on the move became exposed to new foods and wartime scarcity required food substitutions. Food in general was central to the war, with hunger used as a key tool of warfare. The diverse agricultural production of the North, mechanization in farming and food processing, and railroad construction for food distribution were all key factors in the United States' eventual victory—though this outcome was by no means inevitable at the start of the war.

When secession began in 1860, the South was quite wealthy, but its economy was dominated by cotton and was very unevenly distributed. The emphasis on cotton agriculture in the antebellum period meant that the South had to import much of its food supply from the Midwest and North. As the war began, many white Southern farmers left to fight and were thus unable to produce more food, and even those who stayed behind and tried to grow food were often limited by the lack of transportation to distribute their goods. The North had 70 percent of the country's railroad mileage, and six times the number of factories.[6] The Confederates hoped that their cotton production would still save them, by bringing Britain and France—whose textile industries depended on that cotton—aboard as allies, leading to a quick end to the war with a Confederate victory. But this was not to be. Instead, Europe turned to increased cotton production in Brazil, Egypt, and India to supply its needs, even as the South continued to grow more cotton during the war instead of increasing food production and distribution.

The North, meanwhile, had invested heavily in food production and distribution in the antebellum period. Grain production had soared with the adoption of McCormick's reaper and other machines; urbanization in the northeast had created a demand for farmers to grow food for regional markets rather than export crops; new immigrants to the North provided inexpensive labor and military manpower; a Chicago meatpacking industry supported by Great Lakes ice for food preservation made beef and pork cheaper and more widely available; and a Northern canning industry began to grow. Further, railroad mileage had expanded to support the distribution of this abundance. All of this development and mechanization meant that more food could be grown with less labor, which both created surplus that the United States could ship abroad to maintain European support and freed up farmworkers to enlist in the US army.

In April 1861, President Lincoln declared a blockade of Southern ports to prevent exports of cotton and other cash crops and to prevent imports of food and other supplies, both from abroad and from the Northern United States. This was part of a US strategy of "starving the South," along the lines of the proposed Anaconda Plan, which hoped to squeeze the Confederacy from all sides. In order to police the 3,500 miles of Southern coastline, Lincoln recalled naval ships, converted merchant ships into gunboats, and directed vast ship-building efforts.[7]

Confederates tried to get around the blockade by using private ships, called blockade runners, to access imported goods. Wealthy Southerners were willing to pay high prices for luxury goods from the blockade runners, which meant those ships focused more on specialty items than on staple goods to support a wider population. Southerners turned to food substitutes and attempts at local cultivation. A schoolteacher in Southern Alabama later recalled: "When the blockade had inclosed the South, our planters set about in earnest to grow wheat, rye, rice, oats, corn, peas, pumpkin, and groundpeas …. Rarely grown before the war, [ground peas] were generally called 'goobers' [or peanuts]."[8] Peanuts were also a versatile substitute, providing oil that could be used in cooking and baking, soap-making, burning for illumination, or as a lubricant in a wide range of machinery. The little legume was one of many substitutes used in place of imported coffee, in addition to okra seeds, acorns, beets, cotton seeds, and many others. One 1863 cookbook, the *Confederate Receipt Book,* offered substitute coffee recipes along with ways to make "bread without yeast and piecrusts out of potatoes … apple pie without apples, [and] artificial oysters made from green corn."[9] The blockade also limited Southern access to salt, which was critical to meat preservation, vegetable brining, and feeding draft animals.

Following Lincoln's declaration of the blockade after the first shots were fired at Fort Sumter, early battles made clear that the war would not be over quickly. The capture of New Orleans by the US Army in April 1862 meant that the United States now controlled the mouth of the Mississippi River, through which agricultural goods could be transported. A few months later, the US Army won a decisive enough victory at Antietam, Maryland— the bloodiest single day in American history and the first battle fought on Northern soil—that President Lincoln felt emboldened enough to issue the Emancipation Proclamation to take effect January 1, 1863, freeing enslaved peoples in Confederate areas. Although described as a military measure, this proclamation signaled a turning point in both Lincoln's views on slavery and the aim of the Civil War—making it not just about keeping the nation together, but about ending slavery. After this, Black Americans served in the US Army, where they were sometimes put in menial roles. They were treated poorly and often fed inferior food, though even this was better than what they left behind for those fleeing slavery. One formerly enslaved person was asked whether the Emancipation Proclamation had prompted his joining the US Army. "No, missus," he replied, "we never hear nothing like it. We's starving, and we come to get somfin' to eat. Dat's what we come for."[10]

Even as battles continued in 1862, the US Congress took advantage of the absence of states' rights Southerners who had previously blocked federal legislation to pass a number of critical acts that would shape US food and agriculture into the future. These included the creation of the US Department of Agriculture; the passage of the Morrill Land Grant College Act, which sold Western lands taken from Native Americans in order to fund the creation of agricultural colleges in every state; the Homestead Act, which encouraged western expansion by offering free 160-acre plots of land to farmers; and the Pacific Railway Act, which supported the creation of a transcontinental railroad across the entire country as a distribution network for food, crops, and people. These moves dramatically increased the size and power of the federal government and economy. All of these acts, and the Civil War as a whole, also had devastating effects on Native American populations. At the beginning of the war, troops stationed in the west to protect Indian lands were recalled; the resulting conflicts led to the US-Dakota War of 1862 and the largest official execution in American history, of thirty-eight Dakota people in Minnesota.

As US Army soldiers from the North encountered new environments in the South, they also encountered new foods. Peanut cultivation before the war was centered in eastern Virginia, such that soldiers stationed there developed a taste for the legumes, which they brought home with them, leading to a tripling of peanut production between 1865 and 1870 after the war, with much of those peanuts destined for northern cities.[11] Tastes for other foods also developed due to wartime exposure, like canned foods, which, although not part of soldiers' standard rations, were common in camps of the US army, often sold by traveling merchants called sutlers. The standard rations for soldiers—though officers ate better—included a dense cracker called hardtack, small amounts of preserved meat, corn meal, dried beans, coffee, sugar, and salt. As one soldier commented, "these ... boys ... out-Graham Sylvester Graham himself, in his most radical ideas of simplicity in diet ... Coarse meal, cold water and salt have been the ingredients composing many a meal for us."[12] This paltry food supply combined with food that was often spoiled contributed to the high death rates from diseases like dysentery, scurvy, and typhoid. Some soldiers lived off the land by foraging for "scallions, dandelions, and groundnuts [peanuts]." Others "foraged" for food in a different way, in some cases supported by the Confederate policy of impressment—which meant seizing food from local farmers and civilians, often without pay.[13] Still, even in the midst of terrible conditions, food could sometimes offer a place of community, as described in the most famous peanut-related relic of the Civil War, the folk song "Goober Peas," which describes, "Sitting by the roadside on a summer's day/Chatting with my mess-mates, passing time away ... /Goodness, how delicious, eating goober peas."[14]

Goober peas or not, the winter of 1862–3 was especially difficult for the Confederate rebels, as they struggled to keep supply lines open to feed their soldiers. The US army had captured the major food-producing parts of the South and had been conducting raids through the lower South after capturing central Tennessee. By February 1863, a Mississippi newspaper wrote, "There is more to fear from a dearth of food than from all the Federal armies in existence."[15] In April 1863, desperate white women in Richmond, Virginia, the capital of the Confederacy, organized a food riot when they felt that the Confederate government ignored their hunger and the rampant inflation caused by hoarding and speculation. Thousands of women "armed with hatchets, pistols, clubs," screaming "bread or blood," descended on downtown businesses and a government storehouse.[16] This riot, and many others that took place throughout the South, symbolized the political mobilization of white women driven by desperation, despite prevailing antebellum gender expectations.

July 1863 brought two pivotal battles, at Gettysburg, Pennsylvania and Vicksburg, Mississippi—both with food at their center. The Confederate General Robert E. Lee decided to invade Pennsylvania at Gettysburg in part because he "hoped to find more abundant provisions" for his men who had been reduced to "collecting wild onions and sassafras buds to survive." Despite heavy casualties on both sides, the US Army prevailed. Meanwhile, after a six-week siege of Vicksburg, food supplies had been so depleted that the Confederate army surrendered, giving the United States full control of the Mississippi River and splitting the Confederacy in half. Soldiers of the US Army, however, acknowledged that the Confederates had "surrendered to famine, not to them."[17]

After these turning points, the war continued for nearly two more years, with grueling hunger and deadly battles. The US Army plundered the Shenandoah Valley in Virginia, the Confederacy's breadbasket, removing it as a source of subsistence. Then, General William Sherman marched through the Carolinas and Georgia, capturing Atlanta and leaving a path of destruction. Along the way, Sherman's 60,000 soldiers "took the thirty tons of food they needed each day from the farm and homes of Southern civilians" based on "special maps drawn up from the 1860 census that showed the crop yields for each county in Georgia."[18] These events boosted Northern morale, fostering Lincoln's re-election in November 1864 and the subsequent passage by Congress of the Thirteenth Amendment in January 1865, officially abolishing slavery. By March 1865, Robert E. Lee was feeling discouraged and frustrated by the lack of support from the Confederate government, saying to his son, "I have been up to see the Congress and they do not seem to be able to do anything except to eat peanuts and chew tobacco, while my army is starving."[19] As his soldiers in the Army of Northern Virginia deserted due to their own hunger and that of their families back home, and were reduced to eating horse feed, Lee surrendered at Appomattox Courthouse on April 9, 1865. The US Army General Ulysses S. Grant accepted the surrender and then sent three days of rations to the starving former Confederate soldiers.[20] As a tragic coda to the war's end, Confederate sympathizer John Wilkes Booth assassinated President Lincoln five days later, leaving Vice President Andrew Johnson to assume the Presidency and the dramatic challenge of rebuilding a broken nation.

A Period of Attempted Reconstruction

At the end of the war, the United States had defeated rebellion and abolished slavery. But the country faced very challenging prospects: destroyed Southern urban and agricultural landscapes; formerly enslaved people who were technically "free" but lacked land, education, and opportunities; conflicting plans for how the treasonous Confederate states could rejoin the Union; and numerous southern governments that quickly passed "Black Codes," which severely limited Black freedoms. George Washington Carver, the agricultural scientist who would become "Peanut Man" due to his agricultural innovations around peanuts and other crops in the early twentieth century, was born at the end of the Civil War.[21] His early life thus offers a useful lens for understanding this postwar period of Reconstruction (1865–77), which held revolutionary potential that was tragically left unfulfilled.

Carver was born in enslavement, the property of Moses Carver in Missouri. At the war's end, he was freed, but remained in his former enslaver's care, as George Carver's mother and father had recently died. Other freedpeople also frequently remained on the land they had previously worked under slavery, with few other options provided to them. In early 1865, even before the war had ended, General Sherman ordered forty-acre plots of land to be set aside for Black families on the South Carolina and Georgia coasts, along with broken-down army mules, to be used for farming. This "forty acres and a mule" offered hope of real economic independence through land reform. But when the racist and states'-rights Southerner Andrew Johnson came to power after Lincoln's assassination, he ordered the army to forcibly evict these Black farmers who had settled on "Sherman land." Freedmen from South Carolina pleaded with Johnson, writing, "with deep sorrow and Painful hearts [we have learned] of the possibility of government restoring These lands to the former owners .... Here is where we have toiled nearly all Our lives as slaves and treated like dumb Driven cattle. This is our home, we have made These lands what they were. we are the only true and Loyal people ... Land monopoly is injurious to the advancement of the course of freedom."[22] Despite these pleas, and later efforts by the Freedmen's Bureau and Radical Republicans in Congress, no significant land redistribution efforts took place. In fact, formerly enslaved people became trapped in a system of sharecropping, often based on the same cotton agriculture which had bound them in the antebellum period. They came to farm the land of large landowners and paid rent through a share of the crop at harvest time. Frequently, sharecroppers—both Black and white—went into debt, and were thus trapped on the land.

There were other signs of hope during Reconstruction, however. Against Johnson's opposition, Congress passed the three Reconstruction

Amendments—the Thirteenth to abolish slavery; the Fourteenth to grant citizenship and equal protection to all people, which entrenched the 1866 Civil Rights Act and overrode the previous Black Codes; and the Fifteenth to give all men (but not women) the right to vote. The federal government also created the Freedmen's Bureau, which lasted from 1865 to 1870, and worked to offer education, legal and financial support, and dispute resolution to freedpeople. With limited funds and agents, however, the Bureau faced "Hercules' task," according to General Sherman.[23] But Black people in the South did establish schools to satisfy their immense thirst for education after so many years of deprivation. Like George Carver, who would travel throughout the Midwest in search of better schooling, freedpeople everywhere intensely desired education. Author Harriet Beecher Stowe observed that freedpeople rushed "to the schoolroom—they cried for the spelling-book as bread, and pleaded for teachers as a necessity of life."[24] The Black school movement also laid the foundation for the broader public school system throughout the South. Furthermore, Black people gained real—if limited—political power during Reconstruction, with some 2,000 Black public office-holders and a number of Black legislators in the South not seen again until the 1990s.[25]

But the temporary success of the biracial democratic government soon triggered immense backlash. By 1875, for example, segregation had become state policy in Missouri, where Carver lived, such that he had to travel eight miles south to Neosho to attend a school that would accept him. Just as violence had been used under slavery to enforce white supremacy, so too did white vigilante groups like the Ku Klux Klan and others emerge to terrorize Blacks, through savage beatings, rapes, and lynchings. Soon after moving to Kansas to go to a better school, Carver witnessed a lynching of a young Black man by an "immense crowd of people numbering fully 1,000." Carver later recalled at the end of his life: "the horror haunted me and does even now."[26] Acts of terror like this sought to destroy the Republican Party in the South, and to suppress Black political and economic participation. Although the federal government intervened to help suppress the terror around 1870, by 1877 the so-called "Redeemers" had reclaimed control of Southern politics, further subjugated Black people, and undermined much of the progress of Reconstruction. These events, combined with an 1873 depression that weakened Northern support for financial investment in the South, led to the Compromise of 1877, in which the Southern Democrats agreed to concede a contested presidential election to the Republican Rutherford B. Hayes if he ordered the end of Reconstruction. And thus, a period of potential revolution went unfinished, with significant backsliding in the years to come.

The Peanut Begins Its Ascent

Even as Reconstruction ended, the peanut—once a food of enslaved people and hogs—began to rise in popularity, achieving a mainstream acceptance that Black Americans were themselves denied. The Civil War prompted a wider exposure to the peanut, both through its use as a substitute and through soldiers' exposure to the little legume while stationed in Virginia. Production rose from 150,000 bushels in 1860, to two million by 1883, to eight million by 1895.[27] This embrace of the peanut amidst accelerating racism can be considered a part of the postwar rise of a "Lost Cause" narrative, which romanticized the antebellum South, minimized slavery's brutality, pictured the Civil War as a "war between brothers" over state's rights rather than about slavery, and painted Reconstruction as a failure because of Black political power. Peanuts, decoupled from their links to Black people, were one of many foods of the Old South embraced as part of an ahistorical fantasy in which "the culinary contributions of African Americans went the way of the indigenous influences: ingredients, techniques, and dishes were celebrated as uniquely Southern, but the labor, traditions, and cultures from which these meals emerged were often left out of the discussion."[28]

As peanut production increased, the author of an 1871 *Scientific American* article wondered, "But who eats them?" A peanut vendor responded to the author's skeptical question, reporting confidently that "everybody ate them, 'from the wealthy banker to the homeless newsboy.'"[29] Even as journalists and others would continue to question the social status of peanuts for the next several decades, actual consumption continued to increase and diversify, for many intertwined reasons, explored below.

In the years after the Civil War, peanut promoters around Norfolk, Virginia who wanted to revive the postwar Southern economy—Thomas B. Rowland central among them—encouraged local farmers to grow peanuts and encouraged merchants in New York City to buy and sell them. Politicians stepped in to help out: Virginia Representative James H. Platt introduced a peanut tariff in 1879, though "a large majority of the members of that august body hardly knew what a peanut was."[30] The rise of the railroad created a distribution network for peanuts and helped move people into cities, which became burgeoning markets. Mechanization of agriculture during the war not only allowed the North to produce food surpluses but also meant that when soldiers went home after the war, their labor was no longer needed, which spurred urbanization. By 1885, one commentator observed, "One cannot pass along the streets of any of our larger cities and towns, without encountering, at every turn, the little peanut stands, where roasted peanuts are sold by the pint. They are kept for sale in numerous shops, they are peddled on the railroad cars, and sold to the loungers at every depot."[31] Once in the cities, Americans who had previously spent all their time on farms working and eating along with the rhythms of the sun and the seasons found themselves detached from food production and in search of entertainment. The rise of snacking, and places for snacking—theaters, circuses, baseball arenas—were a boon for peanut consumption. Legend has it that an Italian man named Petroni convinced P. T. Barnum to let him sell peanuts at the great circus, creating a longstanding association.[32]

Throughout the late nineteenth century, peanut production improved through the development of machines that reduced the crop's labor-intensiveness—planting, picking, cleaning, shelling, roasting, etc. Though of course the need for labor continued, as with the peanut factories "where thousands of colored women are employed in assorting the peanuts in grades and getting them ready for market."[33] Agricultural and nutrition science began to turn its attention to the peanut, solving its agricultural problems and promoting its healthfulness, at a high point for agricultural science, after the passage of the federal Hatch Act of 1887 established agricultural experiment stations at state land-grant universities. Soon, companies joined together to form trade organizations, like the 1895 Virginia Peanut Association, to promote the general interests of the industry. And by 1900, peanut butter had been developed and then popularized through the work of John Harvey Kellogg at the Battle Creek Sanitarium, which catered to vegetarians and those looking for health cures. This movement also promoted the incorporation of peanuts into "mock meats" like Ella Eaton Kellogg's Protose and Almeda Lambert's recipes in her 1899 *Guide for Nut Cookery.*[34]

Throughout this period of urbanization and mechanization, it was immigrant peanut vendors who were the conduit between these production changes and consumers themselves. Following the path of African American vendors who had often sold their goods in antebellum cities, immigrant vendors, especially from Italy, found work in peddling peanuts and other wares bought from commission men and distributed via pushcart throughout big cities like New York and Boston. In a time when few large grocery stores existed and grocers "considered peanuts beneath their dignity," street vendors were crucial.[35] But they were also often derided, for their "aggressive, often insolent salesmanship" and for being "undesirable citizen[s]" and general nuisances. This was against a broader backdrop of nativism, in which many feared that the influx of so-called "new immigrants" from Asia and Southern and Eastern Europe posed a threat to white America—culminating in the 1882 Chinese Exclusion Act, the 1894 founding of the Immigration Restriction League, and other anti-immigrant movements. In a time when "whiteness" was not a monolithic category, Italians were subject to racist attacks tied to anti-Black sentiment, as they were described as "'swarthy,' 'kinky haired' members of a criminal race" who were "links in a descending chain of evolution."[36] Such racist attacks, along with menial labor tied to peanuts and other agricultural products, however, found their fullest form in relation to Black Americans in the later nineteenth century.

Black Life and Labor after Reconstruction

As the peanut market grew, it was mostly African American labor that supported the industry. The agricultural work was "at best a dusty and laborious task."[37] And in the summer months, "The weather is hot, close, and enervating; the frequent stopping and picking makes it doubly laborious."[38] A characteristic image from 1911 shows seven Black people—mostly women and children—picking peanuts by hand in southern Virginia, as they squint into the sun or focus on their task, with dusty fields behind them.[39] For the most part, Black farmworkers made little profit off of peanuts and other crops. A 1905 article described those who come to the peanut-cleaning factories: "There is the old negro farmer, with one or two bags, which constitutes his entire crop, as well as his more prosperous neighbor, with several hundred bags."[40] The "more prosperous neighbor" is assumed to be a white man, by contrast. Although Black landownership did increase around the turn of the twentieth century, it was disproportionately distributed, with Black farmers in the Lower South—the center of sharecropping—actually owning relatively less land in 1900 as compared with the end of Reconstruction.[41]

This land poverty was tied to the broader rise of Black disenfranchisement, segregation, and lynching that characterized Black life until the civil rights movement. A group of Black people who left North Carolina for Indiana in 1881 explained to a journalist that "although nominally free since the war, our condition in the South was in fact one of servitude, and was each year becoming worse," with low wages, discriminatory laws, imprisonment, and increasing deprivation of their "political rights, by fraud if not by violence."[42] Between 1890 and 1906, southern states limited Black voting through indirect means, using poll taxes, discriminatory literacy tests, and grandfather clauses. In one dramatic example, the number of Black registered voters in Louisiana went from 130,000 in 1894 to 1,342 by 1904.[43] De facto segregation across many institutions—schools, hospitals, bathrooms, public transportation—became codified with the 1896 *Plessy v. Ferguson* case, with Black facilities far inferior. The public murder of Black people through lynching was widespread, especially in the South, with more than 4,400 documented lynching victims between 1877 and 1950.[44] Reformer Ida B. Wells-Barnett railed against "the United States government [which] stands by [protecting] those who stone and burn [the Negro] to death literally and politically."[45]

It was in this context that the Black leader Booker T. Washington hired George Washington Carver to come to the Tuskegee Institute, which served Black students in rural Alabama, in 1896 to lead its new agricultural department. Although Washington has been criticized for his "accommodationist" approach to Black uplift that tolerated segregation, his vision of education and agricultural improvement "helped millions of black farmers and created the capacity for autonomous agrarian community."[46] In 1896, Carver was the only Black person in the whole country with a graduate degree in the agricultural sciences. He came to Alabama with a unified ecological and justice-oriented vision that sought to empower the regions' Black farmers to abandon the tyranny of cotton by "looking to the resources of local landscapes to restore fertility and rejuvenate their lands."[47] An early proponent of what we now call sustainable agriculture, Carver argued that cover crops and nitrogen-fixing legumes—like peanuts—could restore the soil. Although he didn't turn his devoted attention to peanuts until after 1915, they embodied his lifelong focus on thoughtful agriculture as a tool of enrichment.

A final story in this tale of the peanut is that of Ben Hicks, a Black farmer and blacksmith in turn-of-the-century Virginia who invented a number of mechanical devices for peanut agriculture (Figure 6). Despite the power of his innovation, his social and racial position meant that his ideas were co-opted by white businessmen and Hicks has been largely lost to history. The records that remain are from a court case in which the Benthall Machinery Company of Suffolk, Virginia sued Hicks for use of a peanut picking machine that they had patented, and an appeal in which Hicks proved that he had actually patented an identical machine earlier. The problem had arisen because Hicks, who was illiterate, had hired a patent attorney to draw up a patent in 1901. The attorney had failed to include two key aspects of Hicks's complex machine, which the Benthall company tried to exploit in making its own case for originality. In the appeal in 1916, Hicks's attorney brought witnesses to testify that Hicks's original machine was functionally identical to the Benthall machine, contradicting the incomplete patent application and suggesting that it was in fact Benthall who stole the idea from Hicks. Many witnesses were available to testify on Hicks's behalf because, as Hicks testified, "there was so many came there to see such a curiosity, a piece of n——r enterprise; I can't tell you." In this quote and others, Hicks diminished his own accomplishments, seeming deferential and nervous in a white court of law. For their part, the Benthall company insisted that "the construction of the Ben Hicks machine was crude, and therefore did not rise to the dignity of an invention."[48] The appeals court, thankfully, found otherwise, and overturned the lawsuit against Hicks. But Hicks never received the recognition or fortune he was owed for his tremendous innovation.

FIGURE 6 *Historical marker and portrait of Ben Hicks, a Black farmer and blacksmith who never received proper credit for his invention of a mechanical peanut picking machine (Courtesy of Anne W. Bryant and the Southampton Heritage Village/Agriculture & Forestry Museum).*

Thus, Black laborers picked and processed peanuts, Carver helped create consumer demand for peanuts and used peanut agriculture to try to improve Black lives in the rural South, and Ben Hicks revolutionized mechanized peanut farming. All of these contributions, along with the Civil War stimulus, postwar transformations, and immigrant vendors, led to the "social rise of the peanut" by the early twentieth century. A 1902 *Good Housekeeping* article of the same name featured a cartoon peanut wearing a top hat, monocle, and white gloves—presaging Planters' Mr. Peanut.[49] This "patrician" image stood in shockingly stark contrast to the social position of Black Americans around 1900. Though they helped bring peanuts to prominence, their own lives continued to be shackled by racism and discrimination.

7

Jell-O:

Industrialization in the Gilded Age and Progressive Era

In 1902, the first magazine advertisement for Jell-O appeared in the pages of *Ladies Home Journal*. "No boiling! No baking!," the ad read, "Simply add boiling water and set to cool"[1] (Figure 7). These instructions underscored the fact that this was a new product, promising a dessert quite unlike any Americans had experienced before. The many Jell-O ads that flooded the American media scene in the years to follow referred to a wide range of the new product's strengths: it was pure, dainty, colorful, adaptable, available in a range of flavors, easy to prepare, easy to digest, good for the sick, good for children, accessible for the rich and poor alike, produced by happy American workers who never had labor troubles, and endorsed by leading home economists. But one thing that was rarely mentioned in these ads was *what Jell-O actually was*.

A rare 1909 recipe booklet tiptoed around the question: "The base of Jell-O, the chief ingredient, is crystal gelatine—delicate white, translucent, and pure and clean as falling snow, combined with extra-fine granulated sugar. The fruit elements ... are added by the nicest of modern scientific processes in one of the finest food factories in the world."[2] Even more unusually, another booklet from the 1910s delved farther into where that snowy gelatin came from: "Starting from the cartilaginous parts, this pure food product is obtained by a long series of boilings and filterings in the form of a delicate, colorless and transparent jelly from which every trace of grossness has been removed ..."[3] And, of course, the "cartilaginous parts" referred to parts of animals, of cows and pigs who had been slaughtered for meat production. As the meatpacking industry grew in size and sophistication, it found the key to its profitability in selling its many byproducts—gelatin among them.

FIGURE 7 *This Jell-O advertisement from a June 1902 issue of* Ladies Home Journal *introduced a new food product that embodied industrialization at the turn of the twentieth century.*

The rise of Jell-O is a story of the Progressive Era pure food movement in the early twentieth century, of the development of domestic science, and of the emergence of food advertising and branding. But as the link to gelatin's origins indicates, it is also a story of meatpacking and its byproducts, of industrial cattle displacing the indigenous bison on the Great Plains to supply the meatpackers, and of a broader industrialized food system that took hold around 1900, and has never let go in the years since.

It wasn't just food that was industrializing in these transformative years, but practically everything in the United States, in both rural and urban areas. New transportation and communication technologies like the railroad and the telegraph brought mobility and the development of huge corporations, which extracted natural resources from the West and funneled them eastward, destroying Indigenous communities and biota in the process. Cities grew rapidly, filling with millions of immigrants and with rural people displaced by agricultural mechanization. These people worked in the new smoke-bellowing factories, lived in crowded slums, and struggled with immense inequality. Some of them organized in a blossoming labor movement to push against the concentration of wealth and the exploitation of workers. The significant problems that emerged from all this change were often hidden beneath the facade of new wealth and technologies, giving the era between about the 1870s and 1900 its name: the Gilded Age. The surface may have seemed golden, or gilded, but troubles lay beneath. By the late nineteenth century, reformers proposed a wide range of solutions to these problems of industrialization and urbanization, their progressive vision giving its name to this period between about the 1890s and 1910s: the Progressive Era. Progressive reformers took up issues as diverse as labor reform, food safety, prohibition of alcohol, women's suffrage, public health, corrupt politics and business practices, environmental conservation, and more. They had faith in science, expertise, efficiency, and were optimistic about modifying existing systems, rather than calling for more radical or systemic change.

Jell-O, the hard-to-define new dessert that emerged around 1900, was a product of some of the problems created by industrialization and a solution to others. The same domestic scientists and food industry advertising executives who created Jell-O also molded and defined a new era in American history.

The Creation of Jell-O

Before Jell-O was trademarked in 1897, gelatin had been an ingredient in cooking for several centuries. But isolating it was an arduous process, involving slaughtering animals (usually cows or pigs), cutting off their feet *for rich - bc of hard labor*

(or other parts like bones or connective tissues), scalding them to remove hair, extracting the fat within, and then boiling and clarifying for many hours and repetitions before straining through homemade jelly bags. Because of this difficult and dirty labor, gelatin was typically a food of the rich, eaten by those who could afford servants to prepare it and the refrigeration needed to cool and set it. Otherwise, it was to be avoided. As Mary Henderson wrote in her 1881 cookbook: "I have made calf's-foot jelly twice, and never intend to make it again."[4]

Made from animals

In 1845, Peter Cooper, inventor of America's first steam-powered locomotive, filed a patent for pre-made gelatin sheets. But his invention foundered until the later nineteenth century, when several firms took up the project of commercial gelatin production, an early convenience food product. Most of them sold a kind of gelatin powder that could be mixed with flavors and colorings at home. But Pearle and May Wait, of LeRoy, New York, had the idea to pre-mix the gelatin, sugar, color, and fruit flavor and sell the resulting unified product. Likely inspired by the coffee substitute Grain-O, marketed by their neighbor Orator Woodward, the Waits called their product "Jell-O." A couple of years later, failing to make any money off of Jell-O, the Waits sold the rights to Jell-O to that same neighbor, Orator Woodward, president of the Genesee Pure Food Company. By 1906, Genesee was selling $1 million worth of Jell-O.[5]

Oservants

memory of a product

But where was all this gelatin coming from in the first place? Even if housewives were no longer boiling calves' feet themselves, animal body parts were still needed to supply the production of Jell-O. To answer this question, we have to travel back in time and into the US West.

The Trade in Animal Byproducts

A ready supply of gelatin required lots of animal parts, which the emerging meatpacking industry was more than happy to provide. The meatpackers, for their part, required lots of cows and pigs. In the case of cows, land had to be cleared to raise cattle. As historian Joshua Specht writes, "The land and its inhabitations had to be pacified, the canvas cleared, for the coming of the Cattle Kingdom."[6] A key to that "pacification" was the railroad. In 1869, the transcontinental railroad was completed, spanning the entire United States in one continuous rail line. Settlers, businesses, and the federal government made use of the railroad, with revolutionary effects: opening up the West to population settlement and food production, leading to a national distribution system and national culinary style, increasing the extraction of natural resources, and furthering the displacement of Native Americans. Continuous

Dawes Act 1887.

with the ways that white settlers had encroached upon Native American land and life for centuries, the US government passed the Dawes Act in 1887 to splinter Native American reservations and traditional tribal units, violently subdued Native American resistance as in the 1890 Wounded Knee Massacre, and forced Indigenous children to attend assimilationist boarding schools.

Killing Bison but not taking all of it

The great bison herds that had long lived symbiotically with Plains Indians were another target of Western expansion—their destruction led to widespread hunger and starvation, which weakened Indian resistance. Tens of millions of bison had lived on the Plains as late as 1800, gathering in such large numbers "as literally to blacken the prairies for miles together."[7] But as the bison trade developed in the nineteenth century and railroad access grew, market hunters poured onto the prairies, shipping back mountains of bison hides and tongues to be processed and sold in the east. They killed with abandon, thoroughly destroying the thundering herds by the early 1880s. Colonel Richard Dodge wrote in 1877, "The air was foul with a sickening stench, and the vast plain which only a short twelvemonth before teemed with animal life, was a dead, solitary, putrid desert."[8]

SHOCKING COWBOYS

The "grass-bison-nomad system" that had previously predominated now shifted to a "grass-cattle-rancher one," with cattle filling the former eco-niches of the bison.[9] Cowboys served as a critical linchpin between human population centers in the east and cattle in the west. In the 1860s and 1870s, these iconic workers drove herds from Texas to railheads in Kansas, where they were then shipped to Chicago for slaughter, reduction to meat and byproducts like gelatin, and distribution. These cowboys were celebrated and popularized in the vaudeville shows and dime-store novels of the turn of the twentieth century as masculine white men who embodied an idealized frontier spirit. In reality, however, cowboys were hardly independent, but intertwined with the urbanized, national economic networks. As historian William Cronon argues, "far from being a loner or a rugged individualist, [the cowboy] was a wageworker whose task was to ship meat to the cities—above all, to Chicago."[10] Moreover, contrary to the prevailing image, around a quarter of cowboys were Black, and at least as many were of Mexican heritage.

Chicago was the new center of the meatpacking industry, outpacing the previous leader Cincinnati (aka "Porkopolis") in the years after the Civil War. The city grew spectacularly, from 200 residents in 1833 to more than a million by 1890. The meatpacking business quickly consolidated, with four companies—Armour, Swift, Morris, and Hammond—controlling most of Chicago's meat supply, which produced 82 percent of all meat in the United States. These industrial giants were drawn to Chicago by the Union Stock Yard, a centralized stockyard served by railroads that shipped meat products to the rest of the country. In that square mile just south of the city, animals entered, mooing and oinking, and then met their fate with a knock to the head and swinging knives that separated the once-living animals into blood, skin, hoofs, hides, head, intestines, and meat products through an efficient "disassembly line." As one visitor noted, "the whole business [is] ... tainted with cruelty and brutality."[11] In this space, animals' lives and connections to the lands from where they came were devalued and forgotten.

Once animals were killed in Chicago, their meat had to be delivered to consumers in cities, most of which were located on the East Coast, before it spoiled. In earlier eras, transporting meat was more easily done with pig flesh, the muscle fibers of which could be salted and smoked and therefore preserved for transport. But beef required a different touch. The invention of refrigerated railcars by the early 1870s, with major innovations by Gustavus Swift, led to a new market in refrigerated, or "dressed," beef. Cooled by ice cut from nearby lakes, and then resupplied by icing stations all along the route to New York City, beef could be shipped from a slaughterhouse in Chicago without spoiling on the days-long journey. Because only about half of a steer's weight was actually edible meat, shipping 550 pounds of animal flesh instead of a 1000-pound steer was much less expensive. This substantially lowered the price of beef, making it more available to working-class people and stimulating an increase in meat consumption.

To bring us back to gelatin and Jell-O, in the early days of Chicago meatpacking, the majority of non-edible animal parts were discarded, polluting nearby lands and waterways like Chicago's notorious Bubbly Creek, which Upton Sinclair described as "a great open sewer a hundred or two feet wide."[12] But as the scale of slaughter increased, those byproducts like gelatin were present in sufficient quantity for the packers to find markets for their use, and indeed to earn the majority of their profit from the sale of these by-products. As one industry journal wrote in 1916, "today not a single element of what was formerly spoken of as 'packers' waste' is discarded as of no value. Indeed, it is upon the very items that were formerly discarded that the big packing concerns now depend for the greater part of their profits."[13] Gelatin and glue came from bones, hooves, and calves' ears; fertilizer from dried blood; margarine from beef tallow; pharmaceuticals from glands; "combs, buttons, hairpins, umbrella handles, napkins rings, tobacco boxes and many other articles" from hoofs and horns; leather from hides; upholstery from hair; paintbrushes from fine inner ear hairs; sausage casings of bladders and intestines; drumheads from the "skins of unborn calves, of which there are many in the course of a week" and much more.[14] The packers launched chemical research laboratories by the 1880s to foster all these industrial transformations.

So, this explains the production side of things—the large supply of gelatin and other animal byproducts that became available by the 1880s. But what about consumption? Who was going to eat or use all these products?

When it came to Jell-O, a consumers' market developed through two main factors explored in each of the next two sections: the rise of the Progressive movement and significant investment in advertising.

Jell-O as a Progressive Solution

Jell-O was embedded in at least three major strands of Progressivism: the rise of domestic science, attention to inequality, and pure food reform. First, Jell-O was the perfect product to embody the scientific convenience of, and food industry entanglement with, the domestic science movement and the attendant involvement of women in public life. Second, Jell-O ads insisted that its workers were treated well against a broader backdrop of inequality and that its inexpensive cost made it accessible to all. And finally, Jell-O's promise of "purity," and its dependence on a meatpacking industry that became the center of food adulteration scandals, connected it to movements for pure food.

By the later nineteenth century, the domestic science movement sought to transfer the principles of science and efficiency from the factories and offices to the home and kitchen. The women leading the movement, like Progressive reformers in other fields, believed that relatively small changes in how people lived their lives could help address the social miseries wrought by industrialization, including poverty, crime, alcoholism, and unemployment. They also wanted to help solve the so-called "servant problem" that dominated among middle-class white women in the 1890s, as these women struggled to find laborers to take on housekeeping and had to learn how to do it themselves. The domestic science advocates published cookbooks and housekeeping manuals, wrote for women's magazines, gave lectures around the country, organized clubs, and founded schools like the Boston Cooking School in 1879—all with little knowledge of the science of nutrition or vitamins.

By 1899, some domestic scientists began to professionalize into the discipline of home economics, challenging hierarchies of expertise and gender by offering opportunities for professional middle-class white women. They established the American Home Economics Association by 1908 and the *Journal of Home Economics* in 1909, with Ellen Swallow Richards at the helm. Richards, the first woman to attend the Massachusetts Institute of Technology and an expert in chemistry and water quality, oversaw the incorporation of the "male" domains of fields like bacteriology, family psychology, dietetics, and food science into the women's domain of the home. Another woman who was part of this growing field was Ella Eaton Kellogg who, with her husband John Harvey Kellogg, oversaw the Battle Creek Sanitarium, where Americans who were concerned about the pace of modern life came to eat unprocessed, vegetarian foods (some made from peanuts) and participate in fad diets—directly influenced by early-nineteenth-century reformer Sylvester Graham.

As the discipline established itself, home economists became entangled with the growing food industry, uniting their interests in common cause. Many home economists went to work for food processors after finishing their degrees, and they lent their authority and expertise to branded foods. One mid-twentieth-century article suggested that the rise of Jell-O "was perhaps one of the greatest factors in fostering the wide growth of home-economics test kitchens in industry." [15] The packaged food industry and home economics research went hand in hand. As historian Laura Shapiro argues, "uniformity, sterility, predictability—the values inherent in machine-age cuisine—were always at the heart of scientific cookery, so the era of manufactured and processed food descended upon the domestic-science movement like a millennium." [16] Mass production also offered the convenience necessary to solve the "servant problem." Jell-O was central among these new food products that took advantage of these home economist influencers. A 1915 brochure featured "six famous author cooks" including Marion Harland and her daughter Christine Herrick; Sarah Tyson Rorer, the head of the Philadelphia Cooking School; and Mary J. Lincoln, the editor of *New England Kitchens* magazine. These experts "told American housewives why they themselves used Jell-O for desserts and why other women should use it, especially the women who have little time to spare and must make every penny count." [17] Another Jell-O ad quoted Rorer, asking, "Why should any woman stand for hours over a hot fire, mixing compounds to make people ill, when in two minutes, with an expense of ten cents, she can produce such an attractive, delicious dessert?" [18]

Domestic science was one strand of the broader Progressive era and was intricately woven into other movements around women's issues, food, inequality, and labor. The number of women entering public life around the turn of the twentieth century grew dramatically, both among those who entered the workforce and those who took up social and political work outside their homes. Whether implicitly or explicitly, they began to push against the ideology of "separate spheres," which had kept them homebound in past generations. Some middle-class women—both white and Black, though segregated—joined the women's clubs that flourished by the 1890s. Others took up settlement house work, living among poor and immigrant communities to provide social services, with Jane Addams and her Chicago Hull House among the most famous. Some leveraged their increasing public engagement toward furthering the campaign for women's right to vote that had been brewing for nearly a century but became a mass movement after 1900 (even though it would take until 1920 for the Nineteenth Amendment to be passed).

Still others took up more radical work, like Margaret Sanger's push to increase access to birth control and Charlotte Perkins Gilman's utopian feminism and socialism. While domestic science advocates were more conservative in their approach and would not have called themselves feminists, they benefitted from and accelerated the new position of women in American society.

The domestic science leaders thought an American standard of living could be achieved by even the most modest households by reducing the cost of household food budgets. They suggested that economic inequality could be solved by smarter choices in the kitchen, rather than boosting wages or challenging political hierarchies. But this glib response belied the serious inequalities stemming from the Gilded Age, with "the richest 1 percent of Americans receiv[ing] the same total income as the bottom half of the population and own[ing] more property than the remaining 99 percent" by 1890.[19] As critic Henry George wrote in *Progress and Poverty*, "The gulf between the employed and the employer is growing wider; social contrasts are becoming sharper; as liveried carriages appear, so do barefooted children."[20] Businessmen like steel magnate Andrew Carnegie and Standard Oil's John. D. Rockefeller amassed enormous fortunes, while exploitative labor practices and major economic depressions in 1873 and 1893 drove many working-class people into desperate poverty. Meanwhile, Jell-O ads insisted that its workers never experienced this distress, claiming that the workers were "happy, prosperous and content" and that "The Jell-O employees are all Americans. Strikes or labor troubles do not occur. ... Their work reminds one of a big sociable sort of jelling-bee."[21] Questionable though these claims may have been, they showcased the broader environment of labor concerns.

Food companies, in keeping with their home economist allies, suggested that cheaper prices and the democratization of food would help alleviate inequalities. Whereas gelatin-based desserts had been limited to the upper classes in the nineteenth century, the invention of products like Jell-O made them more accessible. One Jell-O ad, drawing on the romantic imagery of the Old South as part of the pro-Confederacy Lost Cause narrative, wrote, "Jell-O, in its role of 'America's Most Famous Dessert,' is confined to no one class of people. It is as much at home in the mountain cabin as in the stately 'big house' on the old plantation."[22] But even though a packet of Jell-O may have only been ten cents, it benefitted from amenities like running water, access to refrigeration, and fuel to heat stoves for boiling water. Those living in tenements or other accommodations for the poor rarely had indoor plumbing, well into the twentieth century.

A final significant way that food, labor, and Progressive reform—and also the meatpacking industry—came together was in concerns around pure food reform. An early 1905 Jell-O cookbooklet announced "Approved by Pure Food Commissioners" at the bottom of each page, at a time when purity in industrial food was by no means a foregone conclusion.[23] In the late nineteenth century, food adulteration was rampant, with manufacturers using all kinds of chemical additives to lower their costs, with no oversight or government regulation. The country had been exposed to the great "embalmed beef" scandal during the Spanish-American war in 1898, when soldiers fighting in this first war for American overseas empire—in which the U.S. took control of Puerto Rico, Guam, Cuba, and the Philippines—were fed spoiled canned beef, rumored to be preserved with embalming fluids like formaldehyde. Two of the most well-known reformers who took up these adulteration problems were Harvey Wiley and Upton Sinclair. Wiley was the chief chemist for the US Department of Agriculture, crusading against food preservatives and launching research projects like his infamous Poison Squad, in which volunteers ate increasing amounts of food additives like borax to evaluate the effects. Aided by women's activism, he had also tried to get measures for food safety regulations through Congress for many years.

Sinclair, by contrast, was a "muckracker," one of the many journalists who sought to expose corrupt business practices and inequality. He was a Socialist, moved by the strong labor movement and the influential strikes of the late nineteenth and early twentieth centuries, alongside the rise of the Populist Party in the 1890s, to advocate for ordinary people against the forces of capitalism. He became interested in the meatpacking industry, the byproducts of which made Jell-O possible, after packinghouse workers went on strike in July 1904. He spent seven weeks in Chicago's Union Stockyards, living in a settlement house, shadowing and interviewing workers, before producing the writings that would become his based-on-real-life novel, *The Jungle*. The novel followed a Lithuanian immigrant family, whose "American dream" was crushed by the inhumanity of the slaughterhouses. The book included horrific descriptions of the packing plants, as with one account of an exhausted worker who slipped into a vat and then was "overlooked for days till all but the bones of them had gone out to the world as Durham's Pure Leaf Lard."[24] Sinclair hoped that readers would feel sympathy for these abused workers and push for socialism, but most instead focused on their own plates, feeling horror at the thought of what was in their food. As Sinclair poignantly said, "I aimed for the public's heart, and by accident hit its stomach."[25] Although Sinclair first struggled to get his book published, when it came out in 1906, it became a sensation. Outcry from worried consumers and angry meatpacking industry leaders led President Theodore Roosevelt to send independent investigators to Chicago, who confirmed the truth of Sinclair's accounts. This publicity, along with Wiley's ongoing work and campaigns from women's clubs, pure food advocates, and the American Medical Association, finally culminated in the passage of the Meat Inspection Act and Pure Food and Drug Act in June 1906.

This regulation was an embodiment of how Progressive reform moved beyond the local level to shape federal policy. Roosevelt was the first of several "Progressive presidents" who used their platforms to push for measures like "trust-busting" by breaking up large monopolies, environmental conservation and the establishment of national parks, and the graduated income tax through the Sixteenth Amendment. As far as regulating the meat industry, however, the effects of the 1906 Acts did little to improve conditions for workers and instead encouraged the growth of big business, as the federal oversight restored confidence in meat and byproducts like gelatin, leading to even higher rates of meat consumption.

Creating a Desire for Jell-O

Jell-O also captured the spirit of the early twentieth century in its pioneering use of advertising and merchandising. Advertising emerged as a way for businesses to project their stories and create desires, to convince consumers to purchase their products as a way of participating in the national marketplace. Jell-O was one of America's first novel processed foods. It was a thoroughly industrial product, but that industrialized nature—especially its link to meatpacking—was hidden. Then and now, it is "a slightly alien substance— both in its actual form and in the open secret of its essence."[26] It resulted from a kind of magical transformation, from meat byproduct to fruity dessert.

To make people want this new packaged food, Jell-O used a variety of innovative merchandising methods. Drawing from the home economists' commitment to written instructions and cookbooks, Jell-O produced recipe booklets to be distributed by "nattily dressed salesmen," who slipped one "under the door of every house in town." Afterward, they would "visit the grocer to advise him of the impending demand" and pressure him to buy large quantities of Jell-O. Before the first self-service grocery store opened in the United States in 1916, food purchases were mediated by a grocer, whose recommendation was especially influential. The sharp Jell-O salesmen would also visit community events throughout the countryside with free samples and promotional items. Their reach was extended by print advertisements in magazines, posters, and billboards. One especially popular 1915 booklet had a twelve-million copy print run, "enough to supply two-thirds of all American homes then in existence." To appeal to new immigrants, versions of the booklets were printed in Yiddish, German, Spanish, and French.[27]

In building a national taste, the Genesee Pure Food Company relied heavily on the Jell-O brand to create positive associations, and in particular to tie industrial production to purity. As historian Helen Veit argues about Crisco, marketing campaigns in the Progressive Era took advantage "of consumers' growing confidence in highly processed food and their growing comfort with ignorance about the ingredients that went into it."[28] In Crisco's case, the hidden ingredient was cottonseed oil; in Jell-O's, gelatin. Jell-O relied on the new printing technologies that were becoming available to produce high-quality color ads for magazines and cookbooks, and rode a wave of larger investments in food advertising. To give one example, N. W. Ayer, the largest ad agency at the time, spent less than 1 percent of its budget on food in 1877, but nearly 15 percent by 1901, with food remaining "the single most advertised class of commodity until the 1930s."[29] In addition to securing endorsements from leading domestic advisors, as described above, the company hired famous artists like Rose O'Neill and Norman Rockwell to illustrate their ads, sent out recipe books and jelly molds free of charge, and conveyed the approval of influential people, as in a 1905 booklet that read, "endorsed by physicians and approved by the Pure Food Commissioners. Received highest award, Gold Medals at both the St. Louis and Portland Expositions."[30]

These many Jell-O ads featured a variety of recurring themes that further help us to understand the values of the period. In addition to purity and scientific origins, ads from the first two decades of the twentieth century emphasized how easy, convenient, adaptable, flavorful, digestible, and health-giving Jell-O was. The Jell-O Girl character, introduced in 1904, and modeled after the daughter of the advertising artist Franklin King, conveyed that Jell-O was so easy a child could make it (despite the need to pour boiling water). Many ads suggested that the ease of Jell-O would overcome the general incompetence of women in the kitchen. One 1904 ad read, "How often some ingredient is forgotten or not rightly proportioned and the dessert spoiled. That will never occur if you use Jell-O." Another in 1911 offered an image of an anxious housewife pulling a burning dish out of the oven had the headline "Keeping Trouble Out of the Kitchen."[31] A 1905 booklet touting convenience assured readers that "Jell-O will save nine-tenths of the time the cook now spends preparing desserts."[32]

That same booklet conveyed the range of dishes that could be made with the ever-adaptable food product, including recipes for Jellied Apples, Date Dessert, Strawberry Conserve, Chicken Salad (with lemon Jell-O, nuts, parsley, and mayonnaise), Wine Jelly, and much more. At first, Jell-O offered four flavors, but grew to offer more as the company developed. A 1917 ad wrote, "what flavors! They come from fresh ripe fruits–crimson strawberries, luscious raspberries, great golden oranges, pale, tart lemons, cherries bursting with sweetness!"[33] Jell-O biographer Carolyn Wyman writes that "In pre-Environmental Protection Agency days, townspeople would identify the flavor of the day by checking the color of the creek that ran behind the LeRoy plant."[34]

Further, Jell-O ads convinced consumers that it was easier to digest than traditional desserts, producing less "dyspepsia" (indigestion) than the pies of yore. A 1913 testimonial from domestic scientists Sarah Tyson Rorer wrote that "Elaborate desserts, such as boiled and baked puddings and dyspepsia-producing pies, have given place to the more attractive and healthful desserts made from Jell-O."[35] And if you did get sick, from indigestion or otherwise, Jell-O was an ideal food to eat in a sanitarium or hospital, offering much to even the most "delicate invalid."[36]

In tying all of these positive values to a simple box of sweet flavored gelatin powder, Jell-O and the processed food industry that it fostered created a new kind of modern American eater. No longer did one have to engage with butchery and animals' deaths and the dirty work of cutting off calves' feet to produce a fancy gelatin dessert. As the Progressive Era came to an end, the former bison range and cattle drives and Chicago slaughterhouses receded from view as modern values of scientific expertise, industrialization, and branding came to shape engagement with the food supply. Jell-O was one magic ingredient in ushering in this new era.

8

Spaghetti:

Immigrants and Consumers in the 1910s and 1920s

In 1919, Maria Gentile published *The Italian Cook Book*, helping to introduce Italian cuisine to broader American audiences. In the preface, she anchored the timing of the book's publication to the recent "Great War" (later known as the First World War), which was responsible for "the teaching of thrift to the American housewife" and attention to food that was "palatable, nourishing and economical." Italian cuisine, she argued, embodied all three of these qualities: "That it is palatable, all those who have partaken of food in an Italian trattoria or at the home of an Italian family can testify, that it is healthy the splendid manhood and womanhood of Italy is a proof more than sufficient. And who could deny, knowing the thriftiness of the Italian race, that it is economical?"[1]

The Italian "race" and its food proliferated throughout the United States in the early twentieth century, as did the millions of other immigrants who reshaped the nation during this time. Around 23 million immigrants came to the United States between 1890 and 1924, crowding into ethnic neighborhoods and transforming American cities. By 1890, 80 percent of Chicago and New York City residents were either foreign-born or the children of immigrants. By 1900, there were more than 1,000 foreign-language newspapers in circulation.[2] Although most immigrants earned more money than was possible in the impoverished regions from which they came, they endured low wages, long hours, and dangerous working conditions. Earlier in the nineteenth century, immigrants came mostly from northern and western Europe, and thus assimilated more easily with the native-born (though one large exception were the Chinese immigrants who came to the west coast to build railroads and support mining operations). But the later nineteenth-century waves of immigration originated in southern and eastern Europe, introducing large groups of Italians and Russian Jews whose language, religion, poverty, and food practices set them further apart from native-born Americans. The migrants came to the United States in search of better wages and an escape from hunger. They fled poverty, declining economies, and religious oppression. Many were "birds of passage," single men who hoped to earn enough to return home to their families with more financial security.

Immigrants and their foodways were the target of Americanization efforts in the home economics movements of the 1910s, contributed to domestic food efforts during the First World War, and were woven into both the consumerism and repression of the 1920s. Italians were highly represented, making up about a quarter of all immigrants between 1900 and the First World War. Because of this and because their food traditions were so iconic and steadfast—not to mention palatable, nourishing, and economical—Italian immigrants and their spaghetti anchor our story.

Americanization Efforts in the 1910s

Many native-born Americans considered the new immigrants arriving on the nation's shores with disdain, worrying about their influence and recoiling at their strange ways. Some reformers approached this disdain with a condescending sense of optimism—perhaps the strangeness could be "fixed," the immigrants assimilated, the foreign practices abandoned. This move to "Americanize" the foreign-born fit neatly into the Progressive Era mold of standardization, efficiency, and rationality. It also fit with other assimilationist education programs of the early twentieth century. In Indian boarding schools, reformers coercively disrupted Native American food and agricultural practices. In some public schools, cooks served up carefully calculated standardized menus. And in rural communities, cooperative extension agents urged families to grow crops and serve meals according to recommendations of crop science and nutrition, instead of passed-on tradition. Similarly, immigrant diets were a central target of Americanization campaigns, as Progressive reformers sought to use the new sciences of home economics and nutrition to create and enforce a national way of eating.

Progressive reformers criticized immigrant foodways for a wide variety of reasons: it was too spicy and too flavorful (too much garlic or chili peppers), it featured too many mixed components that taxed the digestive system (like stews and stir fries and saucy pastas), and it was too messy. They blamed Italian immigrants for using small amounts of imported ingredients like cheeses and olive oil, considering them unnecessary expensive luxuries, even as they ignored the fact that the immigrants' mixed, highly flavored dishes that the reformers discouraged were themselves evolved strategies to economize by stretching costly ingredients, making bland items palatable, and using up small quantities of any remaining foods. The reformers had their own vision of what immigrants *should* be eating, and blamed them for making choices deemed unreasonable. They believed that as long as immigrants clung to their foreign foods, they resisted American ways and ideas.

In order to tell immigrants what they should be eating instead of their traditional foods, culinary reformers had to figure out what "American food" actually was. In this, they took inspiration from the diets of Northeastern elites and a mythologized vision of American ancestors to decide on a plain, unseasoned diet of meat and wheat, in separate dishes. But, in fact, Americans had long relied on mixed and flavored foods, for the same reasons that immigrants did: it was a way to stretch meat and use up ingredients. As historian Helen Veit argues, Americans ate an "inexhaustible variety of stews, hashes, mushes, souses, scrapples, meat pies, and puddings," and nineteenth-century cookbooks invariably had "long sections on homemade pickles, ketchups, vinegars, sweetmeats, slaws, and other pungent relishes."[3]

Although some immigrants welcomed assimilation as a way of fitting in, others resisted the patronizing reform efforts. Italian immigrants in particular had little interest in cooking instruction even as they attended settlement house classes and clubs on other subjects. One reformer wrote of the Italians, "People of this nationality … cling to their native dietary habits with extraordinary persistence."[4] Italians celebrated their food knowledge as central to their identities and felt confident in traditional techniques. In general, Progressive era food reforms had a much larger effect on middle-class populations than on the working class.

At the same time that these Americanization schemes were underway, the increasing diversity of American cities and immigrants' continued adherence to traditional foods led to a slow influence in both directions. The 1908 play *The Melting Pot,* by Jewish immigrant Israel Zangwill, gave a name to a process by which immigrant habits began to mix into American culture, rather than being wholly transformed. Foreign dishes began to show up even more commonly in American cookbooks, with "macaroni and tomato sauce" proliferating—at a time when "macaroni" could refer to a variety of pasta shapes. The slow acceptance of some foreign foods was promoted by the maturation of nutrition science, along with the discovery of vitamins by the 1910s, which led nutritionists to see foods as the sum of their component parts and thus substitutable based on their calorie, protein, carbohydrate, and vitamin content. One extension of this was that "immigrant fare like pasta with tomato sauce and cheese could equal pork chops and potatoes," based on their ability to convey the same nutrients, turning food "into a variable in a kind of cultural algebra."[5]

Despite the devotion of many immigrants to their customary diets, the move to the United States *did* significantly affect the way they ate. For many, America was a land of plenty that could offer a reprieve from hunger. As Fievel the Russian-Jewish mouse sings in the film *Fievel: An American Tail* before his emigration, "there are no cats in America, and the streets are paved with cheese." Though the streets may not have quite been paved with cheese, the move to the United States did offer more plentiful and less expensive food for many immigrants, who could now eat more like the wealthy did back home. Working-class Americans had greater access to a wide range of foods in the United States, thanks to the nation's agricultural abundance and the recent developments in infrastructure and food manufacturing that delivered foods efficiently to grocers' shelves. For example, whereas southern Italians had spent three-quarters of their income on food in Italy, they spent only a quarter in the United States.[6] In Italy, the macaroni vendor on the street sold piles of spaghetti with rich tomato sauce and grated cheese to the wealthy, while the poor could only afford "a little water from the pot."[7] In America, those poor immigrants could eat the spaghetti for themselves. They could even top spaghetti with meatballs—a food that was rare in Italy but would become a staple of Italian-American restaurants. In 1900, Italian immigrant Antonio Ranciglio wrote back to his family and friends at home, boasting, "Here I eat meat three times a day, not three times a year."[8] And the *Americani*—Italians who came to the United States temporarily and then returned to Italy— told wondrous tales of America, "of wheat fields so vast that no fast train could traverse them in a single day; of meats and sweets and fine clothes so universally enjoyed that it was impossible to distinguish the rich from the poor."[9] Despite these exaggerations and the deep inequalities that continued to run through American society, many immigrant workers indeed felt fortunate as compared with their peers in their home countries.

Many immigrants embraced not only the plentiful meat, but the other luxuries of this new land—more sugar, coffee, canned foods, and packaged goods. Italians, however, especially those from Southern Italy, largely resisted assimilation and industrialized American food. One writer recalled his Italian grandmother's attitude toward the packaged foods of the 1920s: "One summer night my mother committed a sacrilege by bringing home a Betty Crocker apple pie mix. My grandmother, seeing Betty Crocker as a threat to both her sovereignty and her ability to run the house, started a tremendous fight." Cooking from scratch was a way of maintaining identity and showing love for the family. Italian immigrants' pride in food production and their commitment to fresh vegetables and imported pastas, oils, and cheese led many to reject commercially processed foods and instead to grow gardens, forage for greens, and start their own food businesses based on vegetable farming and pasta production. Before the discovery of vitamins, many native-born Americans *canned food in war*

Prohibition → during spaghetti

rejected the Italian embrace of fresh fruits and vegetables. But after, they began singing a different tune, supporting the wide network of Italian farms that spread across the country, bringing produce to American tables through a variety of "pushcarts, stands, outdoor urban fruit and vegetable markets, and stores of every size."[10] Merchants like these often extended credit to their customers, allowing even the poorest immigrants to eat well in hard times. But these venues also exposed non-Italians to vegetables like lentils, zucchini, broccoli, and garlic, to a wider appreciation for tomatoes and, of course, to spaghetti.

pushcart + stand

More than any other, spaghetti (or macaroni, as it was often interchangeably called) embodied Italian food. The long strands hung outside of macaroni shops in cities "almost as flags to proclaim the Italian presence."[11] Spaghetti gave rise to immigrant food businesses—import companies, pasta factories, and restaurants. Until the First World War cut off the Italian supply of pasta and tomato products, immigrant entrepreneurs imported large amounts of these products. Afterward, domestic production doubled. Pasta manufacturers in the United States—both those led by immigrants and by the native-born— made use of new varieties of durum wheat, introduced from Southern Russia and grown in the Upper Midwest. The manufacturers banded together to create the National Macaroni Manufacturers Association in 1904, and used the platform of this trade organization to tout their products in the media in the following decades.[12] The non-Italian members of this organization wanted to grow the taste for its products among native-born Americans, using the divisive strategies of distancing from its Italian origins. Foulds, an early brand, advertised its products as "American food for American people" and "Cleanly Made by Americans"—drawing on negative associations with especially southern Italian immigrants as unclean and undesirable.[13] They also touted the nutritious qualities of pasta to appeal to scientifically-minded Americans.

1st world war cut off supply of spaghetti

National Macaroni Manufacturers Association

Italian restaurants further popularized Italian food and created a cohesive Italian cuisine by the 1920s. Italy itself had only unified in 1860, but was still made up of distinctive regions with varying geography, foodways, and cultures. The iconic diet of tomatoes, olive oil, cheese, and garlic that Americans came to associate with all Italians was really the food of the southern city of Naples and the island of Sicily.[14] Even there, serving pasta with tomato sauce was a relatively recent innovation.[15] But as Italian restaurants rose in big cities, staffed by immigrant labor, they standardized this version of Italian cuisine. The first non-Italian groups these restaurants attracted were Greenwich Village bohemians and radicals seeking nonconformity around 1910, then office workers who wanted a quick meal or diners seeking wine during Prohibition, and finally a broader segment of middle-class Americans who were drawn in by the crafted image of appealing Italian food that these restaurants succeeded in conjuring by the 1920s. As historian Simone Cinotto writes, the restaurants

FIGURE 8 *This Van Camp's "Italian style" canned spaghetti advertisement from an April 1920 issue of* Good Housekeeping *asserted the superiority of its recipe to traditional Italian spaghetti.*

constructed "an irresistible narrative of Italianità, mixing images of [Southern] 'black Italy' (primitivism, maternalism, and Mediterranean sensuality) with those of [Northern] 'white Italy' (Rome, the Renaissance, and opera)."[16] These entrepreneurs took advantage of complex racial and symbolic associations to create new tastes.

A final sector that fostered an acceptance of spaghetti and other foreign foods was the canning industry. Industrially canned foods benefitted from the mechanization and transportation booms of the nineteenth century to achieve widespread use by the 1920s. These factories, often staffed by poorly paid immigrant workers (like many of the farms where the food-to-be-canned originated), churned out standardized food products that helped to create a national diet. Beginning around 1900, major food producers like Heinz, Franco-American (later, Campbell's), Van Camp's, and Chef Boy-ar-dee began to manufacture canned spaghetti. They drew on the food's Italian origin, but also distanced themselves from it. Van Camp's touted its recipe, introduced by a "foreign chef," but perfected by "culinary experts, college trained," creating a dish so delicious that "even native Italians concede it supremacy"[17] (Figure 8). Chef Boy-ar-dee was the brainchild of Ettore Boiardi, who changed the name of his products to make it more accessible for non-Italian consumers. And a 1914 guide to selling canned spaghetti assured readers that it was seasoned only "slightly—very slightly—with garlic or onion juice," in case anyone feared too much foreign flavor.[18]

Through pasta manufacturers, restaurants, and canners, spaghetti became one of the most common immigrant foods in the early twentieth century. As Maria Gentile wrote in 1919, "the lovers of spaghetti are just as enthusiastic and numerous outside of Italy as within the boundaries of that blessed country."[19] And, as native-born Americans learned to eat spaghetti, they also learned to make space for other foreign foods.

Food Will Win the War

The First World War was a significant turning point in American relationships to immigrant foods, and to food in general. Although the United States didn't enter the war until April 1917, it supported the Allies (primarily Britain, France, Russia, Japan, and Italy) financially from the war's beginning in July 1914, in their fight against the Central Powers (primarily Germany, Austria-Hungary, and the Ottoman Empire). Through the war's end in November 1918, food became a way to assert global power as Europe experienced food shortages. The United States was a clear global leader in agricultural productivity and used this advantage to provide international food aid, simultaneously as a way of saving starving Europeans, preventing anarchy, and projecting the superiority of American politics and culture.

The wartime US Food Administration (USFA), founded in 1917, first used "Food Will Win the War" as its motto, but by the end of the war instead suggested "Food Will Win the World," significantly expanding its scope.[20] The USFA was concerned with poor nutrition as a threat to national security, especially after nearly 30 percent of American men were rejected as military recruits because of malnourishment. And the USFA was concerned with rising food prices. International demand for food after the war began sent consumer food prices even higher than they had already been, leading to food price riots prices in cities throughout the nation—as had also happened during the Civil War. Thousands of women, most of them Jewish immigrants, marched in the streets of New York City in 1917 to protest high food prices and boycott expensive foods.

Under director Herbert Hoover, the USFA worked to provide nutrient-dense foods like beef, white flour, butter, and sugar to Allies by both encouraging American farmers to produce more and encouraging American consumers to eat less of these items by switching to substitutes. Although there was no official rationing, the USFA worked through a variety of means to encourage voluntary action, asking Americans to observe Meatless Mondays, Wheatless Wednesdays, and to learn to cook with unfamiliar substitute protein foods like peanut butter or cottage cheese (in place of red meat) and grain foods like cornbread and spaghetti (in place of white flour). In order to cultivate these tastes, the USFA propaganda campaigns had to decouple any negative associations middle-class white Americans may have had, like linking peanuts or corn with poor (often Black) Southerners or spaghetti with maligned Italians. In the case of corn, administrators looked back to romanticized American origins to label corn the food of the "Indians, hardiest of races" and the food that allowed early white colonists to have "conquered a continent."[21] As for spaghetti, home economists ignored their past criticisms of Italian diets, now suggesting that the United States could learn from "the food of the allies" in eating pasta, which could be eaten with little meat. A 1918 *Good Housekeeping* article wrote, "Meatless days to the Italian housewife are no problem ... All her days have been meatless days from her bambinohood up."[22] This way of viewing foods as a vector for substitutable nutrients further entrenched nutrition science and home economics, introducing a wide swath of Americans to such ways of reducing food—aided by home economists' new recipe books, conservation courses, and extension programs.

The foreign-born received special attention from the USFA. One poster appealed to immigrants, reading "you came here seeking Freedom, you must now help preserve it." The organization printed its materials in dozens of languages. While the USFA reported that about 70 percent of Americans voluntarily joined the food conservation efforts, many immigrants and other working-class people were not among them. Although native-born Americans blamed this on immigrants' wasteful tendencies, open antagonism, or "disloyal inclinations," more often it was a matter of government efforts not taking working-class considerations into account. Many poor Americans already had frequent "meatless" days simply because they couldn't afford meat, nor could they often afford many of the substitutes the USFA recommended, like chicken, eggs, and cheese. One Administrator in Louisiana wrote that poor Italians he encountered were not "impressed by pleas to conserve a little bread, butter, milk, and fat, because [they are] forced to economize on these items all the time."[23] And the government efforts to promote "liberty gardens" felt redundant to working-class people, many Italians among them, who cultivated gardens just to survive. Indeed, food conservation demonstrators who visited a Boston settlement house in an Italian neighborhood in 1917 found that "the audience was able to give the teacher instructions."[24]

Even as the USFA was disbanded after the end of the war, it had long-lasting consequences, including expanding the reach of the federal government into American foodways and linking patriotism and dietary self-control. As Helen Veit argues, the wartime emphasis on self-discipline and rational food choices led to a downgrading of the sensual pleasures of eating, a linkage between self-control and political maturity, and an idealization of thin-ness as an outward expression of that maturity. Some white Americans especially embraced this approach, seeing their self-denial as one of the "distinguishing traits of whiteness, while wholehearted joy in the pleasures of food was a characteristic that whites ascribed to nonwhites."[25]

This same desire to impose normative "American" values on other populations and to link self-control to morality animated Prohibition, the federal ban on alcohol which lasted from the passage of the 18th Amendment in 1920 to its abolition by the 21st Amendment in 1933. Prohibition followed from the temperance movement that had been in full swing for over a century, driven by social reformers who wanted to protect women and children from alcoholic fathers and promote orderly cities, by business owners who wanted a more reliable labor force, and by Protestant reformers who wanted to control the behavior of heavy-drinking immigrants. Furthermore, under the wartime conservation mentality, distilling grain into liquor instead of using it for food seemed wasteful to many. Unfortunately, like so many things in American history, Prohibition had disproportionate effects and furthered injustices, as wealthy white Americans found ways to access alcohol on the black market or in places like Italian restaurants, while police cracked down on poor, often Black and immigrant, communities for alcohol possession.

Prohibition was joined by other repressive measures amid a tumultuous period during the war and in the years after. The government's patriotic wartime propaganda worked so well that anyone who criticized the war was seen as an enemy of democracy itself. The passage of the Espionage Act in 1917 and the Sedition Act in 1918 made it illegal to impede the war effort by saying or printing anything against the war or government, limiting the freedom of speech. Many foreign-language newspapers, most socialist publications, and other intellectuals were shut down and prosecuted. Contributing to the sense of upheaval, in the midst of the war, a deadly influenza outbreak emerged in 1918 that spread throughout the globe, killing up to 50 million people and infecting a staggering one-third of the world's population. The removal of wartime price controls left the economy—and especially farmers—reeling. Finally, despite President Wilson's proposal of an ambitious peace-promoting Fourteen Points as part of the Treaty of Versailles that ended the war, the final treaty was much more vindictive toward Germany, laying the foundation for Adolf Hitler's rise to power in the following decades. Partisan infighting in the United States prevented it from joining the crown jewel of Wilson's proposals—the League of Nations, an organization to promote worldwide peace. The League was formed, but without US participation, leaving the nation that fought to make the "world safe for democracy," instead turning inward and abandoning its Progressive values.

1920s Consumerism and Repression

The end of the First World War ushered in a pro-business decade, where the restraints of the war period gave way to a consumerist and conformist culture. In this environment, food became a way both to display social standing and to repress others. The era saw a series of interlinked movements against immigration, alternative politics, racial equality, and secular culture.

The food industry and other businesses flourished in the 1920s, with the support of the federal government. Congress reduced taxes on the wealthy, driving an era of mass consumption. Americans who were less wealthy also participated in the buying frenzy, but often had to go into debt to do so, buying the profusion of consumer goods from new department stores—processed foods, telephones, gas and electric stoves, and especially automobiles—on credit. An influential 1929 study of middle America, *Middletown,* cited an Indiana newspaper, which concluded that the average American's identity "is no longer that of a citizen but that of a consumer."[26] The food industry learned from the USFA's success in changing food habits, launching massive advertising campaigns. As Laura Shapiro writes, marketers created "a new image of the American housewife, ... suitable for a new age of material invention and consumption, ... who could discriminate among canned soups but who couldn't ask too many questions about the ingredients."[27] And, along with advertising, the rise of popular entertainment and leisure activities likewise shaped mass culture through film and radio.

This new consumerism was accompanied by loosening rules about appropriate behavior and some acceptance of new positions for oppressed groups. After nearly a century of activism, and bolstered by the more militant National Woman's Party led by Alice Paul, Congress granted women the right to vote with the passage of the Nineteenth Amendment in 1920. Unfortunately, even then, most Black women's vote continued to be restricted, by Jim Crow limits like literacy tests and poll taxes. Especially in cities of the north, though, white women seized new opportunities not only to vote, but to expand notions of femininity, crafting the image of the "New Woman," who entered the workforce, wore short skirts, and smoked cigarettes. This was also tied to the rise of gay community in the 1920s, especially in New York City and other urban centers, which made space for more open sexuality.

Black Americans, too, carved out new spaces of belonging—however limited by racism—in an expanding society. Radio popularized jazz, a uniquely African-American music that was a key part of the flowering of Black art as part of the New Negro movement. Much of this was centered in the neighborhoods of Harlem, New York, as part of the Harlem Renaissance, in which Black writers, actors, musicians, and artists explored the Black cultural experience through self-expression. The period also saw the rise of Black activism, not only through the more traditional National Association for the Advancement of Colored People (NAACP), but also through the Black nationalist organization the Universal Negro Improvement Association, led by Marcus Garvey, who championed Black pride through his call, "Up, you mighty race," and encouraged a "Back to Africa" movement.

Some White Americans looked to urban Black neighborhoods like Harlem and immigrant neighborhoods like the Italian Bleecker Street as a site for exotic adventure. As one writer recalled, "Back then, to eat a loaf of garlic bread was an act of bravado and to eat a garlic-laden spaghetti sauce was an act of liberation."[28] These cultural tourists visited Harlem jazz clubs and Italian and Chinese restaurants as a way of rebelling, even as they viewed these sites in ways that reduced the complexity of the people themselves. As Simone Cinotto writes, "Black music and Italian cuisine could both be consumed easily, without any need to understand their larger cultural contexts and without the need to carry on meaningful personal relations with actual African Americans or Italians."[29] These moves—along with the creation of blander, sweeter versions of foreign foods as the foods themselves became Americanized—helped lead to an embrace of some ethnic foods by the 1920s and 1930s. For example, Winifred Gibbs, a home economist who led the Americanization charge before the war, convincing Italian immigrants to shun their spaghetti, now in the 1920s turned to collaboration with macaroni manufacturers to promote new ideas of nutrition.[30] Also key to this acceptance was the significant immigration restriction in the early 1920s, as the United States basically shut its doors to immigrants from places like Italy, the Soviet Union, and most of Asia. As the "threat" of immigrants' foreignness diminished and newcomers' influence waned, foreign foods began to feel more palatable.

Immigration restriction captures a second major strand of the 1920s, alongside new consumption patterns: significant repression. The era was animated by eugenic thinking that promoted nativism and racism, a fundamentalist revolt against a rising secular culture, a Red Scare that furthered wartime suppression of labor movements and alternative political views, and deepening inequalities. Eugenics was a pseudoscientific approach to "improving" the human, race, inspired by the idea of social Darwinism, which led to effects like the forced sterilization of groups deemed unfit (disproportionately Black, Latinx, or Native American). Early proponents of the 1924 Johnson-Reed Act, which set immigration quotas, claimed that the new "foreign and unsympathetic element" carrying ideas of "anarchy and bolshevism" will gradually poison "the true spirit of Americanism left us by our fathers."[31] Food, too, was part of eugenic thinking, with reformers arguing that diet was indicative of racial status. In maligning Italian immigrants, for example, slurs referring to their diets—such as "spaghetti benders" or "garlic eaters"—were often used. One 1922 *Saturday Evening Post* short story presented an Italian character with a range of derogatory terms, including "dirty little shrimp" and just plain "Spaghetti."[32]

Black Americans, of course, were also primary targets of the racist thinking of the 1920s. They had been left out of Progressive reforms throughout the early twentieth century, and now experienced a new surge of anti-Black violence. Seeking better employment and an escape from Jim Crow, many African Americans moved northward beginning around 1915. In many Northern cities, they encountered exclusion in work and at home. Dramatic racial violence erupted: for example, white mobs killed up to 250 African-Americans and left another 6,000 homeless in East St. Louis in 1917, nearly twenty-five riots took place in the "Red Summer" of 1919 with the worst in Chicago, and the 1921 Tulsa race massacre left up to 300 people dead and one of the wealthiest Black districts in the country decimated. In response to the East St. Louis violence, 10,000 Black people gathered for a protest parade in New York, carrying signs reading, "Mr. President, Why Not Make America

Safe for Democracy?" The irony of fighting a war to preserve others' rights while ignoring the rights of Black citizens at home was clear.

The Ku Klux Klan, which had been a major destructive force in the Reconstruction period, reemerged around 1915 amid a broader pushback against a rising secular culture. This incarnation spread beyond the South, achieving real political power with an estimated membership of five million. The Klan used violence to protect what they saw as "American values," threatened not only by Black people and Jews, but by immigrants, Catholics, feminists, atheists, and others they deemed a threat to white supremacy. Due to internal scandal, the Klan dissipated in force by the late 1920s, but many of its core tenets remained as part of a broader thrust of fundamentalism and concern about the decline of conservative values.

A final repressive streak of the 1920s manifested as the Red Scare, in a backlash against alternative political views like socialism and anarchism, both of which were often linked with immigrants and the labor movement. Following from wartime repression of dissent and abuse of civil liberties along with an anti-communist reaction to the 1917 Russian Revolution, mainstream Americans suppressed those who sought to remake government and industry to better serve the working class. These phenomena were captured by the case of Sacco and Vanzetti. In May 1920, two Italian anarchists, Nicola Sacco and Bartolomeo Vanzetti, were charged with robbery and murder of a security guard at a Massachusetts factory. After seven years of appeals and worldwide outcry, the men were executed in 1927. Before sentencing, Vanzetti captured what was at stake, saying, "I am suffering because I am a radical and indeed I am a radical; I have suffered because I was an Italian, and indeed I am an Italian."[33] In the minds of those who sentenced the men to death, their immigrant status was linked to anarchism—what became known as "the garlic-smelling creed"—and both conveyed guilt.[34]

These threads further coalesced by the 1928 election, when Democrat Al Smith ran against Republican Herbert Hoover, who had headed the wartime USFA. Smith was the Catholic son of poor Irish immigrants, opposed prohibition and immigrant restrictions, and was from New York City. Hoover, on the other hand, was a Protestant engineer from middle America. One southern newspaper editor wrote, "Hoover is sprung from American soil and stock," while Smith was on the side of "the aliens"—that is, people like the Italians whose spaghetti had for so long conveyed foreignness.[35] In the end, Hoover won easily, but Smith carried most large cities, signaling future shifts in party allegiances.

Hoover, however, despite his popularity as head of the USFA and in the 1928 election, would soon face the most challenging economic crisis in American history. Although the 1920s had been prosperous for some, deep inequalities remained, especially among excluded immigrants, Black Americans, laborers, farmers, and consumers who bought on credit and went into debt. These fault lines would become clear with the onset of the Great Depression. At the same time, although spaghetti and its immigrant associations would come to be more widely accepted by native-born Americans in this era, this was only possible because of the restriction of the very people who brought this delicious food. Like the prosperity of the 1920s, American acceptance of immigrant tastes was only on the surface.

9

Oranges:
Food and Agriculture in the Great Depression

In John Steinbeck's classic 1939 *Grapes of Wrath*, among the narrative chapters about the migrant Joad family, Steinbeck includes a series of place-setting chapters. He uses these breaks to set the scene, to step backward—at times moving almost into the realm of poetry—to evoke in the reader a sense of time and place. The title of his book comes from a passage in one of these exceptional chapters. Here, Steinbeck pauses to paint a picture of the California agricultural and human landscape in the 1930s. At first, the scene is beautiful, filled with heavy golden fruit and fragrance, with human agricultural ingenuity. But then, the picture turns, as the economic reality of the Depression era sets in:

> Carloads of oranges dumped on the ground. The people came for miles to take the fruit, but this could not be. ... And men with hoses squirt kerosene on the oranges, and they are angry at the crime, angry at the people who have come to take the fruit. ... And children dying of pellagra must die because a profit cannot be taken from an orange. ... and in the eyes of the hungry ... the grapes of wrath are filling and growing heavy, growing heavy for the vintage.[1]

What is going on here? Who are the men burning oranges in kerosene, and why are they doing it? Why are children dying of pellagra or malnutrition? What exactly are those "grapes of wrath" growing in the souls of the hungry?

The story of oranges, of these burning golden mountains, takes us into an exploration of the 1930s United States, amidst the Great Depression, a period in American history filled with hunger and desperation, but also with ingenuity and political momentum that changed the foundations of the country and the workings of the economy and federal government.

The Depression and Agricultural Adjustment Administration

To understand the burning oranges, we first have to understand the economic picture as a whole. On October 29, 1929, on the day that came to be known as "Black Tuesday," the stock market collapsed. Although economic depressions had been familiar in nineteenth-century America, the country had never seen anything like what followed Black Tuesday. By 1932, the gross national product was at two-thirds of its 1929 level and over a quarter of the potential labor force was out of work.[2] In some cities, unemployment was as high as 80 percent. Banks failed across the country, as many different borrowers were now unable to repay their loans. In the 1920s, Americans had bought stocks on margin and bought consumer goods on credit, farmers had taken loans from small rural banks to try to keep up with the wave of agricultural mechanization, and European countries had borrowed from American banks to repay the First World War debts. And there were many people suffering financially even before the crash, both in the cities and on farms. Even as the decadence of the 1920s had suggested an era of prosperity, this wealth was concentrated at the top, among relatively few Americans. The majority of families were living below the poverty level, unable to buy consumer goods, which led manufacturers to cut still more jobs, leading to an even bleaker situation for the country's laborers. In the countryside, farmers, too, were struggling before October 1929, as new farm technologies enabled overproduction even as farm product prices remained low.[3]

All of this led to devastation throughout the country, as millions of people were left jobless, hungry, and homeless. In the early days, President Herbert Hoover called on American businesses and private charities to independently help those in need. Following historical precedent and economic beliefs that recessions were normal and necessary under capitalism, he first did not take federal action to provide systemic relief. Americans living on the streets in cobbled-together shacks referred to their shantytowns as "Hoovervilles," reflecting a deep dissatisfaction over President Hoover's response—or lack of response—to their suffering. One woman, recalling what she saw at a Hooverville in Oklahoma City, described "people living in old, rusted-out car bodies .... people living in shacks made of orange crates."[4] The same California orchards that would destroy oranges at the height of the Depression had previously shipped orange crates to Oklahoma. Only now those crates were the building blocks of family homes instead of holding sweet oranges for people to eat.

[Handwritten margin notes:]
- Black Tuesday
- Stock market collapse
- 2/3 ↓ GDP
- over a quarter out of work
- unemployment ~80%!
- new farm tech = overproduction
- millions of ppl hungry
- shantytowns = "Hoovervilles"
- Hoover
- lack of response from Hoover
- would use orange crates for homes

By 1932, Hoover made a last-ditch effort to loan money to failing banks and businesses through the Reconstruction Finance Corporation, but it was too little, too late. In that year's presidential election, Democrat Franklin Delano Roosevelt (FDR) secured nearly 60 percent of the popular vote. Once in office, he quickly launched his plan to pull the country out of Depression, with a host of acts and agencies created as part of his "First New Deal" in his first one hundred days, beginning in March 1933.

In addition to launching agencies directed at banks, industry, housing, and joblessness, a major initiative of the First New Deal sought to address the deep problems of American farmers, with the creation of the Agricultural Adjustment Administration (AAA). The main goal was to reduce agricultural surpluses in order to raise prices and boost the farm economy. There were two ways to actually reduce surplus, depending on seasonal cycles. It is critical to note that the AAA was created in May 1933, when the crops had already been planted and the livestock had already begun breeding. "Reducing surplus" in early summer meant destruction. Oranges were burned down to "putrefying ooze," corn was burned as fuel, potatoes were dumped in the rivers. Pigs were "plowed under" or slaughtered by the thousands. The devastation was everywhere. And in a time of great hunger, the wanton destruction of would-be food seemed callous and malicious in the eyes of hungry Americans who cared not for supply and demand charts, not for abstract economic principles, but for their own rumbling bellies and the sunken cheeks of their children. The food waste contributed to the sense of oppression among these downtrodden people, their sense of injustice and their feelings of "wrath" growing heavier with each pile of burning oranges.

By that fall and winter, though, when the harvest season had passed and the next planting season had yet to begin, the AAA moved to the second method of reducing surplus. This time around, using money generated in part from a tax on processed food companies, the federal government was able to pay subsidies to farmers to keep some of their land and animals out of production. This successfully lowered the supply of farm products, without the waste and damage of the previous cycle. The first list of commodities that were regulated included wheat, field corn, rice, milk, hogs, tobacco, and cotton, and later expanded to other agricultural products.[5] But the waste of food extended beyond these regulated commodities, to include oranges and other fruits and vegetables. The cost of labor to even harvest the fruit exceeded the prices farmers could get. Thus, even when the fruit wasn't intentionally destroyed, so much went to waste.

Farm Labor and the Dust Bowl

Especially with intensive crops like oranges, labor has always been a central issue. During the Depression, even as farm prices sank lower, the number of laborers seeking opportunities to make money through fruit picking in California, and across the West, surged. The labor of orange picking and packing was especially regulated. After 1904, when USDA pomologist—aka fruit scientist—G. Harold Powell came to California to help address blue mold problems in the citrus industry, standardization and control of workers' bodies became the norm. He encouraged managers to guide workers in handling the fruit in rationalized ways, as they fumigated the trees with various acids, considered if an orange was ripe enough to pick, handled their clippers and bags, climbed ladders, loaded boxes weighing fifty to seventy pounds onto a truck or wagon, and as they packed oranges into boxes labeled with bright advertisements in the packing houses (Figure 9). As orange historian Douglas Sackman writes, "The Powell Method reformed the bodies of workers, so that their motions in the groves and in the packing houses would more efficiently preserve the perfect bodies of oranges."[6]

To step back for a moment, California agriculture as a whole took a different path than in the American South, with large commercial farms established as

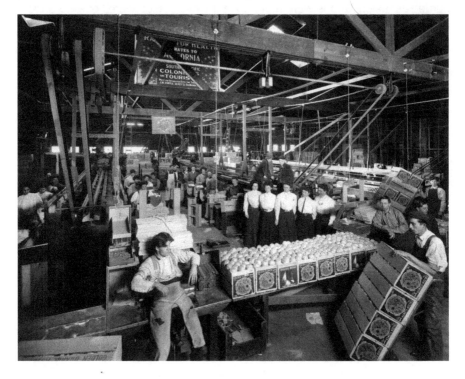

FIGURE 9 *Early-twentieth century photograph of the production line at the Golden Flower Brand Oranges Fruit Packaging Factory in Redlands, California, which displays the organized labor force, wooden crates, and vivid advertising images that characterized the industry. (American Stock/ClassicStock/Getty Images).*

early as the mid-nineteenth century. At a time when the state's population was still relatively small, this created a demand for cheap sources of labor. The state turned, then as now, to immigrants. In a Civil War era report, a committee of the state legislature called for the development of "all inferior races to work out and realize our grand and glorious destiny."[7] This racist vision laid the foundations for an inequitable system from the beginning. The racism was tied to the broader capitalist system of production that predominated in California by the early twentieth century. This system created a divide between the farm owners and those who actually did the work of planting and harvesting. Agricultural reformers throughout the nineteenth century tried to imagine ways that farming could be profitable enough that vulnerable populations wouldn't have to be brought in to work for low wages, that farming could actually be a way for individual farm families to make a living. But large farmers wanted cheap labor, and American consumers came to expect cheap food, leading to a situation where a "caste system" felt inevitable.[8]

Chinese workers were the first to be brought in, helping transform the state's wheat fields into farms of labor-intensive crops. In 1881, a farmer J. W. Gally criticized that the orchard men prefer "the Chinamen because he is their slave, and they can sit in the shade and drive him as the Southern overseer did the negro in the cotton field."[9] In part due to criticism like this, along with broader anti-immigrant sentiment, the US Congress passed the Chinese Exclusion Act in 1882, which prohibited all immigration of Chinese laborers. Japanese workers stepped in to fill the void left by the Chinese, and by 1910, a California Commission of Labor survey "found that Japanese constituted 87.2 percent of the labor force in berries, 66.3 percent in sugar beets ... 45.7 percent in vegetables, 38.1 percent in citrus fruits, and 36.5 percent in deciduous fruits."[10] But through the 1910s and the First World War, anti-Japanese and anti-immigrant attitudes grew stronger, culminating in the passage of the Immigration Act of 1924, which totally excluded Asian immigrants. As a 1910 article in the *Fresno Morning Republican* commented, "to raise oranges is important, but to raise men is more important," describing the belief that cheap labor from Asia wasn't worth the risk of sacrificing the white race.[11]

This Act applied to countries outside the Western hemisphere, preventing immigration from Asia, and setting very restrictive quotas on immigrants from other countries. Due in part to the strength of the agricultural lobby, however, Mexico was exempt from the quotas. Farmers argued that they needed Mexican labor, and that proximity to Mexico increased the chances that Mexicans would come as temporary migrants and then return home, thus reducing their threat. The president of Sunkist furthered the racial myth that Mexicans were "naturally adapted to agricultural work, particularly in the handling of fruits and vegetables."[12]

By the 1930s, then, there was no shortage of farm labor in California, with a large number of Mexican and Filipino workers. One source reported that, in 1933, there were 2.36 workers available for each agricultural job in California.[13] Still, the Great Depression and the Dust Bowl pushed many more farmers to move West in search of better work and better lives. The verdant orange groves of the San Joaquin Valley lured work-hungry migrants to California. The Golden State as a whole, with its temperate climate and diverse agriculture, pulsed with promise in the popular imagination. One migrant song about California referred to the "shining of your sun / the beauty of your orange groves."[14] State boosters circulated flyers in areas with high unemployment, promising good work to those who would come and get it. Abundant advertising, especially by the Sunkist company, promoted an Edenic vision. In *Grapes of Wrath*, Ma Joad captures this vision of California: "Never cold. An' fruit ever'place, an' people just bein' in the nicest places, little white houses in among the orange trees."[15]

Many of those who moved west in search of work came from the Great Plains, with its overworked land, environmental devastation, and failed farms. The damage that American cities felt after the stock market crash was felt even more strongly in the countryside, which was reeling not only from economic collapse but also from drought. The region of the Southern Plains— stretching across Kansas, Oklahoma, Texas, Colorado, and New Mexico— experienced an unprecedented ecological disaster in what was known as the Dust Bowl. Historian Donald Worster describes the Dust Bowl as "one of the most tragic, revealing, and paradigmatic chapters in our environmental history."[16] In the decades before, the economic imperative had driven white settlers to move to the Plains, where they had uprooted the native vegetation to plant wheat. Then, when drought and heavy winds came, there was no sod left to hold down the sandy dirt. Enormous dust storms began to swirl; Worster writes that, for almost a decade through the 1930s, the people of the Plains endured "day after day, year after year, of sand rattling against the window, of fine powder caking one's lips, of springtime turned to despair, of poverty eating into self-confidence."[17] This environmental disaster, coupled with the economic disaster of the Great Depression, left many Plains farmers searching for a new start, moving even farther West.

Although many of these migrants were, often derogatorily, known as "Okies," they came not only from Oklahoma, but also from states across the Southwest and Midwest. Farmers all over this region suffered from broader economic forces, in addition to the drought and soil loss. Some of those who had owned land lost it to foreclosure as the market collapsed. Even more were tenant farmers and sharecroppers, who had little incentive to continue farming as prices dipped lower. And when the AAA offered subsidies to farmers to keep land out of production in 1933–5, it was typically the tenants' land that was left to lay fallow. The mechanization that characterized agriculture in the first decades of the twentieth century also led to the consolidation of small farms and the reduced need for labor on the large farms that remained. One migrant recalled being "tractored off" his farm: "the landowner bought two dozen tractors and let go nearly a hundred share-cropper families."[18]

But when tens of thousands of Great Plains migrants arrived, California was far from the promised land. One migrant said, "They told me this was the land o' milk an' honey, but Ah guess the cow's gone dry, and the tumblebugs has got in the beehive." There wasn't enough work to go around, and the oversupply of labor pushed wages even lower. With little money to be made, the migrants settled into tents and make-shift communities along irrigation ditches. Native Californians looked down on these poverty-stricken newcomers, with one grower exclaiming, "This isn't a migration—it's an invasion! They're worse than a plague of locusts!"[19] The migrants moved on, following the oranges, the potatoes, the peas, whatever crops were ready for picking, working for unsustainable wages.

Nativists—or those who held anti-immigrant views—also used the Dust Bowl migrants' arrival as further ammunition in their campaign to push Mexican repatriation, or deportation. Over the course of the 1930s, millions of Mexican and Mexican-Americans were deported, though exact numbers are difficult to determine. A combination of outright racism, eugenic concerns about racial contamination, and fears about unemployment motivated this program. Some officials pushed for deportation with claims that poor citizens needed the jobs that Mexican-Americans held. Among those who were forced to leave were US citizens and legal permanent residents. Local governments refused to employ anyone of Mexican descent, and often anyone with brown skin was targeted in raids. Although the word "repatriation" suggested that this was voluntary on the part of the Mexican-Americans, or that it was a humanitarian venture on the part of the US government, research suggests this was instead the largest mass deportation in American history.[20]

Questioning the Orange Empire

Not all were willing to accept the injustices pulsing through the agricultural system of the 1930s. The decade saw a number of efforts—on the part of laborers, the federal government, writers and artists, and politicians—to push back against and reform this system. Within California orange production in particular, "the system" was embodied by the Sunkist company, which was at the head of what Douglas Sackman calls "the Orange Empire." The Sunkist brand was created by the California Fruit Growers Exchange, founded in 1893, and quickly grew to embody the idea of California fruit production. The image

Sunkist projected was one of abundance, natural harmony, and economic growth. All this covered up the low wages, hard labor, racialized workers, and the environmental toll that allowed the Orange Empire to grow.[21] Sunkist took the lead in the 1930s in putting down the agricultural strikes and political movements that evinced dissatisfaction with their model.

In 1933, Upton Sinclair, author of *The Jungle*, became the Democratic candidate for governor of California. He had been a member of the Socialist party, but switched his affiliation to Democrat, buoyed by FDR's success. He ran on an ambitious campaign to End Poverty in California (EPIC), which proposed having unemployed people create worker cooperatives on idle farms and factories seized by the government, along with government-provided pensions and a progressive state income tax. The worker cooperatives were based on existing examples—as when a Santa Monica group of unemployed citizens offered to maintain the University of California's experimental citrus plot in exchange for surplus oranges.[22] EPIC also took aim at the AAA policy that led to mountains of burning oranges, stating that "the destruction of food or other wealth … is economic insanity."[23] The EPIC campaign launched a grassroots movement throughout the state, and laid the foundation for liberalism in California. It also influenced later New Deal programs at the federal level.

Sinclair was joined by other leaders across the nation who criticized President Roosevelt's programs for not going far enough. Louisiana governor and then US senator Huey Long launched the Share Our Wealth movement in 1934. Father Charles Coughlin grew to prominence through a weekly radio program, spouting both calls to nationalize banks and antisemitic paranoia. Dr. Francis Townsend, a public health officer from California, called for old-age pensions. All of these voices of popular discontent pushed FDR to propose the Second New Deal in 1935, moving beyond a focus on economic recovery to promote economic security. The centerpiece was the Social Security Act of 1935, which created a system of support for the unemployed, the elderly, and the disabled. Social Security signaled a departure from how the federal government had functioned throughout the nation's history—the government now took some responsibility for intervening in the economy, and for protecting Americans from economic misfortune.[24]

In addition to these political movements, agricultural laborers also began to resist in the 1930s. In 1933 and again the following year, nearly 50,000 workers were involved in a wave of strikes throughout California, many led by the Cannery and Agricultural Workers' Industrial Union. The union represented migrant workers against the growers. In 1936, Mexicano citrus workers in Orange County went on strike, seeking union recognition, along with higher wages and better treatment from foremen. They were met with "pick handles, shotguns, tear gas, and handcuffs," were jailed and denied food, and were threatened with deportation.[25]

The president of Sunkist, Charles Collins Teague, saw Sinclair's EPIC campaign and farmworker unionization as "kindred menaces."[26] He, along with other state business leaders, led a campaign to quash both of these threats. Teague raised a half million dollars from corporations to carry out a full-on assault against Sinclair, a total smear campaign that launched a modern form of politicking. The opponents published widely distributed pamphlets skewering him, created cartoons and radio shows to depict the dystopian future under Sinclair's governorship, and undermined his authority in all areas.[27] After Sinclair was defeated through these attacks, Teague wanted to redirect the remaining anti-EPIC funds to a group called the Associated Farmers, who were the primary opponents of farmworker unionization. When the citrus workers struck in 1936, it was this group who worked with the press and law enforcement to spread propaganda about the striking workers, and to respond with fierce repression.[28]

In the wake of this blowback, writers, artists, and the federal government took some small steps to draw national attention to the stark inequities in orange growing and other agricultural ventures through their various documentary forms. The government sponsored some of these works through the Resettlement Administration (later, the Farm Security Administration, FSA), a New Deal agency, which was responsible for Dorothea Lange's famous "Migrant Mother" photograph, and Pare Lorentz's groundbreaking film about the ecological collapse of the Dust Bowl, *The Plow That Broke the Plains*. The FSA also opened the first federally operated camp to house migrant laborers in 1937. In 1935, as part of the Second New Deal, the National Labor Relations Act was passed, which offered many workers basic labor protections and supported unionization. But the Act explicitly excluded farm workers, as well as domestic workers, from the protections.[29]

Despite these and other efforts, the Orange Empire and the system in which it was embedded remained strong. As FSA ethnographer Charles Todd wrote in 1939: the "system of absentee and corporation ownership prevailing in California, with its resulting demand for a roving, landless proletariat, must be revamped."[30] His call went unheeded.

Oranges for Happiness and Health

Oranges, those golden globes of promise and conflict, were not just caught up in debates around their production (or growing), but also around their consumption (or eating). Americans ate—and drank—oranges throughout the 1930s, for pleasure, for health, and for convenience.

During an otherwise lean time, when many were hungry and undernourished, oranges were a rare treat. One woman, Peggy Terry, recalled in an oral history interview how she went with her family to a breadline that was giving away potatoes in the early Depression. She saw that "they had a truck of oranges parked in the alley. Somebody asked them who the oranges were for, and they wouldn't tell 'em. So they said, well, we're gonna take those oranges. And they did. My dad was one of the ones that got up on the truck. They called the police, and the police chased us all away. But we got the oranges."[31] Even in a time of want, people sought out not just calories in the form of potatoes, but also brightness, flavor, and indulgence—just what the oranges, even if pilfered, offered. Oranges were also a treat at Christmas time, stuffed into Depression-era stockings. In one oral history interview, Richard Grondin from Ohio recalled, "An orange was a big thing because you couldn't afford one during the year." An Oklahoma folk song compared oranges to Santa Claus, both delightful fictions of the imagination.[32]

The discovery of vitamin C also justified orange consumption for the sake of health. Although people had known for centuries that citrus fruit prevented a disease called scurvy, at least since James Lind's definitive 1753 A Treatise on the Scurvy, it wasn't until the twentieth century that scientists isolated the molecule responsible. The discovery of vitamin C was one in a series of nutritional discoveries in the early twentieth century, coming on the heels of Dr. Joseph Goldberger's linkage of the diseases pellagra—mentioned in the opening vignette of this chapter—to dietary insufficiency in 1926, which was then connected to niacin or vitamin B3 a decade later.[33] In 1927, Hungarian scientist Albert Szent-Györgyi isolated crystals of hexuronic acid, or what came to be known as Vitamin C, for which he won the Nobel Prize in 1937.[34] Quickly, orange growers and physicians alike began to boost the powers of this new vitamin. In California, Sunkist used vitamin C to reinforce the image of "oranges as a gift of nature scientifically proven to promote health and growth—the perfect antidote to all of the pathologies of modern living."[35] Herman N. Bundesen, president of the Chicago Board of Health, called it the "mystic white crystal of health," and called for mothers to "feed their children orange juice, tomato juice, pineapple juice, or cole slaw regularly."[36] Of course, this placed gendered responsibility on mothers and women to be the guardians of health. It was they who were expected to have the knowledge and means to buy the right foods, stay abreast of the new health findings, and devote their lives to protection of their children's well-being.

This new nutritional knowledge combined with emerging technologies to make new forms of orange consumption possible. Since the orange had first traveled from Asia to the area that became the United States around 1700, and then grew to support industries in California and Florida by the late nineteenth century, it had largely been consumed fresh, as a whole orange or juiced at home. But the passage of Prohibition with the enactment of the eighteenth amendment in 1920, which banned alcohol across the country, jumpstarted consumer and business interest in alternate beverages that could be consumed in social settings. Soda fountains flourished. Sunkist stepped in to spread the gospel of orange juice, inventing a heavy-duty electrical juicer in the 1920s that was sold to soda fountains, as well as to restaurants and cafeterias.[37] Orange juice consumption skyrocketed, contributing to a threefold increase in overall citrus consumption between 1920 and 1940. Historian Richard Hooker writes of this new taste for orange juice: "never before had a food habit been adopted so quickly by so many people."[38] This trend was further bolstered by new methods of canning orange juice that were developed in the 1930s, improving the flavor—and sales—of canned juice.[39] This was also the era in which American consumers came to generally trust canned food as a whole, making the acceptance of canned juice easier.[40]

Another 1930s phenomenon provided a new venue for consumers to purchase oranges and orange juice, first canned and later frozen concentrated and refrigerated. The year 1930 saw the opening of what is considered the country's first "Super Market," King Kullen in Jamaica, New York. The huge store with separate departments, low prices on a large number of items, and a self-service model created a new marketing form that would reshape the American consumer landscape. The Great Depression created the right environment for supermarkets to take root: the low prices made up for the cavernous space and impersonal atmosphere. Cash-strapped consumers were willing to trade the personal relationships at their independent grocers in order to save money. Supermarkets boasted dedicated produce departments, where produce managers handled oranges and other fruits and vegetables with care, creating mass displays that lured customers in with their eye appeal.[41] Shoppers flocked to the brightly lit, carefully arranged, and frequently restocked mounds of golden oranges, shipped from California and Florida, where they had been picked by the hands of migrant farm laborers.

The Complexity of Sorrow and Hope

In *Grapes of Wrath*, Grandpa Joad imagines the bounty of California: "Jus' let me get out to California where I can pick me an orange when I want it."[42] In the height of the Great Depression and the Dust Bowl, in Oklahoma, the freedom of the orange represents everything that he doesn't have. It would be a rare treat amid the monotony of a Depression-era diet, its abundance a countervailing force against the limitations and hunger pangs at home.

But, as we've seen in this chapter, this image did not represent reality. While the oranges may have indeed been plentiful in California in the 1930s, access to them was not. They were not free for the taking. Oranges were controlled by corporations like Sunkist as part of the Orange Empire; their supply was regulated by growers who burned mountains of oranges to keep prices up; the labor forces that picked them were racialized and oppressed. As the Joad family traveled west on Route 66, they began to confront these realities, finding California to not be the dreamscape they had pictured. Their images were likely based on the lush green orchards and radiant orange globes advertised on the sides of Sunkist orange crates shipped around the country—the same kinds of crates used to build ramshackle structures in Hoovervilles in the early days of the Depression.

Other Americans shared the Joads' disillusionment, as the country reeled from all of these blows in the 1930s. Agricultural workers went on strike to demand better working conditions. Writers and artists projected the reality of ordinary citizens to broader audiences. And with the election of President Roosevelt in 1932, the federal government took on new responsibilities in shaping the economy. New Deal agencies like the Agricultural Adjustment Administration—controversial though they may have been at first—made clear that the nation's farmers and citizens would not be left to fend for themselves. And FDR responded to critics like Upton Sinclair and others by incorporating their ideas, introducing even farther-reaching programs, like Social Security, as part of the Second New Deal in 1935.

Throughout all of it, oranges themselves—rather than the agricultural system they were caught up in—continued to bring flavor and brightness, acidity and vitamins to Americans. For many who only encountered oranges in the form of juice at their local soda foundation or as part of a supermarket display, the fruit still held the sense of promise and freedom that Grandpa Joad had initially wished for. In a time of economic and environmental devastation, oranges embodied all the complexity of sorrow and hope.

10

Spam:

Eating in the Second World War

During the Second World War, the popular Army magazine *Yank* published a poem titled "SPAM" with the following opening stanza:

Jackson had his acorns, Grant his precious rye,
Teddy had his poisoned beef, worse you couldn't buy.
The doughboy had his hardtack without this Army's jam.
All armies on their stomachs move, and this one moves on spam.[1]

This rhyme highlights both the centrality of food to war in general and of Spam to this war in particular. Of all the iconic war foods on that list, Spam was the only one carrying a particular brand name and the one that was a newly invented food, having only come on the market a few years before the war. The canned pink processed meat product was introduced by Hormel Foods in 1937 and quickly spread around the world, both intensely loved and reviled. The United States' entry into the war led to dramatic transformations in the American diet and its influence abroad, with Spam as a central player, as 150 million pounds of canned pork luncheon meat were sent to the army by the end of the war.[2] As anthropologist Sidney Mintz has argued, "war is probably the single most powerful instrument of dietary change in human experience."[3]

The United States' leading status in food production gave it outsized influence both during the war and after. The rapid industrialization of American agriculture and food processing before the war allowed the United States to feed Allied troops all over the world, to keep its domestic population fed even during food rationing, and to set the country up for dominance on the global stage after the war. And it also ushered in an acceleration toward a diet dominated by processed foods, teaching consumers to appreciate

standardized foods that had been developed with wartime needs in mind—
foods that were shelf-stable, preservative-laden, and easy to transport.
Foods like Spam.

*→ foods needed to
be able to be stored* [handwritten]

Spam and Military Food before Pearl Harbor

But it all began in 1891 when, after years of working in Chicago slaughterhouses,
George Hormel started his own meatpacking and canning company in an
abandoned creamery in Austin, Minnesota. The company quickly became
a success. In 1917, George's son Jay Hormel joined the military in the First
World War. Stationed in central France, he used his knowledge of the family
business to suggest that, rather than sending frozen beef quarters still on
the bone from the United States to Europe, the United States could save 40
percent of the cargo space if meatpackers removed the bones before freezing
and shipping. Shipping meat with the bone was one of many inefficiencies
around food during the First World War, which also included food shipped in
faulty containers, inappropriate portion sizes, a lack of standardized recipes,
and a haphazard reliance on local foods.[4] The US Army Quartermaster Corps,
which supplied military food, took Lieutenant Hormel up on his suggestion
and brought him back to the United States to guide American packers in the
process. With this success under his belt, Hormel returned home to begin
taking over the company from his father.[5] Although animal slaughtering and
selling fresh meat remained central, the company also began to produce
many new canned products: a variety of gourmet French-style soups (inspired
by Jay's French wife Jerry), whole tinned hams and chickens, spiced ham,
beef stew, spaghetti and meatballs, and chili con carne. By one count, Hormel
was making a staggering 315 distinct foods by 1937.[6]

Although canned meats had been sold since the early nineteenth century,
they were not widely used among average consumers at first. But beginning
after the First World War, soldiers who were coming back to the United
States after tasting military-provided canned meats (the quality of which had
improved since the "embalmed beef" scandals of the Spanish-American War
two decades prior) stimulated demand. Many of the early canned meats
were sold in large cans, to be distributed to delicatessens and butcher
shops, which would then slice the meats to order. In so doing, customers
had no idea the company name or brand of the canned meat they were
buying, which meant that low-quality products could drag down the profile
of all canned meats. In response, Hormel decided to instead pack canned
luncheon meat in consumer-sized cans and to label them with a distinctive
trademarked name.

[handwritten left margin: *George Hormel ↳ started his own meatpacking & canning co.*]

[handwritten left margin: *soldiers wanted canned meat*]

[handwritten right margin: *save 40% of space if take out bone*]

To develop the formula for this distinctive product, Jay Hormel turned to pork shoulder, a cut of meat that was routinely wasted in the butchering process. Butchers struggled to remove the meat from the bones in large enough pieces to appeal to consumers, who generally looked for intact cuts of meat. But for grinding down and combining with ham, pork shoulder was perfect. Working with several scientists to solve the technical challenges of canning processed meat, Hormel eventually developed a satisfactory product. The ingredients of pork shoulder, ham, water, salt, sugar, and sodium nitrite (a colorant and preservative) were used in 1937 and remained unchanged until 2009 (despite the frequent association of Spam with "mystery meat"). With the ingredients and process set, Hormel just needed a name. As the story goes, he threw a New Year's Eve party in 1936, with each guest receiving a drink in exchange for a completed name suggestion. One guest, an actor named Kenneth Daigneau, who was the brother of a Hormel Vice President, submitted the winning ticket: Spam. Later, it would be suggested that the name stood for "spiced ham" or "shoulder of pork and ham" (or, less flatteringly, Specially Processed Army Meat, Super Pink Artificial Meat, or Some People Are Missing), but in 1936, it was just "Spam."[8]

To announce the new product, Hormel launched what one observer called "one of the earthiest, corniest, and most successful promotion campaigns in U.S. advertising history," with full-color ads in leading American magazines, a unique jingle and singing commercial, special Spam sales teams across the country, recipe books, and promotion on the popular George Burns and Gracie Allen radio show.[9] When Jay Hormel had first committed to advertising and told his father he had spent $500,000 on advertising contracts, George was shocked, scolding, "I can't imagine spending my father's money in any such fashion." Jay replied, "I'm sure you couldn't … but you didn't have a rich dad like me."[10] This investment paid off, with the distinctive advertising leading to a huge increase in sales for Hormel products. Ads for Spam highlighted the shelf-stability, versatility, and convenience of this new product, using quirky taglines like "Cold or Hot SPAM hits the spot!" and offering recipes for breakfast (SPAM and eggs!), lunch (SPAMwich!), and dinner (SPAMloaf!). Hormel's approach to advertising was part of a broader national elevation of consumerism, with the number of food advertisements in women's magazines nearly doubling between 1940 and 1950.[11]

One remarkable Hormel advertisement, in *Life* magazine in 1939, ran a four-page story about the origins of Spam, marked inconspicuously with the word "Advertisement" in the top right corners of each page. It described the exemplary farmers who raised the pigs, the happy well-paid butchers, and the cutting-edge canning machines—operated by "hundreds of Austin girls"—that ensured food safety.[12] The long ad sold the "narrative" of Spam, making it seem accessible, safe, and part of an all-American story. The ad's attention to the incomes and longevity of Hormel's workers also pointed to the unique labor practices of the company, which had recognized unionization after an earlier strike in 1933. Hormel granted its workers a guaranteed annual wage (when most meatpackers instead paid their employees seasonally and inconsistently), written evaluations, and an employee profit-sharing trust.[13]

Even as Jay Hormel was absorbed with advertising his new products, he also turned some of his attention to keeping the United States out of the

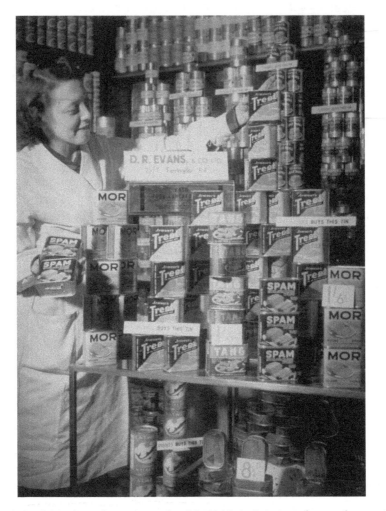

FIGURE 10 *A photo from November 29, 1941, in Britain, where a shop assistant arranges newly arrived canned meats—including Spam, Mor, and Treet—from America, as part of the Lend Lease Act. (Fox Photos/Getty Images).*

Second World War, begun in Europe and Asia by 1939. He was one of the leaders of the America First Committee, the largest and most influential group promoting American isolationism. Hormel even commissioned a Broadway composer to write a song to popularize his view: "This Ain't Our War!"[14] And most Americans agreed with him. Although President Franklin Roosevelt feared the threat of Japanese and German aggression, he responded to popular opinion and waited until after his third presidential victory in 1940 to pass the Lend-Lease Act to support the Allies with food and military equipment, without officially declaring war or violating the Neutrality Acts that Congress had passed several years earlier.

As part of this Lend-Lease Act, Hormel began to ship up to 15 million cans of meat overseas every week, most of it Spam, to Britain and the Soviet Union (Figure 10). By 1944, over 90 percent of Hormel's canned foods were directed for government use.[15] Spam was a boon to hungry populations, sustaining civilians and troops alike. Margaret Thatcher, who would later become the British Prime Minister, recalled Spam as a "war-time delicacy," and a Christmas treat.[16] Journalist Ralph Morse noted that no matter what he ordered at London restaurants, he received some version of "camouflaged Spam": Spam chop suey, Spam in Algerian wine sauce, Spam schnitzel, and so on. (This experience lay the foundation for Monty Python's later 1970 comedy sketch, in which Spam dominates a restaurant menu, and which led to unsolicited email becoming known as "spam.")[17] Soviet leader Nikita Khrushchev wrote that, after losing their "most fertile, food-bearing lands" to the Germans, "without Spam, we wouldn't have been able to feed our army."[18] In these beeleaguered countries, US support in the form of Spam and other supplies was critical.

Fighting the War Abroad

The German strategy of taking over food-bearing lands, as described by Khrushchev, was not incidental. Food and hunger were key tools of belligerents throughout the war, during a time when calorie needs increased alongside the growing challenges of producing and transporting food on a global scale. As historian Lizzie Collingham has described, at least 20 million people died from lack of food in the Second World War, at least as many as died in battle.[19] The desire to command agricultural territory drove both Germany and Japan's aggression, especially as Germany had been driven to defeat in the First World War by food shortages. The National Socialist (Nazi) government of Germany, led by Adolf Hitler, initiated the Second World War with its invasion of Poland in 1939. Britain and France were drawn into the war against Germany, but by

June 1940, the Nazis had overtaken many nations and had joined forces with Italy and Japan to form the Axis Powers. Britain stood alone in Europe for most of 1941 in holding back the Nazi empire, even as the United States sent Lend-Lease support, Spam and all.

On the Eastern front, the Nazis broke their non-aggression pact with the Soviet Union and took the city of Leningrad by September 1941, surrounding it and destroying the city's food warehouses. The siege lasted for nearly two-and-a-half years, with about 1 million people starving to death, and the survivors resorting to eating their pets along with "leather shoes, briefcases, lipstick," and even turning to cannibalism in some desperate cases.[20] Hitler's penetration of eastern Europe also led him to put into action the "final solution" of bringing what he believed to be the master race of Germans to world power. In what came to be known as the Holocaust, the Nazis carried out the horrific genocide of 6 million Jewish people, along with another 6 million people deemed "undesirable"—gypsies, Slavs, homosexuals, disabled people, and others. In the death camps, the Nazis killed these people, who they considered "useless eaters," through forced starvation or poison gas. Writer Primo Levi recalled of his time at Auschwitz, the camp "is hunger: we ourselves are hunger, living hunger."[21]

Soon after the siege of Leningrad began, the United States was drawn directly into the war when Japan attacked US military bases at Pearl Harbor, Hawaii on December 7, 1941. The Japanese continued their offensive throughout the Pacific, taking over US territories and British-controlled islands. In the Philippines, US troops surrendered to the Japanese out of hunger in April 1942, and then the starving Americans were marched to prisoner camps, with more than 5,000 dying during the journey and the remaining prisoners fed starvation rations once they arrived—in significant contrast to the plentiful rations fed to prisoners-of-war held in American camps. After many losses, the United States began to gain the upper hand in the Pacific naval war at the Battle of Midway in June 1942, but continued to fight for three more years before reaching Japan itself. Everywhere the American troops went, but especially in the Pacific, they brought their food with them. Spam's ongoing popularity in the islands of the Pacific—especially in Hawaii, Guam, and South Korea—attests to the enduring value of a food that was nonperishable, easy to trade and gift, contained meat (high-status and often rare in island nations), and was emblematic of American power.[22]

The war in the Pacific continued even after the Allies celebrated victory in Europe (V-E Day) on May 8, 1945, after Hitler took his own life in defeat when US troops reached Germany. By that time, US President Franklin D. Roosevelt had died unexpectedly and Harry S. Truman had assumed the presidency. Upon taking office, Truman learned of the top-secret Manhattan Project, in which US scientists and engineers—many of them Jewish

Atomic Bomb ↑ [handwritten annotation above "atomic bomb"]

European refugees—had been developing the atomic bomb, a weapon of unprecedented scale. Truman made the decision to try to bring the Pacific war to an end by dropping two bombs on Japan, one in Hiroshima on August 6, 1945 and the second in Nagasaki on August 9. The profoundly destructive bombs killed over 200,000 Japanese people, many of them civilians, and left many others with radiation-caused diseases. Thus, the Second World War came to an end.

dropped bombs to end war [handwritten annotation in right margin]

Throughout the war, plentiful food came to symbolize the United States, as the people of both Allied and enemy nations marveled at the American rations. Troops abroad ate large quantities of food—the standard ration was over 4,000 calories a day—including high-status foods like meat. One Armour Meatpacking Company advertisement described the US soldier as "the greatest meat eater in the world."[23] Military-supplied foods were labeled with different letters depending on their intended usage: A rations were fresh foods and B rations were prepared foods, both served at camps and bases; C rations were a replication of a standard meal to be used in the field; D and later K rations were emergency foods. Spam was a frequent component of B rations and its generic version, canned pork luncheon meat, was also included in the K ration—for lunch, along with "a packet of twelve glucose tablets, and a tube of bouillon."[24] Although some troops tried the local foods of the places they were stationed—like a group of Marines who cooked "the best meal" from a discovered stash of Japanese food and saké—most ate the standard American diet of meat and grains supplied by the military.[25]

Despite the abundance, troops were not always delighted with military fare, to put it mildly. They complained that there was too much dehydrated food, too much canned food, too much repetition, that they missed foods from home, and that the army cooks lacked proper training and equipment. One Army Air Force group found Spam on their tables for thirty-one consecutive days, the effect of which, one account drily noted, was that "morale was not raised."[26] One veteran Thomas Clancy recalled of Spam, "You had it fried in the morning with chemical eggs. They burned it black as a painted door. They'd cut it up and put it into stews. They put it in sandwiches. They baked it with tomato sauce. They gave it to us on the beach. You got so you really hated it."[27]

In fact, though, much of the canned pork luncheon meat that the troops were eating wasn't actually Spam, but instead other generic versions made with different ingredients designed to withstand a variety of field conditions. Hormel's advertising campaign and Spam's trademarkable name made it a victim of its own success, however, as all products of this type came to be known as Spam. Hormel tried to clear up this confusion and convey the difference in these products, but the magazine *Yank* summed up the views

— The economy boomed after WWII [handwritten annotation at bottom]

of many soldiers: "What's in a name? That which we call Spam / By any other name would taste as lousy."[28]

At times, the food was so distasteful that the troops avoided it altogether: at Espiritu Santo in the Pacific, "it was not uncommon for men … to enter the mess halls, look at the food, and walk out."[29] Indeed, loss of appetite often accompanied the exhaustion and anxiety of combat, even when the food was desirable. But many refugees and other desperate, hungry people looked to American processed foods as a blessed lifeline. One Warsaw woman who received Spam, chocolate, and soup said they were "a blood transfusion, salvation." And although Jay Hormel received hate mail from American soldiers which he kept in a "Scurrilous File," he also received letters of praise from British housewives describing Spam's "perfect flavour and texture" and attesting that "Only those who have eaten [Spam] at dawn, toasted on the end of a knitting needle at a bomb [shelter], amongst debris, can really know [how good it is]."[30] Even Dwight D. Eisenhower later (sort of) defended Spam—in a letter to Hormel Foods for its seventy-fifth anniversary in 1966, he wrote, "I ate my share of SPAM along with millions of other soldiers. I'll even confess to a few unkind remarks about it … But as former Commander in Chief, I … officially forgive you your only sin: sending us so much of it."[31]

These foods were being directed for military use by the Quartermaster Corps, which worked with companies and scientists to formulate military rations. They had the enormously difficult task of creating a global distribution network that could feed millions of people across varied conditions and environments. The organization invested in research to meet this task, headquartered at the Subsistence Research Laboratory in Chicago. The Lab standardized military food products and processes, updating *The Army Cook* and *The Army Baker* manuals and producing Master Menus to guide field cooks, following the new science of nutrition. They worked in close collaboration with large companies like Hormel, Hershey's, and Coca-Cola to turn production toward military ends—enriching and entrenching those corporations even beyond wartime, even as the smaller companies that didn't have the means to conform to Army requirements languished. The Lab refined and developed methods of canning, dehydrating, and freezing foods, and experimented with new packaging technologies, often in collaboration with powerful trade organizations like the National Canners Association and the National Livestock and Meat Board. And the Lab's work led to a narrowed perception of a national "American" diet, as it created a standardized way of eating that excluded or Americanized regional or ethnic foods—rejecting canned tamales or "hogs and hominy," or cooking spaghetti for 100 soldiers with only three cloves of garlic, for example—and bolstered a meat-and-potatoes-approach in its place.[32]

Fighting the War at Home

Not only did food play a major role in warfare in Europe and Asia, but also in wartime civilian affairs in the United States. Although the United States entered the Second World War later than other nations, it had an outsized influence on the war, in large part because of its industrial and agricultural capacity. Wartime mobilization led to a doubling of the gross national product and eliminated unemployment, ending the Great Depression. New federal agencies acquired enormous power, channeling funds and working closely with big business to stimulate manufacturing, science, technology—and economic concentration. Farmers who had accumulated huge surpluses of food during the Depression now had new markets for their products as the United States moved to feed the military and civilians at home and abroad. This growth at all levels, along with the fact that no fighting took place on US soil, left the nation with unparalleled postwar power. As Ralph Watkins of the US National Resource Planning Board put it in November 1942, "We will emerge from this struggle as the dominant power, dominant in naval power, dominant in air power, dominant in industrial capacity, dominant in mineral production, dominant in agricultural production."[33] And he was right.

Government propaganda linked food and consumption to patriotism. After President Roosevelt introduced the concept of the "Four Freedoms"—freedom of speech and worship, freedom from want and fear—to define what Americans were fighting for in the war, "freedom from want" came to be linked to abundant food and consumer goods. Artist Norman Rockwell illustrated each of the four freedoms, with a huge turkey dinner served by a woman at the table of a middle-class white family symbolizing freedom from want. The Office of War Information produced posters, radio shows, and newsreels to influence public opinion in support of the war. One 1942 war emergency bulletin linked dietary choice to war support asking, "Are you Helping Hitler?" by eating "a poor lunch every day" or "Are You Helping Uncle Sam?" by eating "a hearty lunch every day to help to keep you in top-notch physical condition."[34] Food companies took advantage of tax-exemption for advertising during the war—intended to promote pro-war advertisements—to build their brand names.

By May 1942, the US government's Office of Price Administration (OPA) instituted an official system of rationing to control the food supply and allow for surplus to be shipped abroad, after learning in the First World War that voluntary rationing had not really worked. Sugar was the first food to be rationed, followed by butter, canned and processed goods, and red meat. Spam, however, was not rationed even when other canned goods were, offering Americans an alternative to the rationed red meat. One ad read, "Uncle Sam has okayed the use of tin for Spam … enough [for] you as well as the armed forces and our allies … try one of Spam's delightful Victory Meals pictured below."[35] Rationed goods could only be purchased with ration booklets allocated to each citizen, with a complex point system for different foods. The system offered a way for Americans—and especially women as the presumed cooks—to feel that they were contributing to the war effort, even from home. Historian Amy Bentley describes how this idealized image of the "Wartime Homemaker" who maintained stability in times of crisis reinforced gender hierarchies as a counterpoint to the "Rosie the Riveter" image of women working in traditionally male roles in factories, thus reassuring Americans that things could go back to "normal" after the war, with women returning to the kitchen.[36]

Despite rationing, the amount of food that Americans ate was little affected, though the *kinds* of foods they ate did shift. Women's magazines came on board to help promote recipes using non-rationed ingredients. The US Department of Agriculture introduced the "basic seven" food groups to help guide American understanding of nutrition. This guidance, along with that of a new Committee on Food Habits, sought to influence Americans in making substitutions based on similar nutrient profiles, as nutritionists had tried to do in the First World War. Some substitution practices, like using frozen instead of canned vegetables and using baking mixes instead of adding sugar, succeeded and became common after the war. While others, like the soybeans that nutritionists urged Americans to try as a protein alternative, were too much of a threat to a meat-centered way of life and were thus rejected. Chicken, however, was a more acceptable alternative, rising in popularity when red meat was rationed. Americans also enthusiastically responded to the government's promotion of "victory gardens" and home canning, with about 20 million households producing some 40 percent of the nation's vegetables on small plots in 1943, much of which they canned for the next season.[37]

Much of this food conservation was done in the name of making the world "safe for democracy," but as Indian leader Mahatma Gandhi made clear in a 1942 letter to Roosevelt, this notion "seems hollow, so long as India, and for that matter, Africa, are exploited by Great Britain, and America has the Negro problem in her own home."[38] Colonialism and ongoing racism in the United States undermined the Allies' claims of moral virtue. Nazi Germany even upheld American race policies in support of their own genocidal practices. As one observer put it, it was foolish for the United States "to be *against* park benches marked 'Jude' [Jew] in Berlin, but to be *for* park benches marked 'Colored' in Tallahassee, Florida."[39] The US military was segregated, with Black men disproportionately assigned to kitchen duty or other demoted positions. At home, even as Black migrants moved North as part of the second Great Migration, in search of wartime work and to escape Southern segregation, they were first excluded from defense employment. Only after Black leader A. Philip Randolph and other activists threatened a March on Washington in 1941 and launched the double-V campaign—victory over the Axis Powers abroad and over segregation and racism at home—did Roosevelt issue Executive Order 8802, which forbade discrimination in defense jobs. Alongside these conditions for Black people, the US government, influenced by antisemitism, rejected thousands of Jewish immigrants seeking refuge during the Holocaust. And the United States also intensified its use of exploitative agricultural labor with the launch of the bracero program in 1942, which brought in 150,000 Mexican immigrants to work on farms producing the food on which victory in the war depended.

But among the most shameful acts by the US government in the Second World War was the forced relocation and incarceration of over 110,000 Japanese-Americans in internment camps, beginning in 1942. People were forcibly removed from their homes, mostly in California, and transferred to inhospitable camps throughout the west and as far east as Arkansas. Two-thirds of these were American-born—many of them spoke only English and had never traveled to Japan. But ongoing anti-Japanese propaganda and racist imagery made Americans view all Japanese-descended people with fierce suspicion, even as German-Americans and Italian-Americans were largely left alone. White farmers in California also supported internment as a way of taking over Japanese farms, which produced 10 percent of the state's fruits and vegetables on only 1 percent of the state's land.[40] Many Japanese-Americans farmers had to leave their farms behind, and were never able to recover them after the war. In Hawaii, although nearly 40 percent of the population was of Japanese descent, there was no internment, as the economy would have collapsed without this crucial labor. But Japanese-American fishermen were restricted from deep-sea fishing; in many cases they turned to canned fish and Spam to replace their critical source of protein, contributing to the ongoing popularity of Spam in Hawaii today. On the mainland, the Japanese internees had to eat largely what was served in the dining halls and came from government warehouses, far from familiar Japanese foodways. According to some accounts, Spam musubi—a highly popular dish in present-day Hawaii in which grilled Spam and rice are wrapped with seaweed—has its origins in internment camps, where internees used culinary inventiveness to adapt the processed foods like Spam that they were served into something more familiar and palatable.[41]

Bringing the War to a Close

Even as the war came to an end with Japanese surrender in August 1945, the influence of wartime—not least in the realm of food and power—would extend for many decades to come. Actress and food writer Madhur Jaffrey recalls her early teen years when her hometown of Delhi, India was flooded with US Army "leftovers in the form of mysterious boxes known as K-Rations ... Thus I was introduced to my first olive, my first fruit cocktail and my first taste of Spam. I rolled mouthfuls around my tongue and pronounced each of them to be exotic and wonderful."[42] This movement of processed military food around the globe points first to how the United States became a global power—often with food as a medium of that power—as the Cold War began and, second, to how industrialized foods like Spam and others intended for wartime use transferred to the domestic marketplace.

The United States reached the end of its war with its economy, agriculture, and infrastructure intact and even strengthened, in great contrast to much of the rest of the world. Britain, with the Lend-Lease shipments ending in August 1945, endured even more severe rationing after the war. Crop failure and flooding plagued much of Europe and Asia, with an estimated 500 million people facing famine, worsened by war-related homelessness. The US government and public engaged in debates about whether to continue rationing in order to help end starvation abroad, but ultimately decided against it, though agencies like the Red Cross did send Spam-bearing food packages to starving European refugees. Overall, American-produced grain was directed toward feeding livestock to supply a meat-dependent citizenry at home rather than toward famine relief. Soon, as relations between the United States (and its democratic capitalist system) and the Soviet Union (under communism) worsened as each sought to exert its influence over the postwar world, food became a weapon in the emerging Cold War. The Marshall Plan was passed in 1948, offering billions of dollars in aid, much of it food and agriculture-related, to help European nations rebuild—but only those nations that resisted Soviet communism. The Soviet Union, which sustained the highest wartime casualties of any country, with about 20 million people dead from warfare or starvation, and had its agricultural system destroyed, considered the Marshall Plan a tool of US imperialism.

The United States and its food system thus made inroads throughout the globe, spreading an increasingly industrialized way of eating. Many of the innovations in packaging and processing that had emerged from the Subsistence Research Lab to better feed troops in the field now transferred into the domestic sphere. Before the war, there had been about 1,000 types of processed foods on the market; after the war, the number grew to nearly 5,000 new products—including canned meats inspired by Spam, dried mixes of all sorts, frozen orange juice concentrate, and ready-to-eat meals.[43] Food scientist Emil Mrak observed, "A lot of the foods we have today, the idea of acceptability and convenience, and stability, all came out of the war, the Quartermaster Corps."[44] These new foods also relied on the new large-scale distribution networks that the military had created. They provided convenient options for women who remained in the workforce even after the war. In the end, food companies profited most, with Americans shifting from spending $20 billion for food in 1941 to $60 billion by 1953, with more and higher-priced processed foods in their shopping carts.[45]

And among those processed foods, Spam continued to reign supreme. Despite the negativity hurled at it by American soldiers, many of them came home with a taste for Spam, a nostalgic memory for the food of war. This popularity was bolstered by the creation of the Hormel Girls in 1946, a troupe of sixty female musicians who had served in the war and now starred in a top-rated radio show, traveling around the country promoting and distributing Spam to eager audiences. Spam thus continued to spread, around the country and around the globe, supplying a shelf-stable and nonperishable meat product, a canned messenger that conveyed America's new position as a world power, with plenty of processed food.

11

Green Bean Casserole:

Postwar Foodways

In 1955, in the Campbell Soup Company's test kitchen in Camden, New Jersey, a new recipe was born. It was called Green Bean Bake, and it had three basic ingredients: canned green beans, Campbell's cream of mushroom soup, and French's canned fried onions—staples that most 1950s homes would have on their canned-food-laden shelves. The home economist team that settled on this winning recipe tinkered with different seasonings, trying celery salt, black pepper, Worcestershire sauce, and ham slices before finally settling on soy sauce. When one experimental baking session led to the conclusion that dish needed "more pep," the home economists "stirred in extra soy sauce," until the dish was just right.[1]

Soon, the recipe, with the new name "green bean casserole," was printed on the back of Campbell's soup cans and published in recipe booklets that the company distributed as part of its marketing campaigns. This humble recipe was one of the hundreds produced in that test kitchen, all with the goal of creating tastes for Campbell's products and cementing the idea of using soup as an ingredient in a broad range of dishes. Dorcas Reilly, the lead home economist who oversaw the green bean casserole development process, could also claim tomato-soup meatloaf, a tomato soup cake, and Sloppy Joe "souperburgers." But none of these other dishes would reach the level of fame of green bean casserole which, after being featured in an Associated Press holiday feature as part of a Thanksgiving spread, grew to become an integral holiday dish, gracing the tables of more than 20 million Americans a half-century later. Campbell's reports that the casserole is the most popular recipe to ever come out of its corporate kitchen and its most-requested, with about 40 percent of all condensed cream of mushroom soup ending up in green bean casseroles across the nation.[2]

typical

Despite its popularity today, the green bean casserole is a quintessential food of the 1950s, capturing the transformations that were taking place in politics and global affairs, women's role in the home, and the dominance of the food industry. In the years after the Second World War, the United States took on a larger role on the world stage. The country used the economic boost the war had provided, and the ideological victory of having helped make the world "safe for democracy," to assert the dominance of capitalism. As the country engaged in the Cold War against the Soviet Union and its Communist system, food and its trappings became evidence of American superiority. The nation's leaders showed off middle-class suburban homes with shiny kitchens and new technologies, put-together housewives whose labor was reduced through packaged foods, and the abundance of the food supply. The green bean casserole embodied all of these qualities. It was easy enough for any housewife to prepare, made of ubiquitous canned foods, and produced through the marriage of home economics and the food industry. It was thus a potent ideological weapon, alongside other processed food dishes. To understand the dramatic global affairs context for these changes in American society and foodways in the 1950s, let's first step back to understand the picture of the early cold war.

The Cold War Abroad and at Home

The United States and the Soviet Union, allied during the war against a shared enemy, came into conflict soon after the war's end, as each sought to exert influence throughout Europe. These tensions yielded the decades-long conflict known as the Cold War, in which the two countries never directly went to battle, but waged war through proxy conflicts in other nations and through a battle of ideas about whether communism or a capitalistic democracy yielded a better way of life. Throughout the Cold War, food was used as a weapon in the fight. The United States flexed its agricultural and technological muscles as evidence of its superiority. One example in the early years after the Second World War was the launch of the Marshall Plan, which funneled $13 billion in aid to European nations between 1948 and 1952, with the goal of not only feeding hungry people but also loosening trade barriers and preventing Communist takeover.

In the midst of this, the United States and the Soviet Union came into conflict over the city of Berlin, which had been divided among the Allied powers at the end of the war. To prevent the consolidation of economic power among the United States, Britain, and France, the Soviets established a rail blockade of the city in 1948, preventing any food or other resources from entering. In response, the United States airlifted food and supplies to the blockaded city via aircraft for nearly a year, until the Soviet Union finally lifted the blockade. Much of this food was the same canned and processed food that had fed soldiers during the war and would come to define 1950s foods like the green bean casserole. In the Berlin blockade, the ability to stop hunger was the decisive act. In the years following, in addition to food aid, the two warring nations also engaged in the nuclear arms race and the space race, each trying to develop more powerful nuclear weapons and superior space exploration.

By 1950, American fears about the spread of communism extended from Europe out to Asia and Latin America, leading to a series of proxy wars, in which the United States supported anti-communist regimes—no matter how undemocratic—as a way of battling what it saw as Soviet influence. Again, food and agricultural control led the way. In Venezuela, for example, businessman Nelson A. Rockefeller Foundation launched American-style supermarkets and efforts at industrializing Venezuelan agriculture as anticommunist weapons.[3] The United States also supported the overthrow of democratically elected Jacobo Árbenz in Guatemala, purportedly to prevent Communist power, but also to support the business interests of the American United Fruit company, which benefitted from industry control of agricultural lands and opposed Árbenz's land reform proposals, which would have returned land to poor peasants. Attention turned to Asia when Mao Zedong and his Chinese Communist Party took over China, with its quarter of the world's population, in October 1949. The next year, the Korean war began when, after Communist North Korea invaded South Korea, the United States sent troops to fight against North Korea. After several years of fighting and over a million combat casualties, the war ended in a stalemate, with no clear victory.

In the United States, these global engagements had significant ramifications, as the so-called "second red scare" swept through American politics and culture. A polished housewife serving her family green bean casserole each evening came to embody a kind of American conformity in which not only communism but any kind of unorthodox views or social status were seen as suspect. White norms, traditional gender roles, domesticity, patriotism, celebration of capitalism, and religiosity were held up as ultimate "American values" and talismans against communism. As politician James O'Connel said in 1960, "When a woman comes to be viewed first as a source of manpower, second as a mother, then I think we are losing much that supposedly separates us from the Communist world."[4] Infamous Senator Joseph McCarthy claimed that the country was in an "all-out battle between communistic atheism and Christianity," underlining the religious conservatism of the decade.[5] In 1954, the words "one nation, under God" were added to the pledge of allegiance and in 1956, "In God We Trust" became the national motto. These notions of the "right" ways to believe, behave, and eat were central to the larger political battle.

(margin notes: nuclear arms race & space race; US helped stopped spread of communism; women → gender roles; communist world is where women are manpower → communism is not christianity)

At the national level, security agencies—especially the FBI under director J. Edgar Hoover—and the propaganda-driven US Information Agency produced anti-communist publications and films, and whitewashed American history to downplay poor treatment of Native and African Americans. These messages boosted a uniform notion of American patriotism and cultivated an age of anxiety, in which secret communist spies could be lurking anywhere. The House Un-American Activities Committee and McCarthy led inquiries into people's potential communist sympathies, leading to imprisonment and blacklisting. The height of McCarthy's fame only lasted from about 1950 to 1954, but his name and the term "McCarthyism" became synonymous with the anticommunist witch hunts and hysteria that led to abuses of power. Although the official Communist Party of the United States had never had a large membership, it had been allied with many leftist movements for social justice, such as civil rights, feminism, and gay rights, all of which were weakened by anti-communist panic. These highly publicized anticommunist activities retrenched a sense of the importance of domestic conformity.

Despite the repression of leftist activism and the celebration of white norms, the 1950s saw a significant groundswell that launched the civil rights movement. A number of overlapping strands helped give this movement new impetus: the economic growth that brought so many white Americans into the middle class while leaving Black Americans behind, the horror in response to Nazi ideas of racial purity, the linking of the Black freedom struggle with global efforts for decolonization, and the Cold War impetus for the United States to better align its claims of freedom through democracy with its actual treatment of Black Americans, which served as an embarrassment on the international stage. The major landmarks in the 1950s civil rights movement took on segregation, buoyed by the 1954 Supreme Court decision *Brown v. Board of Education*, which determined that separate schools were inherently unequal and violated the Fourteenth Amendment. Then, in December 1955, Black activist Rosa Parks refused to give up her seat to a white person on a bus in Montgomery, Alabama, launching the yearlong Montgomery bus boycott. The boycott led the Supreme Court to rule public transportation segregation unconstitutional and launched the career of Martin Luther King Jr. Alongside these victories, the ongoing virulent racism of many Americans was on full display with the 1955 brutal murder of fourteen-year-old Emmett Till in Mississippi (and the lack of a conviction for his murderers) and the 1957 protests against the integration of Little Rock's Central High School, with angry white people holding signs reading "race mixing is communism" and spitting on the nine Black children who bravely tried to enter the school.[6] These events brought international attention to racial policies in the United States.

Many Americans reacted to the sense of upheaval that cold war fears and racial inequality brought by trying to exert control, even in small ways.

canned food

→ Being prepared for nuclear attacks

These efforts often circulated around food, home, and family. Just as schools organized "duck and cover" drills to direct kids to hide under their desks in case of nuclear attack (never mind that wooden desks would offer little protection in such a scenario), so too did families build fallout shelters that they hoped would protect them from radioactive residue after a nuclear explosion. And among the most important parts of stocking the fallout shelter was making sure it had plenty of canned foods, underlining how these processed foods became necessary both in times of peace and war. A photograph of one Michigan fallout shelter featured a variety of Campbell's soups, Del Monte canned pineapple, and canned spaghetti; another printed in the Associated Press had one large box labeled "Canned Food" and another "Canned Water"; and one from Tennessee showed Premium Nabisco crackers, Coca-Cola, and Spam, along with a variety of home-canned jars of food.[7] These foods offered at least a semblance of preparedness in a time of turmoil.

Although this sense of fear pervaded much of the 1950s, the Cold War alternately heated up and cooled off over the course of the decade. The summer of 1959 offered a particular moment of reduced tensions and set the scene for the so-called "kitchen debate" between Vice President Richard Nixon and Soviet Premier Nikita Khrushchev—a most iconic episode that highlighted how politics, culture, gender, domesticity, and food were intimately tied together during the Cold War. When Khrushchev took over the Soviet leadership after Joseph Stalin's death in 1953, he expressed a desire for the nations to compete in the production of food and consumer goods rather than in the production of weaponry—as he later said, "Let there be more corn and more meat and let there be no hydrogen bombs at all."[8] Toward this end, the United States put on the American National Exhibition in Moscow to showcase American consumer goods as the fruits of capitalism, with the hope that Soviet visitors would envy the American way of life, full of green bean casseroles, and grow dissatisfied with Communist Party rule.

less bombs → / More food ↑

Among the many displays at the Exhibition were a number of model kitchens, filled with packaged foods and technological innovations and home economist demonstrators. One General Mills advertisement announced that "an estimated 3½ million persons" will see in the Exhibition kitchen "the part that 'convenience foods,' the mixes and frozen products, play in the life of the average American homemaker and her family."[9] It was in the General Mills kitchen that the infamous debate took place, as Nixon pulled Khrushchev aside, saying "I want to show you this kitchen." Despite the fact that the model kitchen wasn't representative of what was accessible to average Americans, Nixon held up this space, its technologies and abundant processed foods, and the feminine women staffing it, as proof of American superiority. But Khrushchev wasn't having it, retorting, "Don't you have a machine that puts food into the mouth and pushes it down? Many things you've shown us are interesting but they are not needed in life. They have no useful purpose. They are merely gadgets." Many Soviet observers agreed, leaving negative comments, such as "We expected that the American Exhibition would show something grandiose, something similar to Soviet sputniks [satellites] … and you Americans want to surprise us with the glitter of your kitchen pans."[10]

Despite this expressed skepticism, Khrushchev actually admired American industrial agriculture and sought to replicate it in the Soviet Union. In the postwar years, American agriculture underwent a dramatic revolution, using mechanization, automation, genetic breeding, and chemical inputs (such as fertilizers, herbicides, pesticides, antibiotics, and hormones) to increase output by 50 percent while decreasing prices and consolidating farms. Khrushchev wanted to see it for himself. A few months after the American National Exhibition, he visited the United States, touring Iowa corn farms, tasting a hot dog, and marveling at American supermarkets. He vowed to set his nation on the course to outproduce American farmers, both to produce abundance and to prove Communist dominance. As he said in 1955, "The people put it this way: Will there be meat to eat, or not? Will there be milk, or not? Will there be decent pairs of pants? This isn't ideology, of course, but what good does it do if everyone is ideologically correct but goes around without trousers?"[11] In other words, the Cold War was fought over ideology, but often that ideology manifested in everyday consumer products, like trousers and meat and canned foods.

Remaking American Society

As green bean casserole came into existence and rose in popularity in the mid-1950s, not only was the country contending with all of political implications of the Cold War, but it was also undergoing a parallel seismic shift in economic and cultural trends. The end of the Second World War brought three decades of economic growth, in which prices stabilized, unemployment was low, and the gap between the rich and the poor narrowed. Some commentators suggested that the United States was moving toward a "classless society," an idea upheld by the food industry who pointed out that dishes like tuna noodle or green bean casserole transcended class lines, with processed food as the great uniter.[12] And indeed many Americans experienced a rising standard of living, complete with new homes in the new suburbs and a full spate of technologies to make those homes more comfortable. Between 1945 and 1949, Americans bought 20 million refrigerators and even more cars.[13] Despite an emphasis on the free market under capitalism, much of this growth was driven by government spending: the GI bill for veterans supported college attendance, business loans, and unemployment benefits; federal spending on the interstate highway system promoted western development and shipping of food and other materials, and military contracts funneled federal dollars into the military-industrial complex.

The suburbs—the new residential areas just outside of cities, neither urban nor rural—represented much of the prosperity of this period, taking "cultural center stage as the postwar embodiment of the American dream and its emblematic consumer market."[14] The unprecedented spike in births after the war, known as the baby boom, created an urgency for these growing families to find homes. A combination of government house-building programs and private developments—like the pioneering Levittown of assembly-line homes built in 1946 in Long Island—created the suburbs, filled with young families, stations wagons, ranch houses, and white picket fences. These suburbs demanded new spatial arrangements. Expanses of private green lawns replaced the urban open spaces that had long provided a location for civic engagement. Centralized supermarkets and their parking lots replaced the corner store, bakery, and fruit vendor. And highways replaced commutes by foot or trolley as fast food and roadside diners replaced city restaurants.

But the shiny veneer of these suburbs and the 1950s affluent society belied much of the inequality that lay beneath. The original Levittowns excluded Black families. And many African Americans were systematically denied home loans and other services through the process of "redlining," in which majority Black neighborhoods were marked with a red line on a map to indicate that they were "high-risk" lending areas to banks and other organizations. As wealthier white families moved to the suburbs with their shiny kitchens, many poor residents were left behind, with "urban decay and suburban sprawl remain[ing] two sides of the same coin."[15] And of course segregation continued across the Jim Crow South. Inequality across racial lines was also prominent, with private consumption celebrated at the expense of public investment in education, health, and welfare.

As Americans turned toward private spending, in the kitchen as much as anywhere, this consumerism was held up as a testament to American freedom, replacing democratic participation as a central responsibility of citizenship. President Eisenhower promoted that idea that enabling every American to "own his comfortable home and a car" was the way to fight communism.[16] The new televisions that took over American homes—with the percentage of American homes owning at least one television increasing from 9 percent to 87 percent between 1950 and 1960—were filled with advertisements that encouraged consumption and with conformist shows like Leave It to Beaver that portrayed a white, middle-class domestic ideal with "traditional" gender roles.[17]

The new suburban kitchens became the heart of the home for "Mrs. Consumer." A 1956 *Better Homes and Gardens* magazine article gushed, "Once an afterthought, the kitchen is rapidly becoming the most important room in the home."[18] This newly important room was filled with processed food from the store to make green bean casseroles and the like, and with a range of new consumer items—from the new Formica counters and Tupperware containers made possible by plastics innovation, to a cornucopia of appliances that promised to make a housewife's life easier, turning her from "Mrs. Drudge" to "Mrs. Modern."[19] Never mind that ever-higher standards meant that women spent as much time on household chores in the 1950s as they had in the 1920s, around fifty-two hours a week.[20]

This consumer ideology was also very gendered, with women being held up not only as moral guardians but also as the ultimate consumers, able to whip up a nourishing meal on command while wearing high heels. Despite the fact that women were working in significant numbers—in 1955, 33 percent of white women worked, and 44 percent of women of color, with those numbers continuing to grow—media and the government idealized nuclear families with men as the working head of household and women staying at home.[21] Historians Shane Hamilton and Sarah Phillips argue that the "tenacity of [the] domestic ideology" was a response to the anxiety of the period: "Marriage and babies, in short, offered security and reassurance in a world still haunted by a genocidal world war and now faced with the real threat of nuclear annihilation."[22] FBI Director J. Edgar Hoover, comparing American housewives with Soviet women who worked in factories, declared that mothers did "not need to put on overalls to prove [their] patriotism … There should be a hot meal ready to serve" when the children and husbands come home.[23] And of course, food companies were happy to step in and help women with these unreasonable expectations, providing ready-to-eat foods with "built-in maid service" that housewives could whip up in a jiffy, easily mixing a can of green beans with a can of cream of mushroom soup before Dad and the kids got home.

Of course, this media representation of housewives and of the broader 1950s conformist culture does not tell the whole story. Many women worked— as those outside the white middle class long had—and not all women cooked by mixing cans of food. Indeed, the editors of *McCall's* expressed surprise in 1954 when their readers clamored for the magazine to republish a complex spaghetti recipe: "We *knew* it made the best spaghetti we ever tasted," they wrote, "but we also knew it took a lot of time and an assortment of ingredients."[24] As this and the rise of Julia Child's complex French cuisine by the early 1960s demonstrated, the demand for convenience foods was not uniform. Nor was the embrace of a religious, gendered, capitalist brand of American patriotism. Elvis Presley and his sensual rock 'n' roll spurred a

FIGURE 11 *This classic image of the happy white housewife, with her high heels, styled hair, pretty clothes and apron, and most up-to-date kitchen appliances conveys the heart of patriotic Cold War era arguments about how the role of American food and women bolstered the nation's claims to superiority. (Getty Images).*

rebellious youth identity, furthered by the Beat movement's countercultural behavior and criticisms of mass society. Gay communities found a place to be themselves in some large cities. And popular books published during the 1950s offered critiques of inequality, suburban life, the modern workplace, and the influence of advertising. But through it all, media continued to elevate a narrow interpretation of Cold War American families, complete with a housewife in the kitchen with her pearls, styled hairdo, and frilly apron as she made canned food casseroles, with pleasure (Figure 11).

large cities gay women.

The Food Industry Ascendant

Let's now return to Dorcas Reilly in that Campbell's test kitchen in 1955, tinkering with her Green Bean Bake recipe. She had graduated from the Home Economics program at the Drexel Institute of Technology in 1947 and then used that degree to secure a spot as a professional home economist at the Campbell Soup Company, by then a major processed food producer. The close relationship between home economics and the food industry that had begun around the turn of the twentieth century when Jell-O was rising in popularity had further solidified by mid-century. For the next decade, until she married and left Campbell's to raise her children, Reilly was one of two full-time employees who developed recipes for the company, in the test kitchen that was a "modern technological wonder," a "sparkling laboratory ... [that] had "a wall of refrigerators, the best mixers and kitchen utensils, and both gas and electric ranges."[25] This laboratory-kitchen space captured the marriage of the science with the home, in order to promote the food industry—much as the General Mills kitchen at the American National Exhibition did. Although Reilly's son recalled after her death that "she was not a flashy person ... she just went in and did her job every day, like most blue-collar people," Reilly's role as home economist was less a blue-collar job than a highly professionalized position for educated women at a time when many women were denied professional status.[26]

Home economics offered a place for women—especially white women—to position themselves as experts. Although a few Black women, like Flemmie Kitrrell and Freda De Knight, achieved prominence in the field, state chapters of the American Home Economics Association continued to reject Black applicants throughout the 1950s.[27] Those home economists who could find work were typically hired by food companies, which meant that many of the dishes these professional women touted were a hodgepodge of processed foods that sometimes hardly seemed palatable, like the General Foods "Salad Pie" published in the *Journal of Home Economics* in 1959, which consisted of a pie shell filled "a combination of lemon Jell-O, frozen mixed vegetables, and cottage cheese, [and topped] with a layer of lemon Jell-O mixed with tomato sauce."[28] This partnership also transferred into public schools, where home ec teachers taught students how to bake only from mixes, to prevent failure—and promote the companies that sold baking mixes while they were at it. Campbell's formed its first home economics unit in the late 1930s, charged with learning "what housewives like in food products," "encouraging the use of Campbell's products," and writing Campbell cookbooks.[29]

One of Campbell's most popular cookbooks was "Cooking with Condensed Soup," which promoted the common strategy of using soups as an ingredient in other dishes, in some ways mimicking the use of white sauces in fancy French foods, in contrast to more common American condiments like gravy and ketchup. The cream of mushroom soup had been commonly used as a "cooking soup" since its introduction in 1934. It had grown in popularity especially in the Midwest, where it came to be known by some as the "Lutheran binder" and was often used as a filler in a casserole, or "hot dish."[30] The tuna noodle casserole came to embody 1950s foodways alongside the green bean casserole, reportedly serving as the favorite meal of President Harry Truman, as prepared by his wife Bess. Both of these iconic dishes used canned cream of mushroom—or sometimes the less popular cream of celery—soup to hold it all together. They, like all casseroles, were thrifty ways to use up whatever small bits you had on hand, in whatever proportions. And both casseroles also had a crunchy topping that added texture and visual interest to the top of the creamy gloppy contents: crumbled potato chips in the case of tuna casserole, canned fried onion rings in the case of green bean casserole. In the words of author Laura Shapiro, the crispy onions were "the touch of genius" that offered glamour to the dish—a common food industry strategy.[31]

The green bean casserole was a dish that displayed canned foods in all their glory, as they came into their prime. The canning industry had operated in the United States for more than a century and had already been widely popular for several decades, but finally reached its heyday in the 1950s, when canned foods dominated grocery store shelves and Poppy Cannon's 1953 *The Can-Opener Cookbook* was all the rage. Canned foods were now joined by a dizzying array of new processed foods, which built upon the foundation the canning industry had laid.[32]

Primary among these new products were frozen foods which, after a rocky start with pioneering work by Clarence Birdseye in the 1920s, began to achieve prominence in the 1950s, when supermarkets and home kitchens began to install freezers that could handle the new products and mechanically refrigerated transportation addressed distribution issues. Wartime rationing of canned foods also gave frozen foods a boost as an unrationed alternative. By the mid-1950s, frozen orange juice concentrate, frozen fish sticks, and frozen TV dinners had achieved substantial market share. TV dinners were a particular hit after Swanson's began selling these marvels in 1954, linking them to the magic of television.[33] By 1955, in a testament to their market success, the leading processor Campbell's acquired Swanson's, marrying two canning and freezing giants together.

Even as these canned and frozen and boxed foods took hold in the marketplace, representing the fruits of capitalism on an international stage, and as the food media breathlessly announced that fresh produce was a "thing of the past," significant skepticism still remained.[34] For one, standardized packaged foods were bland—designed to appeal to a broad cross-section of society, bred to withstand processing rather than for taste, and extended with artificial flavors. For another, the 1950s also saw the rise of gourmet chefs and food writers who decried processed foods. James Beard denounced "the Home Ec side" of cookery and Gael Greene called it "the Velveeta Cocoon."[35] And perhaps most importantly, Americans felt tension between the media representation of cooking as both women's ultimate nurturing task *and* as a tiresome chore that could be conquered through convenience foods. Many women still liked to cook, and felt guilty taking shortcuts.

The food industry sprang into action to address these challenges to its bottom line. It worked with universities to research food science, with the federal government to introduce new products to school lunch programs and other public institutions, and with the chemical industry to devise hundreds of new food preservatives and additives. It also fought against regulators like Congressman James Delaney who brought to light the carcinogenic nature of some chemical additives used in the food industry, like animal hormones, preservatives, and pesticides that left residues on some fruits. And the leaders in the food industry heavily invested in marketing and advertising, recruiting popular television stars to promote their products (Ronald Reagan was a spokesman for Campbell's V8 Juice in 1951 and Campbell's sponsored Lassie in 1954), fueling the impulse buying made possible by self-service supermarkets, flooding magazines with full-color ads after advances in color photography, and touting the "convenience" and "built-in maid service" that Americans were told they now needed.[36] As Laura Shapiro writes, "a manufactured sense of panic began to pervade even day-to-day cooking." General Mills outfitted a researcher with tiny electric lights on her fingers so that a cameraman could track her motions as she made pie from scratch versus using a baking mix—to show how much time she purportedly saved.[37]

A final tool in the industry's arsenal was the use of consumer psychology. A key figure in this work was Ernest Dichter, a psychologist who coined the term "focus group" and who led the Institute for Motivational Research, which informed the advertising campaigns of many food companies. He famously put forth the "egg theory," arguing that women avoided buying pre-packaged cake mixes that had dried eggs because only adding water didn't fulfill their sense of duty to show love through baking; conversely, if companies instead had women add their own fresh eggs, that duty would be met and cake mixes would become more popular. Although the actual outcome of this experiment was less clear, such claims of penetrating the inner psyche of American women appealed to food companies. Similarly, General Mills's Marjorie Husted, who was long the voice of the mythical Betty Crocker, learned from housewives' letters that they felt unnoticed and ignored; she therefore used Crocker's character to make women feel more respected.[38]

From these insights, the food industry developed a new packaged food cuisine that ultimately won over American consumers. Whether it was adding fresh eggs to a cake mix or French fried onions to the top of a green bean casserole, industry men found that giving women a chance to add their own touch, to "glamorize" their cooking, to feel like they were part of the process was key. A 1951 House Beautiful article read, "since most canned foods are still prepared for a very general cross-sectional taste, the trick of using them is

[handwritten left margin: women began to see cooking as a task/chore & felt bad when they took shortcuts to use canned/processed food]

[handwritten right margin: saving time w/ food • food science]

[handwritten bottom: consumer psych
- egg theory
└→ didn't want to buy cake mix
bc it didn't fulfill their duty for]

to treat them like raw materials. Combine them, supplement their flavor, make them into the basis for something else." Poppy Cannon wrote: "armed with a can opener I become the artist-cook, the master, the creative chef," using canned foods as "the basis for any number of prideful, even complicated specialties," bringing haute cuisine into every American kitchen.[39] Processed food could become an ingredient in creativity, a requisite for luxury.

And green bean casserole stood perfectly at these crossroads: a dish made of canned food staples, ingredients (somewhat) creatively combined together to provide any housewife with a sense of satisfaction, a testament to the triumph of the food industry. It was this kind of humble food product that the United States used to showcase the strength of its economy, its suburban homes and housewives, its domestic tranquility, and its industrialized food system as the country competed against the communist threat on an international stage. Green bean casserole became a symbolic weapon to show American superiority at midcentury.

*started using canned food as ingredient to make their own food

↳ casserole fought against comm.

but if they had their own fresh eggs then the duty & cake would be met mixes would be met up.

coolemz

12

Tofu:

Food in the Counterculture and Protest Era, 1960–75

In the popular vegetarian cookbook *The Enchanted Broccoli Forest*, published in 1982, the author Mollie Katzen writes, "So what is this stuff called Tofu? (Are you afraid to ask, because it seems that Everyone Else Knows and they think you aren't cool?)"[1]

By the time of the book's publication, then, tofu had become something everyone in Katzen's presumed audience would have at least heard about—but how much they *understood* about it depended on how "cool" they were. Just eight years earlier, almost no one had known about the "stuff called Tofu." That began to change in 1975, when another cookbook, *The Book of Tofu*, was published and its authors William Shurtleff and Akiko Aoyagi traveled the United States spreading the gospel of tofu and launching tofu businesses all over.[2] After that point, the white soybean product quickly worked its way into natural foodways and countercultural diets across the country. Before 1975, though, tofu was relatively unknown in the United States, except among Asian-Americans who inherited centuries-long knowledge of tofu and among Seventh-Day Adventists whose religiously based vegetarian diets had long endeared them to soybeans.

Well before tofu's arrival on the national stage in 1975, the seeds for its rise were planted and cultivated most centrally in the decade and a half prior, in the heart of the 1960s and early 1970s. The foundation that prepared the fertile soil for tofu's spread was laid by civil rights activists and anti-Vietnam protestors, by the hippie counterculture and environmentalists, and by the new natural and organic foods movements. It was the culmination of the previous decade of cultural, political, and culinary change. The 1960s were a period of dramatic transformation, as the accelerating civil rights movement, catastrophic

Vietnam War, and an environmental reckoning with an unwavering postwar faith in technical fixes led many Americans to lose confidence in traditional systems. Young people were especially at the center of these changes. They recognized the ways that institutions—from partisan politics to the military to corporations—had failed them. As Bob Moses, one of the organizers of the Student Nonviolent Coordinating Committee (SNCC), said, "We can't count on adults. Very few ... are willing to join the struggle .... This leaves the young people to be the organizers, the agents of social and political change."[3] Although he was referring specifically to movements to register Black voters in the South in the early 1960s, this energy from civil rights directly inspired later resistance movements by other marginalized groups.

The attention to tofu emerged out of a number of interconnected phenomena. Leaders developed a heightened concern for hunger both in the United States and abroad. Vegetarianism emerged as an alternative diet and a potential solution for world hunger. Members of the counterculture grew fascinated with Eastern religions alongside a sense of solidarity with Asian peasants and poor people in decolonizing nations around the world. And a commune movement grew out of countercultural disillusionment with mainstream American institutions. Moreover, tofu reflected the way that food had become increasingly political in the protest era of the 1960s. Although, as we have seen throughout this book, food has always been pivotal, the 1960s saw many different groups embracing food identities and food access as central to their political aims. Through food choices, as in the feminist movement, the personal truly became political.

The Fight for Racial Equality

The most iconic rights movements of this period took place in the arena of civil rights. The 1960s saw a new wave of young Black and white activists tackling racism, as manifested through discrimination, segregation, and disenfranchisement, especially in the Jim Crow South. Despite its absence in many mainstream narratives of this movement, food was at the center. Many activists saw access to food—whether through taking a seat at a local lunch counter or the ability to grow food on their own land—as a fundamental right that was denied them by dominant power structures. Using strategies of nonviolent protest, marches, boycotts, and sit-ins, they pressed for social and legislative change. These activists gathered in Black-owned restaurants as central organizing hubs and rallied food resources to literally feed the movement. They helped focus national attention on the problems of hunger, in Black communities and beyond. And although tofu itself was not a part of civil rights, this movement's broader politicization of food laid the groundwork for tofu's rise in the years to follow.

Though there were earlier less-publicized protests, the "sit-in" movement as a national phenomenon began in Greensboro, North Carolina in February 1960, when four Black students sat down at a segregated Woolworth's lunch counter and declined to leave after being denied service due to their race (Figure 12). Their passive resistance led to a six-month long protest, with national attention, in which hundreds of others joined them, even in the face of violent harassment. Restaurants were one venue in which the injustices of segregation were particularly visible. Black cooks prepared much of the

FIGURE 12 *A photo of an early civil rights sit-in that preceded the more well-known 1960 Greensboro protest. This one was led by Clara Luper to desegregate the lunch counter at Katz Drug Store in downtown Oklahoma City, August 26, 1958. It helped establish the centrality of food to the civil rights movement (Johnny Melton/Oklahoma Historical Society/Getty Images).*

food in white restaurants, but they could not eat on the other side of the counter. When Black Americans traveled by car, they typically had to pack their own food and avoid restaurants (in addition to planning their gas stops carefully and finding their own lodging). Lack of access to food was a symbolic representation of injustice. The Greensboro sit-in launched more than one hundred demonstrations in other cities, leading to restaurant desegregation throughout the South.

The protests also catalyzed other student-led direct action. Throughout, civil rights leaders often used Black restaurants as home base—Paschal's in Atlanta, Dooky Chase's in New Orleans, the Big Apple in Jackson—to strategize and fuel the movement.[4] One early campaign was the Freedom Rides launched by the Congress of Racial Equality (CORE) in 1961, in which integrated groups rode on interstate buses to force the Interstate Commerce Commission to desegregate this mode of transportation. Even when the Freedom Riders were met by angry mobs who beat the activists and, in one case, burned a bus, they persisted. In the "Freedom Summer" of 1964, civil rights groups led a widespread voter registration drive in Mississippi, which was again met by violence, with the well-publicized murder of two white men from New York and a local Black man by a Ku Klux Klan lynch mob.

In the midst of this, the pivotal year of 1963 brought high-profile events in the civil rights movement. In April and May, Martin Luther King Jr. and other activists campaigned to desegregate Birmingham, Alabama, despite Police Commissioner Bull Connor viciously retaliating with high-pressure fire hoses and attack dogs. During this, King was jailed and penned his famous "Letter from a Birmingham Jail," in which he poignantly wrote that Black Americans could wait no more, as they saw the majority of "twenty million Negro brothers smothering in an airtight cage of poverty in the midst of an affluent society."[5] In August, King delivered his famous "I Have a Dream" speech during the March on Washington, in which a quarter million people traveled to the nation's capital to call for "Jobs and Freedom" for Black Americans. These kinds of actions, like any time people gathered, required food and water. Organizers put together 80,000 box lunches of cheese sandwiches and apples, and food writer Poppy Cannon urged protestors to bring food that was "light in weight, non-bulky, and non-squashable or drippy."[6] At the year's end, President John F. Kennedy was assassinated in November 1963, bringing his vice president Lyndon Johnson to the presidency.

During his short presidency, Kennedy had focused more on the Cold War (especially managing relations with communist Cuba) than on civil rights. But Johnson concentrated on addressing poverty and injustice, with a focus on hunger. Inspired by the Freedom Summer activists, in 1964, Johnson called on Congress to pass the Civil Rights Act, which prohibited racial, ethnic, religious, and sex-based discrimination. The far-reaching Act was part of Johnson's set of programs known as the "Great Society," which also included the first federal food stamp program, Medicaid and Medicare, investment in education and the arts and humanities, and a range of "War on Poverty" programs. Then, in 1965, after voting rights activists carried out a march from Selma, Alabama to the state capitol in Montgomery on their third try—after being met with violence from white law enforcement on previous attempts, which drew international outrage—President Johnson called for Congress to pass the Voting Rights Act of 1965. This, along with the twenty-fourth amendment that outlawed the poll tax, allowed Black Southerners to finally reclaim the right to vote that had been taken from them after Reconstruction with the rise of the Jim Crow system at the end of the nineteenth century.

These civil rights campaigns concentrated attention on hunger and poverty. John F. Kennedy had been shocked during his 1960 presidential campaign at Appalachian poverty, saying in his first television debate, "I am not satisfied with nine billion dollars' worth of food rotting in storage while millions go hungry."[7] In 1962, *The Other America* by Michael Harrington focused attention on devastating poverty across the nation. Later, the president's brother Bobby Kennedy traveled through the Mississippi Delta and, upon observing children in states of near starvation, said to a reporter, "My God, I didn't know this kind of thing existed. How can a country like this allow this?"[8] In 1968, CBS News aired a documentary *Hunger in America*, which shocked the nation with images of starving children from many regions and races. For organizers who were themselves poor, these images of hunger and poverty were not so shocking; they lived with it every day.

The Mississippi Freedom Democratic Party and SNCC organized food drives when local racist politicians withheld federal food aid as a tool against Black voting rights. Black organizers like Fannie Lou Hamer, who worked on voting rights in Mississippi and founded Freedom Farm Cooperative to create an alternative food system and poverty relief for impoverished farmers, knew that those in power wielded hunger as a means of social control. If the most basic need for food was not met, the underclass could not fight back. As Hamer said, "Down in Mississippi they are killing Negroes of all ages, on the installment plan, through starvation." She wrote that "food is used as a political weapon" and proposed a countermeasure: "if you have a pig in your backyard, if you have some vegetables in your garden, you can feed yourself and your family, and nobody can push you around."[9]

Similarly, critics who thought the nonviolent strategies of the early movement didn't go far enough noted, "we could sit at the lunch counter, but we couldn't afford a hamburger."[10] One strand of the Black rights movement thus took a more radical turn, with "Black Power" as a rallying cry that urged racial pride and an embrace of African-American economic autonomy, style, and food. "Soul food" as an acknowledged cuisine emerged, with food traditions from Africa and from the period of enslavement that showcased resilience becoming a political statement. Malcolm X, one of the figureheads of this movement, was an adherent of the Nation of Islam (NOI), which had its own strict dietary rules that actually avoided soul food. NOI leader Elijah Muhammad wrote that the "commercializing of foods has put forbidden, divinely forbidden, and poison foods on the market for human consumption" and commanded his followers to eat fresh vegetables and whole-wheat bread instead of the pork and traditional southern foods that were reminders of the "slave diet."[11] He also dismissed soybeans and other beans as what "cattle should eat"—no tofu for NOI followers, it seems.[12] The Nation also started a range of farms, food-processing facilities, supermarkets, and restaurants to create Black enterprise and an alternative food system. The Black Panthers, meanwhile, a most prominent group founded in 1966 in Oakland, California, took up food aid as part of its "survival programs," attacking capitalism as the cause of hunger. By 1970, the Panthers' free breakfast program for local schoolchildren fed 10,000 poor kids nationwide each morning. In so doing, historian Mary Potorti argues, the program "resisted the function of hunger in maintaining structures of white privilege and black oppression, politicizing hunger and malnutrition by framing them as intended outcomes of institutional racism."[13]

By 1968, mainstream civil rights leaders had also turned their attention to poverty, with Martin Luther King, Jr. organizing the Poor People's March and supporting a garbage collectors' strike in Memphis. It was in that city that, on April 4, 1968, the beloved leader was killed by a white assassin as King stood on a hotel balcony. Riots followed in the week after, coalescing anger of many Black urban residents, who were multiply oppressed by discriminatory housing policies, police harassment, crumbling urban infrastructure, and underemployment. In the context of other horrors that year—a worsening situation in Vietnam, Bobby Kennedy's assassination, a disastrous Democratic National Convention in Chicago where police and antiwar protestors clashed, the subsequent election of Republican Richard Nixon, and threats of environmental apocalypse—the social fabric seemed to be disintegrating.

Vietnam and the Counterculture

The hope of the early 1960s gave way to a sense of crisis in large part because of the ongoing war in Vietnam. The civil rights movement had already laid bare many of the nation's original sins and Vietnam only deepened the sense for some that the government had betrayed its citizens. These fissures helped spur a far-reaching countercultural movement, which used food as one way to push back against mainstream values and practices, in perceived alignment with oppressed peoples around the world.

American involvement in the Southeast Asian nation of Vietnam had begun in the postwar years as the United States upheld an anti-communist government in South Vietnam against communist independence forces in the North, led by Ho Chi Minh. In the years to follow, America engaged in warfare with little knowledge of Vietnam's history in context, instead reducing a complicated domestic situation to an anti-communist crusade. By 1968, President Johnson had sent half a million American troops to Vietnam, but they were making little progress. The United States employed ever more ruthless measures, dropping bombs, killing civilians, burning food supplies and forests. The *New York Times* published details of the My Lai Massacre in 1969 and then of the Pentagon Papers in 1971, revealing American military cruelty in the former and lack of transparency in the latter. In April 1970, President Nixon ordered an invasion of Cambodia, expanding the unyielding conflict and spurring more intense anti-war protests at home. By 1973, the United States finally admitted defeat, signing the Paris Peace Accords, and by 1975, Vietnam reunified under Communist rule.

American aims in Vietnam had failed, but the war had transformed the United States politically and culturally. The counterculture that emerged was a generational rebellion against the "American values" and patriotic consensus that had animated the 1950s. Many people, especially among the youth, rejected mainstream cultural standards as a way of rejecting the militarism, rigid gender norms, capitalist drive for "success," and industrial power that reigned supreme. In opposing the Vietnam war, protestors also opened a new vision for the nation. On the surface and in popular memory, the counterculture was known for its drug use, sexuality, idealism and rebellion, rock and roll music, bell bottom jeans, and peace symbols—converging in community for events like San Francisco's 1967 Summer of Love and the 1969 Woodstock concert. But the rebellion went deeper than just these lifestyle considerations. Aligned with New Left social movements, which campaigned for political reforms and social justice, many counterculturists saw their personal rebellion as deeply political. In protesting the government, they also confronted other major institutions like big corporations, including the food industry. A leader in the canning industry wrote about his experience listening to speeches at an anti-war rally in 1970, noting their harsh attacks on industry leaders. "What can we do to improve our own credibility?" he asked, acknowledging "the hectic pace of science and the impersonal pressure of feeding the world, along with the growth of the corporate image," which had undermined popular faith in industrial food.[14]

The war also focused attention on broad international issues. Alongside the domestic focus on hunger described above, the 1960s brought concerns

[handwritten margin notes: "Vietnam → burned their food supplies", "rebellion → people"]

about world hunger. Soybeans were heralded as a potential solution to the problem of inadequate global protein resources, with the claim that "meat is vegetation at one remove" and, foreshadowing the environmental vegetarianism arguments of the early 1970s, the encouragement to feed plant protein directly to hungry people rather than feeding it to animals to produce meat.[15] Some counterculturists embraced soy foods, with their origins in Asia, as a way of expressing solidarity with Vietnamese peasants. As historian Harvey Levenstein writes, these ethnic foods "represented an affirmation that the cumulative wisdom of the world's poor brown, yellow, and black folk cultures was superior to that of the rich, white, industrial world."[16] At the same time, the United States itself was diversifying, as immigrants from Asia and Mexico came in record numbers after the 1965 passage of the Hart-Celler Act, which abandoned the quota system that had previously given preference to Northwestern Europeans.

Civil Rights Inspires Others to Fight

Just as the civil rights movement inspired the anti-war protest era, so too did it foster a broader rights revolution, in which many marginalized communities rose up to advocate for themselves. And just as food issues permeated civil rights, such issues were also central to ensuing movements, with feminists pushing back against expectations of women to be ever-willing cooks and housewives, with Cesar Chavez leading a grape boycott to protest the exploitation of farm workers, with Native American fish-ins around Seattle fighting for fishing rights amidst a rising Red Power movement, and with environmentalists decrying pesticides like DDT and other chemicals used in food and agriculture.

One of the early flashpoints in the second-wave feminist movement (following the "first wave" that fought for women's right to vote) was the publication of Betty Friedan's *The Feminine Mystique* in 1963. The book catalyzed a generation of housewives who felt oppressed by "the problem that has no name"—the sense that women were not fulfilled by the restrictive expectations to stay home to cook, clean, and raise a family. This articulation, coupled with the Food and Drug Administration (FDA) approval of birth control in 1960, helped the women's movement to grow. Whereas in 1962, only a third of women felt they were discriminated against on the basis of their sex, by 1974, that number had doubled, as women came to realize the many legal and cultural limitations on their autonomy.[17] The feminist movement introduced consciousness-raising groups in 1967, which spread quickly and allowed women to share their stories with each other to realize how the "personal is political"; that is, how what seemed like individual personal issues (like domestic expectations around cooking and cleaning, sexual assault, abortion rights, or body image issues, for example) were actually reflective of broader sexist problems with the system. The feminist movement also fostered the wider sexual revolution, in which sex outside of marriage, gay rights, non-monogamy, legalized abortion, and other less traditional attitudes toward sexual behavior became more mainstream.

The 1960s also saw the rise of a Chicano movement to support the rights of Mexican-Americans, especially those who worked as farmworkers in the United States. This too was anchored in questions of food and agriculture and was modeled on the nonviolent protest strategies of civil rights. In 1962 Cesar Chavez and Dolores Huerta organized the National Farm Workers Association. A few years later, the organization joined with Filipino grape pickers who had gone on strike to protest working conditions. In December 1965, Chavez asked consumers across the country to boycott California grapes until the grape-growers allowed workers to unionize. As one farmworker said, the alternative would be to "stand still, and in so doing to hand down to their children the bleak frustration they have lived with, with no security, no dignity, and very little hope."[18] This boycott made clear the connections between the food on American plates and the invisible exploited labor that produced it. Eventually, in response to the tactics of boycott and nonviolent protest, the grape-growers agreed to sign labor contracts with the union in 1970.

Meanwhile, Native Americans were also reacting to the centuries-long land dispossession and mistreatment at the hands of the American government by organizing for their own rights, as part of what became known as the Red Power movement. In 1961, students organized the National Indian Youth Council. In 1964, national attention focused on Indigenous people in the Pacific Northwest who had organized a series of "fish-ins," modeled on the civil rights sit-ins, to protest conservation laws that restricted their traditional fishing practices, which were a mainstay of their foodways. By 1968, the American Indian Movement began to stage protests demanding self-determination, and land and resources guaranteed by treaties. The next year, an intertribal group occupied Alcatraz Island, claiming original rights to the land. These events highlighted the ongoing strength and perseverance of groups of people who had lived on American land for the longest time, but under significant oppression since white colonization.

Finally, an environmental movement took shape in the 1960s, questioning the fundamental trust in endless expansion, consumption, and scientific "progress" that had long animated American society and the food system. It connected to the other rights movements by advocating for the truly voiceless: non-human animals and the land itself. In the postwar years, agricultural mechanization and dependence on chemical inputs increased dramatically, with wartime munitions factories pivoting toward producing pesticides, herbicides, fertilizers, antibiotics, and hormones. Gasoline-dependent cars zoomed through the nation's new suburbs, polluting the air. With rising affluence, more Americans found time for outdoor leisure activities, which brought them into closer contact with an increasingly polluted natural world.

The 1962 publication of *Silent Spring* by Rachel Carson served to bring these rising concerns together. In her powerfully written book, Carson raised the red flag about the wildlife and human consequences of the indiscriminate application of DDT, a chemical that had previously been celebrated as a miracle solution for agricultural pests. She showed that DDT caused bird's eggshells to weaken, threatening bird populations and forecasting future springs that were "silent," with no more birds. She accused the FDA of lax oversight and the industry of branding "as fanatics or cultists all who are so perverse as to demand that their food be free of insect poisons."[19] Beyond DDT, *Silent Spring* cautioned that all products of science and technology should be critically studied before being put into use, advocating for a precautionary principle that accounted for unintended consequences—an argument that had far-reaching implications. Although industry leaders condemned Carson's work and called her "hysterical," it raised nationwide concern and action to regulate agricultural chemicals. Then, in 1969, a major oil spill in Santa Barbara and the polluted Cuyahoga River in Ohio catching fire captured the nation. All these events focused youth energies on environmentalism, leading to the first Earth Day on April 22, 1970, with 20 million people advocating for environmental protection. The same year saw the creation of the Environmental Protection Agency, and the years to follow brought the passage of far-reaching environmental legislation, including the Clean Air Act, Clean Water Act, and Endangered Species Act.

Food and Farming as Resistance

Although, throughout the 1960s, food issues emerged in many different contexts, they took fullest form at the end of the decade, alongside the rising environmental movement. As historian Warren Belasco argues, around 1968, "environmentalism was emerging as the left's primary vehicle for outrage and hope, edging aside civil rights, the antiwar movement, and revolutionary socialism."[20] Countercultural youth now turned to alternative food movements to find a sense of purpose and community. Tofu came to mean something bigger. By 1969, the *New York Times* reported that "Some even feel that it may be time to take seriously what many members of the younger generation, especially the hippies, have been saying for quite some time: You Are What You Eat."[21] Members of the New Left who may have previously dismissed those who were focused on food and environmental issues as "wilderness freaks" now saw how those same freaks were bringing necessary attention to undue corporate influence, and that their seemingly faddish food habits had direct progressive connections.

Before this pivotal phase, many precursors had introduced alternative food ideas as part of larger movements. One of those with the deepest roots was the organic food movement, popularized in the United States by J. I. Rodale, who founded *Organic Farming and Gardening* magazine back in 1942. At first, his magazine and its subject were welcomed only by a small niche audience. But the magazine's circulation increased from 60,000 in 1958 to 650,000 by 1970 and Rodale was profiled in the *New York Times* in 1971, testifying to the rising interest in alternative food production following mistrust in agricultural chemicals like DDT.[22] Meanwhile, in San Francisco's Haight-Ashbury neighborhood—the heart of the hippie world—a group of anarchist actors known as the Diggers used free food giveaways beginning in 1966 as a way to denounce private property, linking food production with the problems of capitalism. A final way that food became politicized in this early phase, but in a way more firmly linked to the Washington establishment, was through the 1960s consumer movement. Ralph Nader, the nation's most prominent consumer advocate, who had become well known by advocating for auto safety, raised concern about meatpacking regulations, processed food, and agribusiness more generally in 1969, which led to the publication the following year of *The Chemical Feast*, a searing indictment of the FDA.

All of these precedents fed into the countercultural food movement as a whole, which emerged as a backlash against the highly processed "plastic" diet of the 1950s. As historian Maria McGrath writes, "Eating overprocessed foods seemed tantamount to swallowing modern alienation. Conversely, the smells, tastes, and creation of whole foods conferred authenticity and oppositionality."[23] And because everyone eats three times a day (give or take), every meal became an opportunity for resistance.

The soybean became a particularly valuable symbolic food in this space, as it could be grown outside of the mainstream economy, was ecologically friendly and cheap to grow, could be processed into tofu or sprouts or soy flour, required slow and methodical preparation that stood in stark contrast to "convenience" foods, and connected to the hardworking Asian peasants whose Eastern religions captured the imaginations of the counterculture. Although most of the people involved in this movement were white—and indeed gave little attention to the parallel Black agrarian movements—they were fascinated by ethnic foods as they shopped at small stores in immigrant neighborhoods for "exotic" ingredients and took advantage of airflight advances to travel the world. For these adherents, brown was elevated over white, at least symbolically; as Warren Belasco memorably writes,

Soybean = symbol

"Whiteness meant Wonder Bread, White Tower, Cool Whip, Minute Rice, instant mashed potatoes, peeled apples, White Tornadoes, white coats, white collar, white wash, White House, white racism. Brown meant whole wheat bread, unhulled rice, turbinado sugar, wildflower honey, unsulfured molasses, soy sauce, peasant yams, 'black is beautiful.'"[24]

Among the most important topics within the movement was meat-eating. Many counterculturists advocated vegetarianism—for health, ethical, religious, environmental, or political reasons—while others embraced meat consumption, when it was done mindfully with attention to the act of killing. The question of whether to eat meat was become ever more pressing, as broader trends of meat consumption rose significantly in the postwar period, with the rise of industrial agriculture that lowered the upfront cost of meat, while ignoring the externalized environmental costs of the fast food that spread hamburgers far and wide.

Into this conversation stepped Frances Moore Lappé, with the 1971 publication of *Diet for a Small Planet*, the definitive and widely influential case for environmental vegetarianism. Influenced by fears of worldwide famine spread by books like Paul Ehrlich's 1968 *The Population Bomb* and attention to problems of hunger, Lappé picked up on ideas about the inefficiencies of animal agriculture that had been swirling for decades and made them accessible to a broad audience. With clear calculations, she showed that there was plenty of food in the world, but that most of it was being fed to, or wasted on, animals. She demonstrated that it required 21 pounds of plant protein (often soy) to yield 1 pound of beef protein, and that the latter was not nutritionally superior. To make these arguments easy to apply in readers' everyday lives, Lappé provided vegetarian recipes. The leading plant protein she showcased was the soybean, which showed up in various forms in muffins and waffles, curries and veggie burgers, Mexican pilafs and stir frys. She lauded tofu as well, though noted that it was not widely available in stores. Even though the United States had become the largest soybean producer in the world by 1970, most of the yield was turned into animal feed or oil, and very little was directed toward human consumption. Lappé's book and her promotion of it, as on talk shows where she became known as the "the Julia Child of the soybean circuit," made clear that food choices had far-reaching political dimensions.[25]

As many members of the counterculture considered vegetarianism and other calls to natural foods, some decided to put their ideals into practice by retreating to isolated communes where they could build alternative societies. Between 1965 and 1975, an estimated 10,000 new communes were founded with the goal of reclaiming food production in community.[26] One commune-dweller wrote that he had first tried to make the world a better place, but had failed and decided that "a farm with friends is a very pleasant street corner to hang out on while waiting for the bomb to fall."[27] On these farms, securing food was a central preoccupation and, despite the broader feminist movement's influence on the counterculture, women often ended up doing most of the cooking, recreating patterns of mainstream society. Among the best known of these communes was The Farm, in central Tennessee, founded by Stephen Gaskin, who had had a "psychedelic vision of the soybean, in which he saw it as a great provider for all humankind" in 1964.[28] Following his vision, Gaskin and his many followers left San Francisco in August 1971 to form their vegetarian commune, where they learned how to grow soybeans from their neighboring Tennessee farmers, who had themselves only recently learned how to do so from agricultural extension agents who saw the bean as cheap animal food. On The Farm, however, the soybean was pure human food. To make it more palatable, Farm resident Laurie Praskin studied soy foods, building on the knowledge of Seventh-Day Adventists and research scientists who had themselves studied traditional Asian methods. Using scavenged equipment and through grueling work, Praskin learned how to make soy milk and then, in correspondence with *The Book of Tofu* author William Shurtleff, to coagulate that milk into tofu.

The strands of interest in Eastern religions and customs, concern about meat consumption and global hunger, and commune independence came together in the embrace of tofu by the early 1970s, with Shurtleff at the center. It was he and his partner Akiko Aoyagi who helped mainstream Americans reimagine the soybean, first from animal feed to hippie food, then to an elevated exotic ingredient. Shurtleff traveled to Tokyo from California in 1971 to study Japanese and Zen Buddhism. While there, he read *Diet for a Small Planet* and began to see the tofu being made by local Japanese artisans through new eyes—as a tool for global change. As historian Matthew Roth writes, "Like The Farm, [Shurtleff] looked to soybeans as a way to achieve abundance without recourse to industrial agriculture and its 'rape of the planet.'"[29] He and Aoyagi studied with these local tofu-makers and then became "the soybean's biggest missionaries," publishing *The Book of Tofu* in 1975 to teach anyone how to make tofu using low-tech equipment.[30] The couple then traveled around the United States on an epic book tour, seeding small tofu shops in nearly all the places they went. Between 1975 and 1982, the number of tofu shops grew from fifty-four (all owned by Chinese or Japanese Americans) to more than 170, many white-owned.[31]

Shurtleff and Aoyagi's tofu business proselytization was part of a larger trend of commercializing natural food, which reshaped the countercultural food movement, alongside a shifting cultural context, by the mid-1970s. Although consumerism had been part of the counterculture and the environmental movement earlier, the rise of co-ops, health food stores, alternative food businesses, and natural foods restaurants solidified this link by the early 1970s. As they lost hope in the government, the counterculture turned instead to marketplace solutions to food and political problems. As Maria McGrath argues, "the movement's pocketbook and personalist food politics refreshed and sustained the capitalist order."[32] At the same time, after first rejecting tofu and granola and other natural foods, the mainstream food industry began to see the "natural" label as a money-maker and began to adapt it for themselves. Despite the popularity of *Diet for a Small Planet* and the rise of meat alternatives like tofu, meat consumption continued to rise, with ever more soybeans turned into animal feed to fuel the livestock industry. The hope once embedded in the alternative food movement as a bearer of social change grew ever more dim.

13

Chicken Nuggets:
Cheap Food and Politics in the 1970s and 1980s

In 1984, a *New York Times* headline read "America Goes Chicken Crazy." The article described the dramatic increase in chicken consumption and the advances in chicken production in recent years. "Agribusiness," the author wrote, "has managed to take the old barnyard, worm-eating animal and transform it into a wondrous fast-growing creation bred to live in a synthetic setting."[1] The newest and most popular of products coming from this wondrous development was the chicken nugget, introduced nationwide by McDonald's the previous year. The nugget would reshape the American food industry and diet in the years to come, catapulting chicken into first place as the country's favorite meat.

This shift in consumption habits toward chicken, and especially nuggets and other highly processed versions, was very much a product of its time. A combination of forces all came together to allow the chicken industry to grow unimpeded. These forces included advances in food science and agricultural science, industrial consolidation and vertical integration, government policies that promoted cheap feed for the meat industry, concerns about saturated fat, an economic climate that encouraged "value-added products", and a political climate that reduced the strength of labor unions, worker safety, and environmental protection. Consumers seeking convenience in an era of growing inequality were the final piece of the puzzle.

Chicken nuggets expressed the values of Reagan-era America. Ronald Reagan, taking office in 1980, projected a sunny optimism about reduced government and trickle-down economics—in which tax cuts and other economic benefits for the wealthy would eventually "trickle down" to the working class. Chicken nuggets, for their part, promised a convenient food that had the allure of "healthier" white meat, lower in saturated fats. But just as Reagan's tax cuts led to dramatic increases in income inequality, the rising popularity of chicken nuggets and similar ultra-processed foods contributed to a growing epidemic of diet-related diseases. Further, the chickens were increasingly produced and processed by exploited workers who labored in factory farms and brutal slaughtering facilities that deepened environmental and public health woes. The push for smaller government worsened these problems by undermining worker and environmental protections. Both Reagan's toxic optimism and the golden chicken nuggets were full of empty promises.

"Chicken Fatigue" and Political Fatigue

Even before the nugget, chicken had begun its upward trajectory by 1970, selling at double the rates of the postwar years, alongside a more general rise in meat consumption. The previous decades had seen a range of advances that brought chicken out of the barnyard and into the laboratory and factory. Rationing of red meat during the Second World War had increased demand for poultry and the military's commandeering of chicken from the Delmarva (Delaware-Maryland-Virginia) peninsula—which had been the previous center of the industry—shifted the locus of the chicken production to the South, especially Arkansas and Georgia. The industry became increasingly rationalized, as agricultural science led to innovations in breeding and feeding chickens; wartime chemicals were turned toward the production of antibiotics and growth-promoting hormones; advances in diesel trucking allowed for farther shipping; and the different stages of production became further integrated, with single companies beginning to control the many steps of the process, from hatching to growing feed to slaughtering and processing. The 1948 "Chicken of Tomorrow" contest, staged by Delaware's agricultural extension service and organized by the A&P grocery store chain with partners around the nation, led to the creation of the Vantress breed of chicken, which would become the industry standard thereafter.[2] This bird and its descendants grew quickly, with large breasts to satisfy Americans who wanted white meat and with consistent sizing to allow for mechanization.

By the mid-1960s, 90 percent of broiler chickens were produced by integrated companies, which had outsized control over most steps in the production process. They would breed chickens and hatch eggs, then deliver chicks to contract farmers who had to follow the integrators' specific instructions for the growing stage, then return the full-grown chickens to the company for processing and distribution. Foreshadowing later concerns about contract farming, one grower in 1961 testified before Congress that "the role of the family-size poultry producer has been reduced to 'a cheap hired hand with a large investment.'"[3] By the early 1970s, the largest integrators were companies like Tyson, Perdue, and Holly Farms, which furthered the dramatic shift in animal agriculture from diversified small farms to factory farms, or CAFOs (concentrated animal feeding operations), which had already been ramping up in the decades before. These new institutions removed animals from pasture and moved them indoors, into crowded facilities where they were fed round the clock to produce meat poundage as quickly as possible (Figure 13). By the 1980s, Perdue gave each chicken only three-quarters of a square foot (smaller than the laptop on which I'm typing this). And the "conversion rate," or amount of feed needed to increase an animal's bodyweight decreased dramatically during this period, declining by 57 percent between 1935 and 1995.[4] At the same time, mechanization made the labor of animal killing and processing more efficient, but also more monotonous and dangerous.

Despite these "improvements" in chicken production, sales still lagged behind the more popular beef and pork by 1970. Some consumers suffered from "chicken fatigue," or a sense of boring sameness around eating the

FIGURE 13 *This photo shows the hyper-crowded interior of a chicken factory farm, which characterized most U.S. chicken production by the 1970s, with all the attendant animal welfare, environmental, and food safety costs (Getty Images).*

same broiler chickens in the same ways. A 1962 industry source described "cut-up, tray-packed poultry" as "the whimsical dreams of some poultry men that could become the realities of the future."[5] At the time, chicken was sold largely as whole bone-in birds, which limited its accessibility and appeal. But soon those whimsical dreams came true, as chicken processors began to dismember the birds, remove the skin and bones, and sell a range of pre-packaged cuts. This allowed the companies to sell different products to different groups of customers and to make higher profits, at a time of economic instability. This development was accompanied by a new move toward branding as companies increased their advertising budgets and tried to develop loyal consumer followings.[6] As different kinds of chicken products multiplied, advertising campaigns became ever more important to create distinctions among them in consumers' minds.

These moves by the chicken industry were efforts to find some stability among an uncertain political and economic backdrop. Many Americans in the early 1970s felt deeply distrustful of the government and its ability to solve the nation's problems. Richard Nixon had won the presidency in 1968 by appealing to the "silent majority" who sought "law and order" in contrast to the apparent lawlessness of the urban riots and anti-war protests of the late 1960s. The outright deception of the American government throughout the Vietnam war, as uncovered by the Pentagon Papers and other media revelations, shook American trust. During Nixon's presidency, his administration actively sowed partisan division, taking pride in furthering the fragmentation spurred by the identity politics of the previous decade. Then, in 1973, Nixon's involvement in the Watergate scandal became public knowledge. During the 1972 campaign season, Nixon's colleagues had broken into the Democratic Party headquarters in the Watergate building in Washington, D.C. to install wiretapping equipment. Thereafter, Nixon tried to cover up the burglary and ordered the FBI not to investigate the crime. By July 1974, in response to House Judiciary Committee's move to begin impeachment, Nixon resigned, without an apology. This contributed to an erosion of public support for federal action in the years to come, which undermined regulation of industries like chicken production.

These political crises also kept the government from addressing a series of concurrent economic crises. The first signs of disorder appeared in late 1972, as meat prices began to rise, due to a combination of poor weather and global crop failures, world economic conditions, and a grain deal with the Soviets which led to huge wheat exports and thus higher domestic grain prices. Although the Russian grain sale improved farmer income and won the farmer vote for Nixon in the 1972 election, consumers were less happy. By early 1973, meat prices saw the highest rates of inflation since the Civil War. Housewives across the country organized consumer boycotts and protests, calling on President Nixon to enforce price ceilings. Earl Butz, the head of the US Department of

Agriculture (USDA), used this moment to re-engineer the Farm Bill in ways that would have profound effects on the American food system. He took advantage of concern over high prices to demolish the price supports that had been in place since the New Deal to control supply and demand. By removing these supports, farmers were encouraged and subsidized to produce as much grain as possible, which helped provide the meat industry with cheap animal feed, and food processors with cheap inputs. Butz, not incidentally, had an industry background before coming to the federal government, and he continued to promote industry interests after coming to the USDA.

These moves, along with Butz's calls for American farmers to expand by "plant[ing] fencerow to fencerow," led to the growth of huge farms producing monocultures of corn, soy, and wheat using expensive machinery, the financing of which drove many farmers into debt. The flood of cheap grain that resulted went into producing high-fructose corn syrup—that ubiquitous industrial sweetener—along with a dizzying array of other processed food ingredients that made junk food cheap, and into animals to produce ever-higher amounts of cheap meat. As historian Bryant Simon writes, "corn went into the chicken feed, and it went into the batter that coated nuggets and tenders, into the filler, and into the high fructose corn syrup (HFCS) that sweetened the dipping sauces."[7] Journalist Michael Pollan found that the content of the average Chicken McNugget by 2006 was actually 56 percent corn.[8] All this cheap grain helped fuel unprecedented rates of diet-related diseases.

At the same time that the nation was dealing with high food prices, an oil and energy crisis began. In October 1973, in retaliation for earlier US support of Israel against Egypt and Syria in the Yom Kippur War, the Organization of Petroleum Exporting Countries (OPEC) in the Middle East halted oil export to the United States. The global price of oil quadrupled and American demand far exceeded supply. The fragility of America's fossil-fuel dependence, with its large vehicles and suburban homes and oil-hungry agricultural system, became clear. Even after OPEC lifted the embargo, the United States continued to experience an energy crisis and rising rates of inflation. These events set the tone for the rest of the difficult decade, as Americans contended with a divided culture, economic woes, foreign policy failings, and strong doubts that political leaders could do anything to resolve these issues.

New Products and New Policies

The chicken industry felt these economic conditions acutely, with high feed prices after the Soviet grain sale causing extra expenses and then the lifting of price controls leading to broiler overproduction. Chicken producers reacted by finding ways to stabilize prices and profits, using one of the broader food industry's central tactics: adding value. The price a company could fetch for a whole broiler chicken, on its own, was intimately tied to two factors: labor costs, which were relatively stable, and feed prices, which were quite unstable and fluctuated wildly with market changes. By "adding value" through changing the form of the chicken further, producers could charge more for their products on a stable basis and loosen the connection between the price they charged and the unstable costs of grain commodities. As Tyson's corporate motto from this era stated, "Don't Do More Chickens, Do More to Chicken," prioritizing further processing over higher rates of production. Tyson's specialized products yielded 22 percent profit, nearly three times what they earned from whole broilers.[9] And consumers increasingly sought these value-added products for their convenience.

The new products included things like chicken hot dogs, pre-cooked chicken products, breast patties, chicken bologna, and chicken meatloaf. This product differentiation allowed the industry to reduce waste, by using chicken parts like necks, skins, and backs in bologna and hot dogs, and by sending dark meat chicken legs and thighs to consumers abroad who didn't share Americans' general preference for white meat. Companies relied on food scientists and university researchers like Robert Baker at Cornell University—known as a "chicken Edison"—to help develop a wide range of products. He helped create over fifty chicken-based foods between 1960 and 1980, explaining that his development of "the convenience industry, put[ting] the chicken in different forms" helped make chicken profitable after being a "loss leader" from 1955 to 1970. One of his inventions was the "chicken stick," essentially a proto-chicken nugget.[10] Further, this shift to value-added products also created new labor demands, as tens of thousands of poorly paid workers were brought on to handle the labor-intensive steps of cutting chicken into separate body parts, removing bones, and further processing—steps that resisted mechanization.

Meanwhile, the nation as a whole dealt less successfully with the turbulence of the 1970s than did the chicken processors. Following the 1973 OPEC oil embargo, the United States entered a period of "stagflation," in which both inflation and a recession—typically thought of as opposing phenomena—plagued the country. Even as food like chicken became cheaper due to industrial efficiencies, working-class Americans spent a higher proportion of their dwindling incomes on food. The period of economic expansion that had followed the Second World War came to an end, as manufacturing was outsourced abroad and the country began to import more than export. High rates of unemployment alongside high prices, ongoing oil shortages, and unregulated global trade all contributed to the sense that postwar America's dominance was faltering. At the same time, social division increased, with political strategists making issues like gun control and abortion deeply partisan. The bitter fight over the Equal Rights Amendment divided women and brought conservatism and evangelical Christianity under the banner of "family values" to the fore.

As President Jimmy Carter struggled to address these layered challenges in the 1970s, he moved to cut taxes, reduce government spending on domestic programs, and deregulate a number of industries, hoping to increase competition and investment. Many of these strategies foretold the "trickle-down economics" and deregulation of the Reagan years to come. Under Carter, the federal government moved against regulating a number of pressing issues in the growing meat industry, undermining public health and worker safety. For example, despite evidence that antibiotics and hormone growth promoters could lead to disease outbreaks among humans, Congress prevented the FDA from instituting a ban in 1978.[11] And, despite earlier support of workplace safety through the Occupational Safety and Health Administration (OSHA), soon after his election Carter began to reduce safety standards to appease business interests, agreeing that "we ought to get the Federal Government's nose out of ... private enterprise."[12] Those private enterprises—chicken producers central among them—sought to avoid government oversight however they could, moving their operations to states, especially in the "Sun Belt" area of the South and West, that had less regulation, less support for organized labor, and cheaper raw materials. This region grew more conservative politically, as deindustrialization hollowed out the former-manufacturing centers of the Midwest and East Coast. As Bryant Simon writes, this was all part of a move in the 1970s to embrace "the notion of cheap ... cheap foodstuffs, cheap government, and cheap labor" in a misguided effort to solve the nation's problems.[13]

A final thread of the late 1970s that reshaped the American political and dietary landscape was the increasing national attention to problems of nutrition and diet-related diseases. During this tumultuous period, many Americans began to think of food as something that should be restricted, as part of what some scholars have called "negative nutrition." Historian Warren Belasco writes that "this negation was as political as it was nutritional ... The loss of confidence in America's political superiority was matched by a loss of faith in its food habits."[14] People began to shift toward alternative ways of eating for a variety of reasons: calorie-counting appealed to upper and middle classes as a form of control, radical critics attacked an unhealthful food system, some Black activists maligned "soul food" as the cause of disproportionate disease among Black Americans, and anxieties shifted from the chemical scares of the post-*Silent Spring* era to nutritional scares around calories and fat. A significant turning point in this space was the issuing of the *Dietary Goals for the United States* in 1977, the result of years of discussion by a Senate Committee led by South Dakota Senator and 1972 presidential nominee

George McGovern. The first version of the report called on Americans to reduce red meat and dairy consumption. But after backlash from McGovern's South Dakota ranching constituents and other industry advocates, the report shifted to recommending only that Americans "choose meats, poultry and fish that will reduce saturated fat intake." The emphasis shifted from foods to nutrients, from cutback to active choice.[15] And the call to reduce saturated fat intake suited the chicken industry well, as their poultry products came to be perceived as healthier alternatives to beef, despite the highly processed nature of many chicken products coming on the market.

This shift toward "nutritionism"—a view that sees food only as the sum of its component parts—gave rise to an even more powerful processed food industry, bolstered by advances in food science that made it possible to create a wide variety of ultra-processed foods that were stitched together in the lab.[16] Following on a long history of dietary gurus who made money by promoting questionable diets, the food industry pushed "lite" and "lo-cal" imitation products. Many Americans replaced the saturated fats in their diet with trans fats (later found to be even more damaging), highly sweetened (but low-fat) products with high-fructose corn syrup, and, last but not least, "low-fat" white-meat chicken products like chicken nuggets. Chicken's popularity rose in the 1970s and 1980s not only because industry manipulation made it cheaper than beef, but because consumers came to see chicken as a healthier option in a time of fears about saturated fat—even as chicken would soon be most often consumed in fried form, counteracting its supposed healthfulness. Processors like Perdue took advantage of this perception, as in one ad that showed two larger customers considering some red meat at the grocery store while Perdue called to them, "Come on folks, shape up! Start eating my chickens."[17] By the end of the 1970s, Americans were indeed eating Perdue's chickens, and those produced by many other huge corporations, for reasons of health, marketing, politics, and economics.

Reagonomics and Chicken Nuggets

By 1980, a new political wave emerged, which reshaped the landscape for the chicken industry, and for all Americans. Ronald Reagan defeated the incumbent Jimmy Carter in that year's presidential election. Where Carter had struggled to deal with the layered crises of the late 1970s and had conveyed pessimism, even seeming to blame Americans themselves in his infamous 1979 "crisis of confidence" speech, Reagan approached the challenges with an optimistic frame. Known as the "Teflon president," because of the way that political problems seemed to slide right off of him, the former Hollywood actor was a charismatic speaker who led a wide-ranging conservative coalition. He appealed to many Americans, especially among the white middle and upper classes, who wanted clear solutions to the unraveling of the 1970s. As part of the "Reagan Revolution," he brought together suburbanites with anti-government activists, evangelical Christians with Westerners who rejected environmental regulation on public lands, white Southerners who opposed civil rights with those in Jerry Falwell's "Moral Majority" who believed the sexual revolution had gone too far.

In his 1981 inaugural address, Reagan famously said, "government is not the solution to our problem; government is the problem."[18] Throughout his presidency he sought to "fix" this perceived problem by slashing government funding for most social services, cutting taxes for the wealthiest Americans, discouraging unionization, and reducing regulation. This solidified the shift away from the principles that had guided government action since the New Deal, which had promoted economic equality and social security. "Reagonomics" instead hewed to the idea of "supply-side" economics, which argued that cutting taxes on the wealthy would encourage them to re-invest and establish businesses, allowing their wealth to "trickle down" to poorer folk.

As part of this plan, the federal government slashed the budgets of the agencies tasked with maintaining workplace safety, regulating advertising, protecting food safety and the environment, and reducing businesses monopolies, among others—all of which moved the chicken industry in the direction of causing greater harm. The attack on environmental regulation was especially consequential in the long term, as it prevented government action on climate change at a time when the topic was not yet deeply mired in partisan rhetoric and fossil fuel companies were only beginning their disinformation campaigns. Reagan also set the tone for a backlash against organized labor, after he fired more than 11,000 air traffic controllers who had gone on strike in 1981 against low wages and dangerous working conditions. Private employers followed his lead, becoming increasingly hostile to unions, which had already been eroded by corporate political action committees (PACs), deindustrialization, racism, and overseas competition. The food industry, for one, welcomed these cuts and actions, as industry leaders had been complaining in the 1970s that they were dealing with an "overwhelming blanket of regulatory people" and operating "in a goldfish bowl" of federal oversight.[19] Reagan also cut spending on research and public health, even as the AIDS epidemic tore through American communities, especially among gay men.

On the whole, the effects of Reagonomics were mixed. It did counter inflation, with prices falling; chicken, for example, cost the same by 1983 as it had in 1933.[20] Unemployment fell and the gross domestic product increased—in part because of new technologies and expanded oil production.

Corporations and investors benefited hugely, even as their speculation and consolidation led to destructive job losses and unstable communities. But these economic policies also led to a tripling of the national debt; a set-up for the future collapse of the savings-and-loan industry; a rise in homelessness as the government divested from public housing, welfare, and mental healthcare; and starkly deepening inequalities that exacerbated racial disparities.

One of the colorful episodes in all this budget-slashing that offers insight into the food politics of the era occurred in 1981, when the Food and Nutrition Service, tasked with reducing costs for school nutrition programs by one-third, issued new standards. These standards allowed for certain substitutions—like tofu for meat—and for the inclusion of condiments like tomato concentrate and pickle relish in the "vegetable" category. Soon after, journalists and consumer advocates made headlines by announcing that ketchup was now considered a vegetable. This formulation made sense in a time of rising nutritionism, which allowed an industrial product like ketchup to *equal* a vegetable, in terms of vitamins, minerals, and nutrients, no matter the additional salt and sugar content. Still, there was enough backlash against this proposal that within a few weeks the standards were rescinded. Nevertheless, at a time when school lunch was already being taken over by food processors and was largely used by low-income children, and when Reagonomics was already increasing inequality, the "ketchup as a vegetable" debacle "became a symbol of the 'let them eat cake' attitude" and the partisan division of the period.[21]

But the new food that best embodied this Reagan era with its de-regulation of the food industry, its celebration of processed food, its reductionist view of nutrition, and its culture of convenience was the chicken nugget (which also was often dipped in ketchup). Although Robert Baker had invented the chicken stick in his Cornell lab in the early 1960s, the idea and method had lain dormant until McDonald's decided it needed a convenient, on-the-go, bite-size chicken product around 1980, at a time when rising concerns about saturated fat in beef and an embrace of chicken made the hamburger-dependent fast-food chain nervous. There are a range of origin stories for the McNugget itself, only some acknowledging Baker's early idea, which was never patented but was distributed in free bulletins for decades and conceivably influenced McDonald's. But by 1980, food technologists working for McDonald's had developed a small reconstituted chicken product held together by corn-based binders that was breaded, fried, frozen, and then fried again at each restaurant, this time in beef fat. They test-marketed it in Knoxville, Tennessee where it proved so popular that McDonald's invited Tyson Foods to breed an extra-large-breasted chicken variety—named "Mr. McDonald"—to help meet the demand.[22] McDonald's also worked with Ray Dalio, the founder of Bridgewater Associates, which would become the largest hedge fund in the world, to reduce the volatility of the grain market that produced chicken feed by developing a system of forward pricing for chicken producers so they could offer McDonald's a stable price for chicken.[23] By 1983, the McNugget was introduced across the nation and became a sensation. Within a few years, McDonald's was the second-largest consumer of chickens, just behind Kentucky Fried Chicken.

The McNugget cemented the transition to "further-processed" chicken that the prior "value-added" move had begun. This chicken was an industrial product quite distant from its agricultural roots. After the McNugget's introduction, the percent of chicken consumed in further-processed form grew from 16 percent to 80 percent over the next two decades. The nugget inspired new chicken restaurants, frozen chicken products, and grocery store items. This helped companies like Tyson to grow even bigger as they automated and streamlined the processing of breaded and fried chicken products. These moves helped catapult chicken consumption by 50 percent between 1976 and 1989, overtaking beef as Americans' #1 meat of choice.[24] Even as the McNugget's introduction was motivated by Americans' rising taste for chicken due in part to their perception of its healthfulness, the fatty fried form it took was distinctly unhealthy. Further, nuggets were typically dipped into sweet sauces like ketchup, barbecue sauce, and honey mustard, all flavored with government-subsidized high fructose corn syrup, adding to their unhealthfulness.

The popularity of fried chicken products in the 1980s was underpinned by a number of changing cultural factors. The rise of fast-food franchises and eating out at restaurants in general followed on the postwar innovations in processed food to remove Americans further from scratch-cooking in their kitchens. As part of this move toward convenience, supermarkets began to carry more prepared foods in their deli counters and in the form of microwavable meals in the freezer aisles. The microwave itself burst on the scene: American households owning one increased from less than 10 percent in 1979 to more than 70 percent by 1989.[25] Fried chicken products were perfectly suited both to restaurant deep-fryers and to at-home microwaves. They were also malleable, to fit with a growing taste for ethnic foods—add some General Tso's sauce to make it Chinese, some marinara to make it Italian, some hot sauce to make it Mexican. Convenience foods also fit with the rise of snacking in the 1980s, both of which were welcomed by the rising proportion of married women entering the workforce. That percentage rose from around 40 percent in the mid-1970s to more than 50 percent by 1982.[26] The rise of fast food offered a way out for these women who experienced increased pressures alongside reduced federal support for feeding their children, especially for women living near the poverty line. Fast food restaurants took advantage of this audience with McDonald's urging families to give "Mom a Day Off" and Kentucky Fried Chicken showcasing a bucket of its fried chicken as "Women's Liberation."[27]

The nugget's popularity emerged against a backdrop of a changing poultry industry and larger food industry in the 1980s. Early in the decade, before the McNugget's national roll-out, the chicken industry experienced an economic slump, as part of a broader farm crisis resulting from 1970s overproduction. The decade's politics and gutting of antitrust agencies also encouraged consolidation of huge food companies in the hands of a few large corporations, bringing a certain kind of efficiency but also outsized political power to reduce regulation. The biggest chicken companies in 1984 were ConAgra, Tyson, Gold Kist, Holly Farms, and Perdue. Most of these companies operated in the rural South, with a poor and unionized workforce, which grew to be largely comprised of Central American immigrants beginning in the late 1980s. By 1989, Tyson had acquired nineteen other companies in about as many years. Of course, the millions of dollars that flowed from these acquisitions went to industry leaders, consultants, and lawyers, not to the growers, laborers, and consumers who actually made the industry run.[28]

By 1990, chicken production had become thoroughly industrialized, with all its attendant costs. The industry relied on dependent contract farmers who operated like serfs at the behest of their corporate lords, a break from seasonality as formerly "spring chickens" were raised in confinement year-round, environmental contamination through manure disposal and wastewater discharge, an inhumane process of chicken slaughter that electrocuted and beheaded chickens hanging by their feet, grueling dangerous labor for poultry workers, growing bacterial contamination with salmonella found in more than a third of industrial chicken by 1987, and rising rates of antibiotic use and evidence of antibiotic resistance. These problems resulted directly from the new policies, products, and cultural changes of the past two decades that had made America go chicken crazy.

14

Big Mac:

McDonaldization and Its Discontents, 1990–2008

In 1999, former Soviet president Mikhail Gorbachev wrote the foreword of *To Russia with Fries*, a memoir by the executive who brought McDonald's to Russia in 1990 after the end of the Cold War. Gorbachev fondly describes the popularity of McDonald's, with its "merry clowns, the Big Mac signs, the colourful, unique decorations and ideal cleanliness, ... the welcoming smiles and helpful service."[1] All these features helped make McDonald's—what one journalist called the "ultimate icon of Americana" and also an icon of capitalism— wildly popular in Russia, the former enemy of the United States[2] (Figure 14). The presence of McDonald's in Moscow signaled the triumph of capitalism in these post-Cold War years, spread by new patterns of globalization.

In this period, McDonald's was spreading not only to Russia, but all around the world, with around 15,000 restaurants operating in more than a hundred countries by 2001.[3] In 1998, British commentator Martin Plimmer joked, "There are McDonald's everywhere. ... Soon, if McDonald's goes on expanding at its present rate, there might even be one in your house. You could find Ronald McDonald's boots under your bed. And maybe his red wig, too."[4] Its clean spaces, efficient preparation, standardized offerings, polite service, and satisfying menu full of fatty, salty items made it a hit among average consumers. As it traveled around the world, McDonald's became not just a place to eat, but a representation of the United States itself. As anthropologist James L. Watson wrote in 2000, "like the Stars and Stripes, the Big Mac stands for America."[5] The Big Mac, both in Watson's words and in this chapter, stands in for McDonald's and its pervasive influence. This particular hamburger was introduced in 1968, with its "special sauce, lettuce,

FIGURE 14 *A photo of a McDonald's restaurant—a symbol of American capitalism—in Moscow, the heart of the former Soviet Union (Franck Charel/ Gamma-Rapho via Getty Images).*

cheese, pickles, onions" on two hamburger patties and a three-layer bun. It quickly became one of the restaurant's signature items.

Despite McDonald's rapid growth and popularity, or perhaps because of it, the restaurant also came under attack from a wide range of critics, who cited its significant environmental, labor, cultural, and health costs. During the political and economic turbulence of the 1990s and the first decade of the 2000s, McDonald's and its Big Mac became embedded in broader concerns about globalization, deregulation, corporate growth, cultural conflicts, divisive partisanship, and US imperialism.

Making a Global World after the Cold War

Before McDonald's reached Moscow in 1990, the chain had its origins in the 1940s and began to open franchise locations under the guidance of Ray Kroc by 1954. Kroc's innovation was standardizing and centralizing the fast-food chain, through the creation of Hamburger University in 1961 to train managers (as they earned their Bachelor of Hamburgerology degrees) and the development of strict rules for all franchise operators to follow in their preparation and presentation of menu items. The chain also benefited from the 1946 US Department of Agriculture decree that a "hamburger" by definition

Hamburger can only contain beef & beef fat

could contain only beef and beef fat (no pork or other meat allowed). Because burgers were made of ground meat, the quality mattered less, allowing spent dairy cows, cull animals, and leftover feedlot fat to all go into the grinders together, lowering costs all along the chain and promoting high rates of beef consumption. When it came to the beef industry, hamburger production served as "the gasoline that ma[de] the whole engine run."[6] By the 1970s, even as burger competitors (like Burger King and Hardee's) and more "diverse" fast food (like Taco Bell and Long John Silver's) emerged, McDonald's remained dominant in the United States.

By 1990, the opening of a McDonald's restaurant in Moscow extended this dominance abroad to the United States' longtime rival. This opening represented the definitive end of the Cold War, as the formerly Communist nation embraced a widely recognized embodiment of American capitalism. The surprisingly rapid fall of communism had taken place as the 1980s came to a close. In April 1989, nearly 1 million protestors gathered in China's Tiananmen Square to advocate for democracy. Although the Chinese government reacted with harsh measures, the pro-democratic spirit spread, with German crowds in November 1989 tearing down the Berlin Wall that had long separated democratic West Germany from communist East Germany. Within the year, the first McDonald's in East Germany opened, in the town of Plauen, despite one East German politician calling for a ban on "McDonald's and similar abnormal garbage-makers."[7] Communist governments fell all across eastern Europe. With Gorbachev at the helm, the Soviet Union dissolved into fifteen independent nations. After more than forty years, the ideological warfare between the United States and the Soviet Union ended, with the United States as the world's remaining superpower. Global capitalism took over, as these formerly Communist nations began to transition to market economies. Even China, which remained Communist, introduced economic reforms that allowed foreign investment. McDonald's brought with it tastes for homogenized American products: music, fashion, popular entertainment, and, of course, food.

The export of McDonald's and its values was part of a broader trend of globalization that characterized the 1990s, as the end of the Cold War ushered in a worldwide economy and consciousness that was not limited by the local or national borders that had previously dictated human life. The rise of the Internet and satellite technology—subsidized by American federal dollars—enabled this global spread of information and culture. As market capitalism reigned supreme, politicians increasingly sought to reduce regulations that they believed hampered the free market, even as those regulations also protected workers and the environment. In 2002, Joseph Stiglitz, who had been the chief economist at the World Bank, published *Globalization and Its Discontents*, which argued that international institutions that extended this neoliberal free market ideology globally hurt poor countries.

[margin annotations: Soviet Union = 15 independent nations; US = worlds superpower; communist → market economies; ground meat / cheaper = low quality; Berlin Wall | West Germany vs East Germany; internet & satellite tech; → free market hurt poor countries]

Global perspective

Price of Big Mac as an index of 150 countries

→ control variable for global economic conditions

But globalization pushed forward, with more corporations operating at an international level. McDonald's was often the wedge that opened nations to Western economic development and other franchises. The Big Mac in its all its ubiquity even came to serve as a reference point for comparing the cost of living across different countries when *The Economist* magazine introduced the "Big Mac index" in 1986. This list of adjusted prices for Big Macs around the world provided a way to compare purchasing power among different currencies. Because the standardized Big Mac is sold in so many countries, it offered a control variable of sorts for understanding global economic conditions.

McDonaldization

convenient

assembly line of life

Sociologist George Ritzer introduced one of the most enduring theories of McDonald's effects in his 1993 book *The McDonaldization of Society*, which showed how the restaurant's emphasis on efficiency, calculability, predictability, and control extended beyond McDonald's to affect labor, education, family, and other aspects of American life. Americans came to accept "convenient," fast-paced, low-quality versions not only of food, but of everything: low-paid and insecure "McJobs," McUniversities that handed out standardized curricula and diplomas, McLove in the form of standardized online dating services that reduced love to a formula, and hospital birthing processes that treated each McMother like a cog in a machine. Ritzer argues that all these spaces dehumanize people, moving them through the assembly line of life.[8]

Global Perspective

only upper class naive mcdonalds — convenient

online

To see this McDonaldization in action, consider the case of Asia, where the introduction of McDonald's influenced a wide range of social changes. After opening in Japan, Hong Kong, Taiwan, and South Korea in the 1970s and 1980s, the chain arrived in China in 1990. As an economic boom gave families more disposable income, many of them headed to McDonald's to signal their new social status and desire for culinary adventures. Many Chinese parents saw McDonald's as "an important stop on the way to Harvard Business School or the MIT labs"—prestigious US institutions that embodied success in a connected world.[9] Anthropologist Yunxiang Yan found that children in Beijing described "Uncle McDonald" as "funny, gentle, kind, and ... under[standing] children's hearts."[10] Elements of McDonald's structure began to influence broader business and civic practices, as social norms around waiting patiently in line or expecting clean public bathrooms spread beyond the fast-food restaurant. Local operators opened their own fast-food restaurants to capture some of the McDonald's glow—in Beijing, you could find "McDucks, Mcdonald's, and Mordornal."[11] Soon, many Asian consumers came to see McDonald's as their own cuisine, rather than something foreign. When journalist Nicholas Kristof asked his son, who had grown up in Tokyo, what his favorite Japanese foods were, his son replied, "rice balls and McDonald's."[12]

But even as many consumers in Asia and across the world made McDonald's their own, others were less welcoming of the shift in values it represented.

In South Africa, professor Suzanne Leclerc-Madlala, in reflecting upon the opening of the first McDonald's after the fall of apartheid, wrote: "pressing issues of the struggle, such as land, housing, decent education, and health care, have increasingly been replaced by calls for macroeconomic growth, managed democracy and creating a better environment for investment, Americana in all its forms—from fast foods [to] B-grade TV sitcoms ...." She saw the "tasteless multinational fast-food" as a distraction from the pursuit of social change.[13]

Across the globe, activists in more than fifty countries protested and ransacked McDonald's restaurants, seeing the corporation as "a saturated symbol for everything that environmentalists, protectionists, and anti-capitalist activists find objectionable about American culture."[14] When the first McDonald's opened in Italy in 1986, in the heart of Rome, activists decried the degradation of Italian cuisine and culture. This movement inspired Carlo Petrini to launch the International Slow Food movement, which has since spread to more than 160 countries with its commitment to local foods, regional cultures, ethical buying, and opposition to fast food and industrial agriculture. When California Proposition 187 proposed restricting immigrants' access to state services in 1994, students in Mexico City vandalized a McDonald's, writing "Yankee go home" on the windows.[15] When the US air force accidentally bombed the Chinese embassy in Yugoslavia in 1999, Beijing University activists waved flags reading, "Attack McDonald's, Storm KFC."[16] And perhaps most famously, in 1999, French farmer and activist José Bové demolished a McDonald's under construction to protest US restrictions on the import of Roquefort cheese, which hurt French farmers. The US restrictions were a retaliation against the European Union's move to ban American beef treated with growth hormones. But Bové's actions came to represent much more, as the media depicted the conflict as "a battle between the friends and enemies of globalization."[17]

Another famous event that drew worldwide attention to McDonald's sins was what became known as the "McLibel" case. In 1994, the corporation sued two members of London Greenpeace for libel, for distributing a pamphlet accusing McDonald's of everything from destroying the rainforest to causing cancer. The case came to be a seen as a David and Goliath story, with the powerful company preying on two underfunded activists. In the end, the Judge ruled in the company's favor, but during the year-long trial that had 130 witnesses testify and produced 40,000 pages of documents, it was revealed that McDonald's had hired spies to infiltrate London Greenpeace, and that many of the claims in the pamphlet were true—particularly those about workers' low wages, the exploitation of children through ad campaigns, and cruel treatment of animals.[18]

Much of this attention to McDonald's emphasized the consumption side of the food chain, but many of the critiques extended outward to the broader realm of global agriculture. McDonaldization reshaped industrial agriculture, not only in raising chickens for McNuggets or growing potatoes for French fries, but to all corners of modern production. At the same time, problems with the mid-century Green Revolution and concerns about genetic modification drew international attention. Although global food production had doubled from the 1960s to the 1980s, the new high-yielding varieties that anchored this growth were dependent on American chemicals, seeds, and machinery and were only accessible to better-off farmers. Poorer farmers were displaced from the land, many farmers went into debt (leading to widespread cases of farmer suicides, as in India), and pesticide use skyrocketed, with all its attendant environmental problems. Another technological fix alongside the Green Revolution that began to take hold in the 1990s was the use of genetically modified organisms (GMOs), in which scientists manipulated organisms' DNA to enhance or reduce certain traits. By the early twenty-first century, three-quarters of all US-processed foods contained GMO ingredients such as corn or soy. Many critics expressed concern about the direct health or environmental dangers of GMOs, but the real risks, as with the Green Revolution, came through spreading a global reliance on the fruits of American corporations, like genetically engineered seeds and chemical inputs. Monsanto, the corporation that has most embodied this risk, controls an outsized percent of the world's seed market and patents on genetic material. Alongside McDonald's, powerful corporations have spread the practices of the American agricultural and food system around the globe, with a range of negative consequences.

US Politics and Economics in the 1990s

Meanwhile, against the backdrop of these 1990s global affairs, McDonald's was contending with a changing political, economic, and cultural landscape in the United States. The 1990s economy was characterized by a tech boom, low unemployment, and celebration of the ultra-rich and the wealthy yuppie lifestyle. Even as the real wages of restaurant workers and others at the bottom of the economic ladder stagnated, media portrayed an era of plenty. Advocates of globalization, free trade, and deregulation used the economy's perceived improvement as evidence in favor of their positions.

The rising power of corporations like McDonald's only increased as the long reach of Reagan's small-government influence extended even after the election of Democrat Bill Clinton in 1992. Despite his party affiliation, he took fiscally conservative positions, promoting free trade while cutting taxes and welfare. Nevertheless, conservatives despised Clinton for his social policies, his feminist wife Hillary Rodham Clinton, and his extramarital dalliances (the most infamous of which, with intern Monica Lewinsky, led to his impeachment trial in 1998). Under Hillary's guidance, Clinton's administration tried to pass universal healthcare (partially to address the rapid increase in diet-related diseases, to which the rise in fast food contributed mightily) but failed due to pushback from Republicans and the healthcare industry. But Clinton's policies drifted even further to the right after the 1994 midterm elections, in which Republicans took both houses of Congress, inspired by Newt Gingrich's conservative "Contract with America" platform. This midterm victory pushed Clinton in the direction of his opponents.

Gingrich's platform also spoke to increasing partisanship and cultural conflict. Despite the unified representation of "American values" like cleanliness, control, and standardization that McDonald's exported to the world, the reality of American life was much messier. As Cold War disagreement subsided, it was replaced by partisan fighting over a wide range of issues—immigration, religion, "family values," abortion, guns, gay rights, affirmative action, the environment, multiculturalism. With the erosion of traditional social networks, many Americans turned to new forms of media for their political engagement. The repeal of the Fairness Doctrine in 1987 promoted the rapid spread of polarized talk radio stations, embodied by host Rush Limbaugh. Fox News and MSNBC both began in 1996. And the Internet opened a new vista for unregulated transmission of information, however misleading or conspiratorial. Such ideas sometimes fostered radical action and violence, as with the 1995 Oklahoma City bombing in which Timothy McVeigh, motivated by militant antigovernment sentiment, bombed a federal building and killed 168 people, including nineteen young children in the building's daycare.

Clinton's actions on an international stage only worsened the deindustrialization and outsourcing of American jobs that were a central part of globalization. In 1993, Clinton signed NAFTA, the North American Free Trade Agreement. This treaty created a free-trade zone among the United States, Canada, and Mexico, which led many American companies to relocate to northern Mexico, where labor protections and environmental regulations were weaker. Anti-globalization activists decried NAFTA. Several years later, their anger came to a head in Seattle, where, in 1999, the World Trade Organization (WTO) convened a meeting of international delegates to create global trade agreements. More than 30,000 people—including trade unionists, environmentalists, anarchists, and McDonald's-protestor José Bové—marched in the streets to denounce globalization and its consequences, arguing that free trade harmed poorer countries and poor people within rich countries, that it harmed the environment, and that it eroded American jobs. The "Battle in

Seattle," though not focused on McDonald's specifically, highlighted many of the same issues as fast-food protests.

The food industry as a whole contended with new policies, problems, and strategies in the 1990s. Congress passed the Organic Foods Production Act, creating a US Department of Agriculture (USDA) certification system for organic products, which signaled both the increasing popularity of organic foods and the increasing consolidation of the organic industry, as large-scale farms were better able to handle the costs of the certification process. In 1992, the USDA issued the Food Guide Pyramid to offer nutritional guidance on a balanced diet, under significant pressure from the meat and dairy industries. And the problem of food waste received the critical attention it deserved under the Clinton administration, when the USDA created a Food Recovery and Gleaning Initiative and Congress passed the 1996 Good Samaritan Food Donation Act, which protected organizations from liability when donating food. But critical aspects of the food system remained under-regulated, with proposed food safety legislation weakened by meatpacking industry lobbying. The role of industry money in the federal government was highlighted by the 1994 prosecution of USDA Secretary Mike Espy for corruption due to his accepting gifts from Tyson Food.

Many environmental issues rose to public consciousness in the 1990s, with the 1987 Montreal Protocol focusing attention on the depleting ozone layer, the publication of books like Vice President Al Gore's *Earth in Balance* (1992), and movements to protect the Amazon rainforest, to save the whales, and to fight acid rain. But in a time of limited trust in and support for the federal government, many Americans did not demand government action. They instead focused on individual consumer choices and on corporate behavior. This individual approach and industry's half-hearted attempts at greenwashing failed to adequately address complex environmental problems. For example, concerns about overloaded landfills and the ozone-depleting chemicals in polystyrene packaging led McDonald's to shift away from using Styrofoam hamburger containers. But the packaging got more attention than the hamburger itself, despite the destruction caused by the beef industry. Jeremy Rifkin's 1992 book *Beyond Beef* captured broader criticisms by describing cows as "hooved locusts" whose production was leading to desertification, clearing of the rainforests, feedlot runoff that polluted waterways, global warming, and inefficient consumption of grain. This critique, needless to say, did not lead McDonald's to phase out the use of beef as easily as they had Styrofoam packages. Fast food and meat-eating were too embedded in the American economy and culture.

McDonald's also had to contend with a range of worries about health, with diet-related problems like heart disease, type 2 diabetes, and some forms of cancer becoming the leading causes of death in the United States by the 1990s. The dramatic rise in soda consumption, the use of hydrogenated oils with artery-clogging trans fats, and the use of ads, TV shows, and toys to target children all pointed to a big problem with the Standard American Diet (SAD). Fast food was among the worst offenders. In addition to these nutritional concerns, foodborne illness also plagued the meat industry. A 1993 outbreak of *Escherichia coli* was traced back to hamburgers from Jack in the Box restaurants, causing over 700 people to get sick, 200 to be hospitalized, and four deaths. A 1996 USDA study found that over half of ground beef samples were contaminated with some form of pathogen that could make people sick. Bacteria thrive in cattle feedlots where sewage is omnipresent and where, until 1997, cattle were fed livestock wastes composed of dead sheep and cattle and were fed dead cats and dogs from animal shelters, all of which further spread disease. In that year, the emergence of "mad cow disease" in Britain led the FDA to ban such practices of feeding herbivorous cows the remains of other animals in this fashion.

The food industry scrambled to contain these crises and to push back against advocates who sounded the warning bells. When, in 1996, famed talk-show host Oprah Winfrey had a vegetarian activist on her show to talk about mad cow disease and the problems with meat production, a group of Texas cattlemen decided to sue her for libel, under a new Texas "food-disparagement law." Although the jury ruled in favor of Oprah, the "cattlemen succeeded in demonstrating that the threat of a lawsuit could chill debate about controversial practices of food companies," according to nutritionist Marion Nestle.[19] The same year, food industry advocates created the Center for Consumer Freedom to push against food activism that made consumers question processed food. They insisted that consumers should have "choice" and be "free" to decide what they eat. The problem is that systemic factors— like agricultural subsidies that make processed food cheaper than fresh foods, lack of support for working parents that makes convenience food a near-necessity, and urban planning that makes fast food most accessible to low-income families—deny consumers real "freedom of choice" and instead push us all toward unhealthful foods.

Upheaval and Fast Food in the New Century

As the new century dawned, the United States found itself dealing with new challenges of its own making. The 1990s stock market growth and tech boom had created a bubble that burst in 2000, leading to a recession. Revelations surfaced about the corruption and misdeeds of many in the financial sector— with the energy company Enron and its misreporting of billions of dollars in losses as profits as a prime example. The deregulation of banks, energy, and telecommunications that had taken place in the 1990s, along with the strong political influence of industries, left the government less able to act in the public interest. Globalization and free trade exported jobs abroad, limiting domestic job growth. And the dominance of McDonald's led to widespread health problems.

Then, the 2000 election raised questions about the foundations of democracy and the electoral process. During the campaigns preceding the election, corporations had enormous influence, with agribusiness alone contributing $60 million in support of their preferred candidates—typically Republican—and spending $78 million on lobbying.[20] The election itself became contested when Al Gore won the popular vote against George W. Bush by a half-million votes, but the electoral college majority came down to an uncertain outcome in Florida, where voting machines had caused problems and where Bush's brother Jeb served as governor. Florida began a recount, but then the US Supreme Court ruled to end the recount and Governor Jeb Bush certified his brother's win, on contested terms.

Soon after Bush took office, the country was struck by the deadliest act of terror on US soil, in the attacks of September 11, 2001. That morning, hijackers seized four passenger planes, crashing them into the twin towers of the World Trade Center, a third into the Pentagon, and a fourth into a field near Pittsburgh after passengers fought back and took control. All the passengers aboard the four planes died and the twin towers collapsed, killing 2,977 people. The Bush Administration traced the attacks back to al-Qaeda, a militant Islamic terrorist organization led by Osama bin Laden. He had been radicalized by anger over US support for Israel against the Palestinians, by the presence of American military bases in Saudi Arabia after the end of the Gulf War in 1991, and by a resentment of America's global influence. A 1996 *New York Times* op-ed commented on earlier acts of terror fueled by this resentment, with US cultural imperialism threatening traditionalists: "The cultural messages we transmit through Hollywood and McDonald's go out across the world to capture, and also to undermine, other societies."[21]

In response to the 9/11 attacks, the US turned its enormous military power toward a "war on terrorism," using what became known as the Bush Doctrine to claim the right to make war on anyone who threatened the United States and its citizens. The United States declared war on Afghanistan in October 2001 and on Iraq in March 2003. Although many world leaders saw the Afghanistan war as initially justified, most denounced the preemptive strike against Iraq, considering it a violation of international law. The United Nations refused to extend its approval, and millions of people across the globe protested the war. And, as in earlier times, McDonald's restaurants, as a symbol of the United States, became the target of antiwar protestors—in Ecuador, France, South

Korea, Argentina, Pakistan, and elsewhere. Opponents of the war called for a boycott of McDonald's and other major American brands.[22] Conversely, staunch American defenders of the war blamed France for its lack of support and suggested that French fries should be renamed "Freedom fries." The war also led to long-term instability in Iraq, outrage over the use of torture in US military prisons like Guantánamo in Cuba, the erosion of civil liberties with the passage of the US Patriot Act that gave law enforcement unprecedented powers to spy on American citizens, and the rise of Islamophobia. Already by 2007, a majority of Americans considered the war in Iraq to have been a mistake.[23]

In addition to being maligned as a symbol of an imperialist United States at the start of the war, McDonald's also struggled with its image at home during the early 2000s. Along with the mad cow scare and other protests, McDonald's was now contending with high-profile takedowns like Eric Schlosser's 2001 book *Fast Food Nation* and Morgan Spurlock's 2004 film *Super Size Me*, in which the filmmaker suffered terrible health consequences after eating only McDonald's food for thirty days. The chain also contended with the competition from new fast-casual chains that sold healthier alternatives and appealed to a more affluent audience, such as Panera, Chipotle, and Starbucks. McDonald's leaders sought to address these crises: the company published its first Social Responsibility Report in 2002, sought to engage rather than dismiss Greenpeace and other environmental organizations, tried to allow global franchises to modify their menus and décor to better suit local tastes, brought back the original Big Mac special sauce recipe, and tried to introduce healthier menu options. These halfhearted attempts did little to address the underlying issues.

The country as a whole was also struggling. Although Bush narrowly won re-election in 2004 against John Kerry, his approval ratings were already low when the devastating Hurricane Katrina hit New Orleans and the Gulf region in August 2005. The New Orleans levees broke, flooding most of the city and especially the lowest-lying parts, where mostly poor Black people lived. The federal government was unprepared, and its incompetence worsened the crisis, as many were left stranded, 1,500 people died, and the city was nearly destroyed. The hurricane highlighted the country's racialized poverty. The neighborhoods abandoned during Katrina epitomized the poor areas around the country where food options were limited to fast food and convenience stores, creating layered crises amid numerous kinds of neglect. Katrina also made clear that the erosion of government support had left many people unable to endure disasters, and that inaction on climate change would only make these problems worse in the years to come. Al Gore's film *An Inconvenient Truth* the following year concentrated attention on the growing climate crisis, linking the strength of Hurricane Katrina to warming waters and intensifying climatic effects, exacerbated by the industrial food system.

Then, in the final year of Bush's presidency, the Great Recession began, as the country plunged into the worst economic crisis since the Great Depression. Its causes were many and complex: banks making risky loans that encouraged consumers to go into debt buying houses or consumer products, rampant speculation unchecked by regulatory agencies, the flood of cheap goods from China and the related loss of US manufacturing jobs, and the general misguided faith in an unregulated free market that had reigned since Reagan's presidency. Alan Greenspan, the head of the Federal Reserve Bank from 1987 to 2006 who had overseen much of this change, admitted in 2008 that there was a "flaw" in his long-held free market ideology.[24]

But the recession actually left some institutions stronger than before. A 2009 *Slate* article asked, "Who won the recession?" and answered with, "McDonald's."[25] The company's sales growth was greater in 2008 than in the prior two years, benefitting from consumers' turn toward cheaper comfort food in a time of economic crisis and from seeing the gains of the changes instituted in response to earlier challenges. The company continued to grow even more abroad than domestically, extending its global reach. The Big Mac, it seemed, had found its special sauce again.

The Great Recession

- unregulated free market
- no money so ppl turned to cheap foods
- McDonalds grew most in recession

15

Korean Tacos:

Immigration, Social Media, and America Today

In 2008, a new kind of taco truck hit the streets of Los Angeles, selling Korean tacos—handmade corn tortillas filled with Korean-style barbecued meat, topped with onions, cilantro, lime, and salsa roja. It was called Kogi (with a hard "g") and it was slinging a new Korean-Mexican fusion food in a venue that would soon transform the culinary landscape not only in L.A. but throughout the country. Advertising its location through the new social media tool Twitter, Kogi brought mobility and accessibility together with the richness of US immigrant traditions.

At the same time, a young senator from Illinois, Barack Obama, was campaigning for the Democratic nomination for president with a slogan borrowed from the 1972 United Farm Workers campaign, "Sí, se puede," or "Yes, we can!" The son of a Kenyan immigrant and a white woman from Kansas, he grew up in Hawaii and Indonesia and became the first African American president. When advised to change his name during the campaign to something more "familiar," he refused, maintaining his multicultural background as a central part of his story, touting his family "of every race and every hue, scattered across three continents." "As long as I live," he promised, "I will never forget that in no other country on Earth is my story even possible."[1]

Obama, like the new L.A. street food, came from a fusion of immigrant backgrounds and also used the Internet and social media as a central organizing tool. Both Obama and Kogi rose to popularity due to the same cultural factors. As a *Newsweek* article put it, "youthful, urban, multiethnic, wired and communal, both brands resonate with a grassroots generation that distrusts top-down messaging and prefers to learn from peers, often online."[2] The same article described Kogi as "America's first viral eatery."

However, the cultural moment that paved the way for these newcomers clashed with darker forces that had been brewing for generations. The trends of deregulation and globalization that had gutted the economy and contaminated the environment led to a backlash among Americans who felt left behind. Many Americans increasingly absorbed information through social media and partisan news that fed into pre-existing worldviews. They looked outside the political establishment for leadership. This desire for something different manifested first in Obama's 2008 victory and then, in 2016, in the narrow victory of real-estate mogul and television celebrity Donald Trump. On the campaign trail, Trump pledged to "Make America Great Again" by, in part, building a border wall to block Mexican immigration and banning Muslim immigrants. Trump's election relied on and amplified forces of anti-immigrant nativism, white supremacy, and voter suppression.

Even as Korean tacos and the immigrant-influenced food revolution of which they were a part continued to flourish, the people who brought this culinary diversity to the United States became the targets of a regressive backlash. Immigrants and people from diverse racial and ethnic backgrounds had made the nation what it was from its earliest days. At the beginning of the twenty-first century, a new swell of anti-immigrant sentiment rose alongside—and as part of—a broader destabilization of American democracy.

Korean Tacos on the Rise

Long before Kogi hit the streets in 2008, taco trucks, or *loncheras*, had been common in communities with significant Mexican populations since the 1970s, building on an even longer history of mobile food vendors catering to the working class. Loncheras were typically run by Mexican migrants who came to the United States seeking seasonal work, often pushed out of their home countries due to changing trade policies that undermined local economies. They catered to low-income urban and agricultural workers looking for a quick, inexpensive traditional meal that brought a taste of home. The loncheras' nomadic nature allowed their owners to manage uncertain landscapes and political pressures, as when avoiding raids on undocumented immigrants by Immigration and Customs Enforcement (ICE). Moreover, their presence on city streets, often in poorer neighborhoods, offered public gathering spaces and food for the hungry.

Kogi drew on the long-term popularity of Mexican food among American-born audiences, while popularizing a taste for Korean food. Even as nativists in the past used food-based ethnic slurs like "beaner" or "greaser" against Mexicans, Americans came to broadly embrace Mexican food—from canned foods like chili in the early twentieth century to the rise of Taco Bell after its launch in 1962 to Chipotle burritos by the 1990s. Korean food, for its part, had remained less widely known by mainstream American audiences into the twenty-first century. Although Korean immigration to the United States grew beginning in the late 1960s, alongside Chinese and Japanese immigration, Korean food took longer to spread, in part because Korean restaurateurs made less effort to Americanize their cuisine. But the introduction of Korean food through the more-familiar vessel of a tortilla, along with the broader reach of Korean culture—through K-pop music and Korean skincare products—began to make foods like kimchi and Korean barbecue more mainstream. One Kogi-inspired Korean taco vendor in Indiana reflected, "The meat makes it Korean … The tortilla and toppings are a way to tell our customers that this food is O.K., that this food is American."[3] In his view, the Mexican ingredients had come to represent American food so significantly that they helped make Korean food legible to the average consumer.

Kogi was the brainchild of Mark Manguera and his sister-in-law Alice Shin who, after a night of bar-hopping, started daydreaming about a Korean-Mexican fusion taco truck. Manguera brought his friend Chef Roy Choi aboard to enact the vision, while Shin took to Twitter to build the hype and inform consumers of the truck's location and schedule. With a borrowed truck selling $2 tacos, Kogi hit the streets, targeting late night customers outside of Los Angeles nightclubs. Within a few months, they had lines snaking down the street, with people waiting up to two hours to try the delicious hybrid (Figure 15). The truck earned $2 million in its first year and in 2010 Choi was named best new chef by *Food & Wine* magazine. By 2012, even the all-American chain TGI Fridays had added Korean tacos to its menu.

This wasn't the first time chefs tried to blend Korean and Mexican food, but now the social, economic, and cultural moment was ready for Korean tacos. Alice Shin's knowledge of popular culture and of food studies—she was a graduate student in New York University's leading Food Studies program—allowed her to capitalize on the "upbeat, LOL-speak that drives online dialogue." For example, she announced the launch of a second Kogi truck with the post "KOGIHEADQUARTERSIS TOTALLYPREGGERSAND ISGIVINGBIRTHTOANEW BABYTRUCK" and a request for followers to help name the new truck.[4]

Further, the economic recession of 2008 made food trucks appealing to entrepreneurs, for whom mobile trucks required less capital than restaurants, and for consumers, who appreciated the relatively inexpensive food. The rise of a foodie generation, too, created consumers who valued the innovative food trucks and expanded their palates to accommodate strong Korean flavors like fermented kimchi and gochujang chili paste. Korean food more broadly—with its seasonal flavors, fermented ingredients, and focus on fresh

FIGURE 15 *This photo shows people congregating around the Kogi truck in Los Angeles, perhaps drawn here by the truck's Twitter feed, eager for the cultural fusion and foodie experience of the Korean tacos (Ted Soqui/Corbis via Getty Images).*

meats and vegetables—appealed to health-conscious American consumers. As sociologist Oliver Wang has explored, Kogi targeted these consumers by sticking to wealthier, higher-income neighborhoods, parking its truck in these areas far more often than in the poorer areas of South and East Los Angeles.[5] The communal aspects of eating from a taco truck also satisfied a public hungry for social connection. *The Los Angeles Times* wrote, "The truck and its staff of merry makers have become a sort of roving party, bringing people to neighborhoods they might not normally go to, and allowing for interactions with strangers they might not otherwise talk to."[6]

The effects of Kogi were significant throughout the food world, launching a food truck movement, promoting fusion cuisine, and reshaping the landscape for traditional lonchera taco trucks. After Kogi's runaway popularity, upscale food trucks using social media proliferated throughout the country. Whereas cities had often passed regulations that made it more difficult for loncheras to thrive, consumers welcomed gourmet trucks with open arms. As scholar Robert Lemon writes, of Columbus, Ohio, "the taco trucks, which were so viciously contested ... from 2001 to 2007, are now venerated as contributing to the city's international image."[7] The American-born chefs who ran these gourmet trucks, with their native English and relative procedural savvy, were better able to navigate the system that regulated taco trucks. And the whiter, more middle-class audiences that patronized these trucks made mobile food more palatable to city officials. As Anthony Bourdain wrote, using a derogatory term for loncheras: "Roy Choi first changed the world when he elevated the food-truck concept from 'roach coach' to highly sought-after, ultra-hot-yet-democratic rolling restaurant."[8] With its denigration of the traditional taco truck, this commentary highlights the way that the immigrant roots of the movement have often been dismissed. Loncheras, meanwhile, carved out their own niches, and tried to appeal to new audiences through the incorporation of American flavors. Some cities began to offer "guided tours" of area taco trucks, making them into "sites of culinary tourism for Anglos searching for ethnic exoticism."[9] One lonchera owner described how he began to offer to add sour cream, lettuce, tomato, and cheese for American tastes, "Taco Bell Style," instead of the traditional onion and cilantro.[10]

The Obama Era

This rise of Kogi and its descendants took place against a broader backdrop of food, environmental, and political change under the Obama presidency. In November 2008, Barack Obama decidedly won the election against Republican senator John McCain. As the first Black president, Obama represented hope and change for many Americans. The Democrats also won majorities in the House and the Senate, allowing Obama to make progress in his first months in office, including appointing Sonia Sotomayor as the first woman of color to the Supreme Court, passing a nearly $800 billion stimulus package to restore the economy, bolstering women's reproductive rights, and proposing government support for healthcare reform and clean energy. But he entered office with overwhelming challenges facing him and the country that would define his two terms in office: pressing food and environmental issues, an ongoing economic recession, a broken healthcare system, increasing partisanship, and wars in Iraq and Afghanistan.

In October 2008, just before the election, leading food journalist Michael Pollan wrote "An Open Letter to the Next Farmer in Chief."[11] There, he described how interwoven food issues were with the most pressing questions of the time—climate change, healthcare, national security, and energy independence—even if the food system itself was rarely directly addressed as part of mainstream political dialogue. By 2008, the problems of the food system were countless. Federal policies maximized production of commodity crops like corn and soy that became cheap animal feed to prop up polluting and inhumane factory farms and became ingredients in ultra-processed junk foods. The entire US food system relied on cheap energy, burning up nonrenewable fossil fuels to produce petroleum-based fertilizers, pesticides, and antibiotics, to mechanize food production from farm to factory, and to transport food products enormous distances—all central contributions to greenhouse gas emissions and devastating climate change. Diseases and contamination on factory farms led to outbreaks of foodborne illness, antibiotic resistance, and the development of novel zoonotic diseases (like Covid-19 in the years to come). The food system was dominated by just a few enormously powerful companies that controlled the "$1.5 trillion industry that grows, rears, slaughters, processes, imports, packages and retails most of the food Americans eat" and that had strong political lobbying power in Washington D.C.[12] Laborers in the food system— most of them migrants—were exploited. Nearly 30 percent of all food was wasted, at all levels of production, leading to increased methane emissions in the landfill. And low-income communities had the least access to healthful foods and the highest rates of diet-related diseases.

Pollan called for the incoming president to take action against these problems. He proposed a range of solutions, from federal promotion of sustainable agriculture and farmers' markets to the training of ecologically minded farmers, from a symbolic garden on the South Lawn of the White House to a system of local meat inspectors and a strategic grain reserve. The proposals were many and varied, but they were also specific and actionable.

Obama, once in office, did seem to listen to Pollan and other food activists. His administration passed the Healthy, Hunger-Free Kids Act in 2010 to reform school lunch. First Lady Michelle Obama launched her Let's Move campaign to promote physical fitness and created the Partnership for a Healthier America to attempt to bring the food industry on board with making healthier products. The Obamas even planted an organic garden on the lawn of the White House.

But like so many other efforts Obama made, these were undermined by opposition. For example, in 2010, the administration put forth an ambitious antitrust initiative to reduce the power of the Big Food giants and to support small farmers. The meat industry pushed back with funding, lobbying, and political persuasion, until Agriculture Secretary Tom Vilsack backed down, and no new regulations were put in place. Other efforts to reduce antibiotic dependence in meat production or to enforce nutritional standards were made voluntary, rather than mandatory, giving the industry permission to continue making its own rules. Corporations were given even more power after the Supreme Court ruled in the 2010 *Citizens United* case that limits on corporate campaign spending were unconstitutional, furthering their influence on politics. With political opposition and the lack of an organized food movement, the Obama administration failed to make headway in addressing the many problems of the food system. The new foodies who flocked to buy Korean tacos did not apply that same enthusiasm to advocating for broader systemic change to bring about a more diverse and healthful food supply for the nation as a whole.

This general pattern of attempts at progress stymied by establishment power, indifference, and backlash characterized other dimensions of the Obama presidency. As the Great Recession continued, Obama bailed out the banks to prop up the financial system. This passed the cost on to taxpayers, only deepening entrenched inequality. Few financial executives were held accountable for their roles in the crisis. Even as the economy began to recover, most of the gains went to the wealthy, with 85 percent of new income between 2009 and 2013 going to the top 1 percent of earners.[13] Lower-paid workers faced stagnant wages and the lack of a social safety net in the form of welfare, unemployment insurance, or state aid. And Black Americans were the hardest hit of all, with Black unemployment and poverty rates remaining nearly double that of whites. McDonald's urged its workers, many of whom barely received minimum wage, to weather economic difficulty by going on food stamps.[14]

The Obama administration also made efforts toward nationalizing healthcare and making it more equitable and accessible, with the Affordable Care Act in 2010. But its passage was caught up in bitter partisan fighting, leading to a government shutdown by Republicans in Congress in 2013. This ineffectiveness was worsened by the rise of the Tea Party opposition, a movement of very conservative, mostly white voters who claimed the legacy of the Founding Fathers to argue for limited government, lower taxes, and anti-immigration sentiment. This movement pushed the Republican Party far to the right on these and other issues.

Citizenship issues emerged in attacks on Obama, with the rise of the "birther" conspiracy theory promoted by far-right radio show host Alex Jones and future presidential candidate Donald Trump, which falsely claimed that Obama was born in Africa. Trump, signaling his use of Twitter and bypassing of traditional media sources, tweeted in 2012 that "An 'extremely credible source' has called my office and told me that @BarackObama's birth certificate is a fraud," despite the fact that Obama had released his long-form birth certificate more than a year before this tweet, which showed Hawaii as his birthplace.[15] The same ethnic fusion that had made Obama the bearer of hope and change was now being used against him.

Beyond the specific focus on Obama, immigration more broadly became a major political issue. Even as many Americans gobbled up Korean tacos and becoming more adventurous eaters in exploring diverse international cuisines, a segment of society also turned against the immigrants who brought these new flavors. By 2012, almost a quarter of Americans were immigrants or their children, with half of that population from Latin America.

A new wave of conservative politicians, emboldened by resurgent white national movements, began to target undocumented immigrants and call for immigration restriction. Tighter border controls ironically led to less back-and-forth seasonal migration and encouraged migrants to the United States to stay permanently. The majority of immigrants, especially from Central America, were drawn to the United States by work in the agricultural sector (along with construction and domestic work), performing manual labor for wages too low for many native-born Americans. The American food system by the twenty-first century was utterly dependent on immigrant labor, even as those workers came under attack.

Viral Democracy

Another significant development was the groundswell of protests and democratic movements aided by the new technologies of smartphones and social media, with many movement hashtags "going viral" or spreading rapidly online. Americans took to Twitter not only to get updates on the location of Korean taco trucks, but also to connect to one another in ways that at first seemed to hold promise for true democratic connection. The years between 2004 and 2007 saw the launch of Facebook, YouTube, Twitter, and the iPhone. By 2015, about two-thirds of Americans owned smartphones.[16] They used these new technologies to connect with friends, share status updates, and, increasingly, to follow politics and the news.

As indicated by Kogi's use of Twitter, online platforms aided a new interest in food as part of a "food revolution." A new class of "foodies," inspired in part by Michael Pollan's 2006 *The Omnivore's Dilemma* and related writings, came to see new food tastes and food politics as central to their identities. Though their platforms varied, the movement as a whole spurred the growth of farmers' markets; supported community supported agriculture (CSA) subscription arrangements; advocated for school lunch reform; organized for better conditions for farmworkers; put local, organic, and artisanal food on the map; and linked food problems to other social problems like racial and economic justice and climate change. And sometimes foodies just looked for creative new cuisine, buying from food trucks and other small eateries, indulging in trends like molecular gastronomy, and binge-watching the many cooking shows on the Food Network and Netflix. Although their overall political influence remained small, the food industry did take notice. For example, companies including Monsanto and the National Cattlemen's Beef Association hired the public relations firm Ketchum Communications to combat food movement messages in response to the popularity of the 2008 film *Food, Inc.*[17]

Beyond food, again supported by the connectivity of social media, popular revolts proliferated in the Middle East, toppling dictators in Egypt, Libya, and Tunisia. The United States sought to promote democracy while also protecting its strategic interests. Obama's foreign policy focused heavily on the Middle East throughout his presidency. He successfully withdrew troops from Iraq by 2011, ending an eight-year war that had cost the United States almost $2 trillion and had taken the lives of hundreds of thousands of Iraqis. Earlier that year, Obama directed US forces to Pakistan, where they killed Osama bin Laden, the mastermind behind the 9/11 attacks. But the war in Afghanistan continued, and the Taliban and al-Qaeda remained active. A new terrorist group, the Islamic States, or ISIS, rose to power and claimed territory in Iraq. And despite criticizing the war on terror, Obama continued drone assassinations and the invasive practices of the National Security Administration (NSA).

Social media also fueled domestic popular uprisings, such as those to promote economic equality, gay rights, a reckoning with sexual violence, and racial justice. Inspired in part by Vermont senator Bernie Sanders—whose 8.5-hour Senate-floor speech on poverty in December 2010 was "the most Twittered event in the world on that day"—protestors launched the Occupy movement, which spread throughout the country and the world, protesting the dominance of politics and the economy by the "1 percent" of richest Americans. Then, the Supreme Court ruled in the 2015 *Obergefell v. Hodges* case that state bans on same-sex marriage were unconstitutional, effectively legalizing same-sex marriage. Many Americans celebrated the culmination of decades of gay rights activism and the role of media in creating a culture of greater public acceptance. Others, however, saw the decision as a defeat in the culture wars, a decisive strike against a conservative Christian worldview. These changing norms around sexual behavior, along with anger over evidence of Donald Trump's sexual misconduct, also spurred the viral #MeToo movement, which drew attention to problems of sexual violence. The social media hashtag #MeToo, developed by Black activist Tarana Burke, rose to prominence in October 2017. Within a few days' time, the hashtag had been used nearly a million times on Twitter and in twelve million posts on Facebook, testifying to the widespread experience of sexual assault and harassment among women.[18]

Finally, the Black Lives Matter movement also used social media platforms to organize for racial justice. Beginning around 2013, in response to the acquittal of George Zimmerman, a Florida man who had killed Black teenager Trayvon Martin the year before, Black activists began tweeting using the hashtag #BlackLivesMatter. The rise of smartphones that could capture video of encounters between police and Black men led to a surge in high-profile cases of police misconduct. Far from ushering in a "post-racial era," Obama's election did little to disrupt the nation's long history of racial violence. The murders of Black people by police filled the news in the years to follow: Michael Brown near St. Louis in 2014, twelve-year-old Tamir Rice later that same year, Philando Castile in Minnesota in 2016, Breonna Taylor, killed by police as she slept in her apartment in March 2020, and so many others. The officers were rarely convicted of any crimes. These horrors were compounded by the 2013 Supreme Court *Shelby v. Holder* decision that undermined the 1965 Voting Rights Act and its protections for Black voters, by a 2015 attack on a Black church in Charleston, South Carolina by a white supremacist gunman who killed nine people, and by a violent neo-Nazi rally in Charlottesville, Virginia in 2017 against the removal of a statute of Confederate general Robert E. Lee. The Black Lives Matter movement accelerated, with protests across the country in mid-2020 after the murder of George Floyd by a Minneapolis police officer. Attention to systemic racism, mass incarceration, and police brutality increased, but little policy change resulted to address the deep racial disparities in American society. Black activists have also focused attention on food justice, demanding systemic change—at the agricultural, political, economic, and technological levels—to promote access to healthy, nutritious, and culturally appropriate foods. The fight for justice more broadly is deeply intertwined with the fight for good food.

The Erosion of Democracy under Trump

As part of his campaign, and then into his presidency after the 2016 election, Donald Trump focused on curbing "illegal immigration" as one of his central talking points. The same richness of cultural exchange and ethnic fusion that had brought Korean tacos to popularity was now being weaponized against entire groups of people. One of Trump's favored tools in spreading his ideology was Twitter, where he could speak directly to the people. In contrast to social media's early promise as a tool of democracy and the promotion of new foods, it became increasingly used as an anti-democratic platform, promoting partisanship, false information, and segmented worldviews that allowed for little common ground.

In the 2016 campaign season, former First Lady, New York Senator, and Secretary of State Hillary Clinton vied against the unexpected Republican candidate Donald Trump. His ascendancy, like Obama's, was the result of many Americans' disenchantment with establishment politicians and hunger for a different approach. Trump appealed to Americans who felt left behind and left out, many of them struggling with the fallout from globalization and its attendant effects on wages, unemployment, and immigration—though few understood their sense of unease in these terms.

Trump fired up his supporters by denouncing "political correctness" and by his use of vulgar language. He promised to "Make America Great Again" by returning to some imagined idyllic past—before the sexual, cultural, and civil rights revolution of the 1960s. He branded many Mexican immigrants as "criminals, drug dealers, rapists" and promised to build a border wall.[19] And he claimed that his opponent Hillary Clinton belonged in jail as he led his supporters at huge rallies in chants of "Lock Her Up!" He trumpeted all these sentiments across social media platforms, relying on them instead of the more traditional television ads or newspaper endorsements. Trump's insults and swaggering tweets got more attention than Clinton's detailed and thoughtful policy statements. His one-time campaign manager said they sought to "monopolize the media attention by using social media unlike anybody else," getting Fox News to cover Trump's every tweet.[20] And Russian operatives intervened as well, creating fake Twitter and Facebook accounts that flooded the sites with false information intended to stoke anger and increase support for Trump. Twitter had nearly 48 million fake accounts leading up to the election. Russia's Internet Research Agency bought divisive political ads on Facebook that reached over 126 million Americans.[21]

Mexican food played a role in Trump's rhetoric as well. On Cinco de Mayo in 2016, Trump tweeted a photo of himself eating a taco bowl with the caption "I love Hispanics!"[22] In this case, he intended for his embrace of "ethnic food" to convey a positive message, despite his hate-filled rhetoric against Mexican immigrants. Taco bowls, it should be noted, are an American invention rather than a traditional Mexican food. In another adaptation of the theme, co-founder of Latinos for Trump Marco Gutierrez infamously threatened that "if you don't do something about [Mexican immigration], you're going to have taco trucks on every corner." A public that eagerly patronized loncheras and made Kogi famous responded by launching a nationwide "Guac the Vote" campaign, using taco trucks as voter registration booths, and using the hashtag #TacosOnEveryCorner.[23]

On election day, although Hillary Clinton won the popular vote by nearly three million votes, the decisive electoral votes made Trump the victor. Once in office, Trump carried on his party's legacy by passing huge tax cuts that helped corporations and the wealthiest Americans, removing environmental and worker protections, and trying—but failing—to overturn Obama's Affordable Care Act. And in keeping with his campaign rhetoric, he took anti-immigrant action. He tried to shut down all Muslim immigration by passing a travel ban to the United States from Muslim-majority countries—though the courts limited the ban's reach. And in 2018, the Trump administration began separating young children at the southern border from their parents who were seeking asylum.

The separation policy and images of children being held in what looked like cages led to protests across the country. Trump's administration also detained and deported undocumented immigrants at record levels. These actions were met with anger and disbelief from Trump's opponents, but served to further consolidate his political base.

This anti-immigrant sentiment was also tied to the rise of white supremacy, calling itself by a new name: "the alt-right." This movement embraced white nationalism, railed against immigration of dark-skinned people, and sought to preserve the Confederate legacy. As one of the movement's leaders wrote in 2014, "Immigration is a kind of proxy war—and maybe a last stand—for White Americans who are undergoing a painful recognition that, unless dramatic action is taken, their grandchildren will live in a country that is alien and hostile." These mostly younger white men took to online forums and social media to entrench their views, where they "mocked PC culture, bemoaned the decline of Western civilization, attacked feminism, trolled women, used neo-Nazi memes, and posted pornography," as historian Jill Lepore writes.[24] These online spaces served to deepen the divide between mainstream media and the increasingly conspiracy-theory driven "alternative news sources" that radicalized some Americans. Commentators have warned that social media, with its "likes" and "retweets," its clickbait headlines, and its echo-chamber qualities, has deepened political anger and led to factionalism in ways the nation's architects could not have predicted. Jonathan Haidt and Tobias Rose-Stockwell write that founder James Madison hoped the vast size of the country would mitigate partisanship that "inflamed [men] with mutual animosity." Online platforms, however, have proved adept at overcoming that vastness and "spread[ing] a general conflagration" of animosity throughout the country and the world.[25]

Trump also attacked the mainstream media and peddled his own version of "truth," peppering his statements with distorted perspectives and outright lies. The Washington Post determined that he made 30,573 false or misleading claims during his four years in office.[26] He stoked rage among his supporters with angry and aggressive tweets, and lashed out against anyone who criticized him—breaking many of the norms of the office. He went through two acrimonious impeachment proceedings—once in 2019 for abuse of power and obstruction of Congress and a second time in 2021 for incitement of insurrection—but was acquitted both times.

All of this led to deepened political divisions and a sense of two separate Americas. This division was made clear not only around immigration, but also in fights over topics like climate change and gun control, in which people fought for a more secure future, often using social media to fuel their activism. While many Americans—especially younger generations— recognized climate change as a dire emergency and *the* central issue requiring action to preserve human life on earth, the Trump administration withdrew from the Paris Agreement on climate change in 2017, sought to ramp up coal mining, and appointed a climate denier to the head of the Environmental Protection Agency. When it came to gun control, in March 2018, hundreds of thousands of Americans organized the March for Our Lives after a school shooting in Parkland, Florida left seventeen students and teachers dead, on top of an epidemic of other public shootings. The United States had more private gun owners and homicides than any other affluent nation. But the ideological devotion of many Americans to the Second Amendment's right to "bear arms" and the lobbying power of the National Rifle Association (NRA) prevented any reasonable regulations.

By 2020, many of these trends coalesced in significant threats to American democracy. The Covid-19 pandemic highlighted the lack of central authority, lack of trust in science, and partisan reactions to basic measures of community maintenance. The new respiratory virus emerged in the United States in early 2020, and by the end of the year, it had killed about 385,000 Americans (and about 3 million people worldwide), with twice that number recorded the following year.[27] Beyond these staggering death tolls, the virus wreaked havoc on the economy and caused widespread social trauma. And yet, even when it became clear that wearing face masks helped prevent the spread of this deadly disease (which sometimes manifested asymptomatically) and when the miraculous new technology of Covid-19 vaccines became available by December 2020, significant percentages of Americans refused both actions on partisan grounds, no matter how many fellow citizens they infected in the process. The political divisions sowed in prior years proved deadly.

In the 2020 presidential election, former vice president Joe Biden ran against Donald Trump. After a long campaign season, Biden won the electoral and popular vote. His running mate Kamala Harris, the daughter of Jamaican and Indian parents, became the first woman, first Black, and first South Asian vice president. Biden and his administration faced tremendous challenges, as they fought global authoritarianism and corruption, addressed the Covid-19 global pandemic with mass vaccination efforts, and passed the $1.9 trillion American Rescue Plan and the $1.2 trillion infrastructure bill to jumpstart the economy.

But even after Biden's decisive win, Donald Trump refused to concede the election, and began to tout the "Big Lie" that there had been election fraud. Despite overwhelming evidence to the contrary, many Republicans disseminated his lies, with members of his party working to overturn the election and undermine voting rights. Many of his followers took matters into their own hands, culminating in the violent invasion of the Capitol Building on January 6, 2021, by a mob of more than 2,000 Trump supporters who sought to disrupt the electoral count and undermine the foundation of the country's democratic process.

This insurrection at the capitol was the result of many factors and long-term trends. But, like the Korean tacos with which this chapter began, new attitudes toward immigration, cultural (mis)understandings, and the spread of social media were decisive. Both the insurrection and this new fusion food connect to questions that have been present throughout American history—questions about who is considered an American citizen, how we struggle with one another over ideas and norms, and how cultural products like food shape our sense of belonging. The answers to these questions are still to be determined.

Epilogue

Food as Care and Hope
for the Future

As I began writing a final draft of this epilogue, I traveled a few states over to help some close friends with their new baby, who had been born two months early and with high medical needs. In between tending to the baby and catching up with my old friends, I made meals. The baby's sensitive digestive system required that the mom keep a range of foods out of her breast milk, in addition to her preferred vegetarian diet: no dairy, no soy, no eggs, no beans, no cruciferous vegetables. So, I took this opportunity as a challenge and searched for recipes to accommodate her dietary needs. I traveled to their local grocery store to purchase specific ingredients, and each night I stirred together dishes to feed this tired family. Walnut burgers and roasted potatoes. Vegetable cashew coconut curry. Jambalaya with seitan and mushrooms. Quinoa with eggplant and zucchini. I pulled together quick breakfasts and assembled lunchboxes of PB&J and string cheese for their older child.

As I cooked, the background hum of the baby's oxygen tank and the beeping of his blood sugar and heart rate monitor provided a soundtrack to my thoughts. I thought about this medically fragile baby and his uncertain future. I thought about the litany of global and local horrors on the news, as Russia continued its rampage in Ukraine, as white supremacist violence raged, as Covid-19 continued to claim lives, and as our political, environmental, and social foundations felt ever more tenuous due to years of human destruction (willful or not). And I thought about this book I was writing, about what this food history can teach us not only about the past, but also about the future. How do we find hope in bleak situations? Could this narrative provide reasons for optimism? Given all the other dire challenges of the world, why should we care about food, anyway?

I have to admit that even as someone who spends a lot of time thinking about these questions, answers haven't come easily. I hope that readers of this book will take the time to search for their own answers. But the restricted diet dishes I was creating in my friends' house made me see things a bit more clearly. Food *is* care. The act of feeding has always been, and will continue to be, a way to nourish ourselves and our communities. When faced with terrible circumstances, people put one foot in front of the other, tending to our most fundamental need for sustenance, fostering hope as we care for each other and for the nonhuman world around us.

As we've seen, in previous crises of American history, as during the Civil War, the Great Depression, the World Wars, or the fight for civil rights, food has been a concrete tool for action. Governments, community groups, and individuals have used food as a tool for organizing, for nurturing family and community, and for basic nutrition. The need for food is one of the most fundamental drives of human life. When other foundations start to falter, turning to food offers a sense of shared humanity.

During the Covid-19 pandemic, mutual aid organizations sprouted across the United States and created innovative local solutions to food insecurity as they fed others, regardless of need or political affiliation. Such grassroots efforts have allowed people to help one another directly, without the need for often slow-moving government intervention and with the potential for more attention to the most vulnerable communities. In my small community in Virginia, for example, a Facebook group called "Looking Out for Each Other" connected thousands of people in need with neighbors who had resources to spare or recommend. A related organization called The Future Economy Collective set up a free fridge and pantry, a community garden that donates all its produce, a public seed share, a skill-sharing exchange, and more. Similar efforts spread throughout the country.[1] Hunger is a common enemy and caring for others—through food—remains a critical tool for coping in times of hopelessness.

In August 2021, when the United States withdrew troops from Afghanistan, ending the twenty-year war, tens of thousands of refugees relocated to the United States. According to official US government policy, when they arrived, exhausted and hungry, they were supposed to be met with one "culturally appropriate" meal, a rare government recognition of the cultural needs of different groups of people. After that first meal, though, many refugees faced an uncertain American food landscape that could make them feel even further alienated. To meet that need, restaurateurs (many of them immigrants themselves) and local agencies around the country rallied to provide familiar foods and ones that meet the halal requirements that shape many Muslims' diets. In Houston, an Afghan chef provides fresh breads, fragrant rice, spiced lentils, and grilled lamb or chicken. In Pennsylvania, one refugee agency realized the mashed potatoes and mac and cheese they had been providing were going uneaten, so they shifted their requests to basmati rice, chickpeas, and fresh produce. In Richmond, Virginia, another Afghan chef, Hamidullah Noori, hires refugees to work in his restaurant and cooks thousands of free meals. "This is what humanity is," Noori said, "to hold each other's hand when in need. Everything else is secondary."[2]

After Russia launched a full-scale invasion into Ukraine in February 2022, food needs there have been severe. In addition to the hundreds of millions of dollars of food aid that the United States and entities like the United Nations World Food Programme have committed, many organizations have stepped in to help Ukrainians at home, on the battlefield, and the millions who have fled as refugees. The World Central Kitchen humanitarian nonprofit, headed by chef José Andrés, has served over 27 million meals across eight countries to those affected by Russia's violence in Ukraine. Volunteers make sandwiches on fresh-baked bread, and serve meat, potatoes, and soup, even after a missile destroyed one of their charity kitchens in Kharkiv. Andrés says that when nothing makes sense amid such violence, "At least, feeding people is what makes sense … people working together to make sure that one plate of food at a time we can bring hope of a better tomorrow."[3] Russia's aggression in Ukraine has also led the McDonald's corporation to announce its departure from the country in May 2022, shuttering the restaurants that had begun to open in 1990 at the end of the Cold War.

In May 2022, a white supremacist terrorist, fueled by the racist and antisemitic hate and lies of online forums, shot and killed ten people in a Tops grocery store in Buffalo, New York's predominantly Black East Side. This location was not incidental. The murderer specifically targeted this gathering place, which offered healthier food and community in a city characterized by racial segregation and food apartheid caused by redlining and disinvestment reaching back to the 1930s. Activists like Della Miller had protested the lack of fresh food in the neighborhood and convinced Tops' executives to build the store nearly twenty years before. After the shooting, the store was temporarily closed, and the area was once again without access to groceries. Into this vacuum stepped a wide range of local, Black-led organizations to fill the need, providing and delivering food to the people. The pre-existing social networks supplied the food needed to sustain residents through the work of healing and advocacy.[4]

This theme of care has also taken on larger scales in recent years, as people have extended care to broader agricultural and political systems. There are trends in the United States and around the world toward hopeful anti-corporate or alternative foodways in the increasingly complex and globalized food system. When the United Nations held a Food Systems Summit in September 2021, a wide array of scientists, food producers, and Indigenous groups protested the Summit's focus on maximizing production through corporate agriculture. In India, in 2020 and 2021, tens of thousands of farmers marched in the streets, and the country staged a nationwide general strike against farm laws that would have further opened the nation's agriculture system to the free market, forcing the government to repeal the laws. Activists organizing on behalf of agricultural and food processing workers' rights ramped up their action during the Covid-19 pandemic, highlighting the essential nature of those workers in the food system. Research is under way to develop plant-based meat substitutes and to cultivate cell-based animal flesh, in an attempt to move away from the destructive foundation of animal agriculture and the meat industry.[5] And support for local agriculture through farmers' markets, farm-to-table restaurants, and farm-to-school programs continues to grow.

As in the case of Korean tacos, new tastes and new foods abound. Although it's certainly possible to embrace an immigrant group's cuisine and not welcome the people themselves, eating across cultural lines can foster more cultural understanding. Immigrant foods are an obvious positive influence on American culture from the many waves of people who have come to this country. Eating new foods, when done with respect, can expand empathy. We are what we eat, and in the case of most Americans, we eat multi-ethnically.

Growing food, as well as thinking about where our food comes from, is also a fundamentally hopeful act. Each sprouting seed holds within it the promise of abundance to come. The seasonal rhythms of agricultural production offer a sense of renewal, a suggestion that we can begin again. Life can come from a single seed. The act of planting that seed is an act of hope, in imagining that we or those we care for will reap its harvest in the future.

In the Talmudic story of Honi and the carob tree, Honi asks an old man who is planting a carob seed why he bothers with it, since the tree won't bear fruit for another seventy years. The man replies that he benefited from the abundant carob trees his ancestors had planted for him, so now he plants his own for the generations to come.

When we eat, we benefit from the care of others whose labor and ingenuity make our survival possible, and from the environment that provides material resources. When we stop to think about food, about where it comes from and where it has taken us, we recognize the daily acts of hope that feed us all. No matter how commercialized or industrialized these foodways have become, food is our common denominator, binding us to one another and to the natural world.

Notes

Introduction

1   Poon, Linda. "There Are 200 Million Fewer Hungry People Than 25 Years Ago." *NPR*, June 1, 2015, sec. Goats and Soda. https://www.npr.org/sections/goatsandsoda/2015/06/01/411265021/there-are-200-million-fewer-hungry-people-than-25-years-ago.

Chapter 1

1   George Amos Dorsey and Alfred Louis Kroeber, eds., *Traditions of the Arapaho: Collected under the Auspices of the Field Columbian Museum and of the American Museum of Natural History* (Chicago: Field Columbian Museum, 1903), 46.

2   Bison is the more accurate biological term, but when the Europeans mistakenly referred to the animal as a "buffalo," the name stuck. I thus use the two terms interchangeably in this chapter.

3   George Colpitts, *Pemmican Empire: Food, Trade, and the Last Bison Hunts in the North American Plains, 1780–1882* (Cambridge; New York: Cambridge University Press, 2014).

4   Charles C. Mann, *1491: New Revelations of the Americas before Columbus*, 1st edition (New York: Vintage, 2006), 156.

5   Alfred W. Crosby, *The Columbian Exchange: Biological and Cultural Consequences of 1492* (Westport, CT: Greenwood Pub. Co., 1972), 280.

6   Maria Montoya et al., *Global Americans: A History of the United States*, 1st edition (Boston, MA: Cengage Learning, 2017), 10.

7   Jared Diamond, "The Worst Mistake in the History of the Human Race," *Discover Magazine*, May 1, 1999, https://www.discovermagazine.com/planet-earth/the-worst-mistake-in-the-history-of-the-human-race.

8   Linda Murray Berzok, *American Indian Food*, 1st edition (Westport, CT: Greenwood, 2005), 4.

9   Berzok, *American Indian Food*, 6; Neal Salisbury, "The Indians' Old World: Native Americans and the Coming of Europeans," in *Major Problems in American Indian History: Documents and Essays*, ed. Albert Hurtado and Peter Iverson, 2nd edition (Boston: Cengage Learning, 2000), 36.

10 Montoya et al., *Global Americans*, 23.

11 Colin G. Calloway, *One Vast Winter Count: The Native American West before Lewis and Clark* (Lincoln: University of Nebraska Press, 2003).

12 Berzok, *American Indian Food*, 182.

13 Berzok, *American Indian Food*, 175.

14 Berzok, *American Indian Food*, 172.

15 Mann, *1491*.

16 "The Beginning of the Skagit World," in *Indian Legends of the Pacific Northwest*, ed. Ella E. Clark (Berkeley: University of California Press, 1953), 140.

17 Crosby, *The Columbian Exchange*, 280.

18 Libby H. O'Connell, *American Plate: A Culinary History in 100 Bites* (Naperville, IL: Sourcebooks, 2014), 27; Mann, *1491*, 251.

19 Mann, *1491*, 218.

20 Montoya et al., *Global Americans*, 21; Berzok, *American Indian Food*, 179.

21 "First Peoples Buffalo Jump State Park and National Historic Landmark," Montana Fish, Wildlife & Parks, accessed December 21, 2020, https://stateparks.mt.gov/stateparks/first-peoples-buffalo-jump.

22 Colpitts, *Pemmican Empire*.

23 William Cronon, *Changes in the Land: Indians, Colonists, and the Ecology of New England* (New York: Hill and Wang, 1983), 51–2.

24 Salisbury, "The Indians' Old World," 36.

25 Berzok, *American Indian Food*, xii.

26 Alexander Koch et al., "Earth System Impacts of the European Arrival and Great Dying in the Americas after 1492," *Quaternary Science Reviews* 207 (March 1, 2019): 13–36. I am following Linda Berzok in using the term "invasion."

27 T. Kue Young, *The Health of Native Americans: Towards a Biocultural Epidemiology* (New York: Oxford University Press, 1994), 55.

28 Crosby, *The Columbian Exchange*, 6.

29 Pedro de Castañeda de Nájera, *The Journey of Coronado, 1540–1542*, trans. George Winship (New York: A.S. Barnes & Company, 1904), 112, http://www.americanjourneys.org/aj-086/.

30 Herman J. Viola, "Introducing: 'A Song for the Horse Nation' on the National Mall," *The National Museum of the American Indian* (blog), accessed December 22, 2020, https://blog.nmai.si.edu/main/2011/08/introducing-a-song-for-the-horse-nation-on-the-national-mall.html.

31 Mann, *1491*, 320.

32 "The West: A Wound in the Heart," *PBS*, accessed December 22, 2020, http://www.pbs.org/weta/thewest/program/episodes/five/woundinheart.htm.

33 J. Weston Phippen, "'Kill Every Buffalo You Can! Every Buffalo Dead Is an Indian Gone,'" *The Atlantic*, May 13, 2016; Andrew C. Isenberg, *The Destruction of the Bison: An Environmental History, 1750–1920* (Cambridge: Cambridge University Press, 2000).

Chapter 2

1 Fulmer Mood, "John Winthrop, Jr., on Indian Corn," *The New England Quarterly* 10, no. 1 (March 1937): 121–33.

2 Alan Taylor, *American Colonies: The Settling of North America* (New York: Viking Press, 2001), 72.

3 "The Coronado Expedition 1540–1542, by George Parker Winship, Excerpted from the Fourteenth Annual Report of the Bureau of Ethnology to the Secretary of the Smithsonian Institution, 1892–1893, Part 1. A Project Gutenberg EBook.," accessed January 30, 2021, https://www.gutenberg.org/files/50448/50448-h/50448-h.htm.

4 Taylor, *American Colonies*, 80.

5 Taylor, *American Colonies*, 46.

6 Andrew Lawson, "Smith vs. Wingfield: Remaking the Social Order in the Chesapeake," *The Virginia Magazine of History and Biography* 128, no. 3 (2020): 215.

7 Katherine A. Grandjean, "New World Tempests: Environment, Scarcity, and the Coming of the Pequot War," *The William and Mary Quarterly* 68, no. 1 (2011): 79.

8 John Smith, "'What Can You Get by Warre': Powhatan Exchanges Views with Captain John Smith, 1608," in *The Generall Historie of Virginia, New England & the Summer Isles* (Glasgow: James MacLehose and Sons, 1907), 158–9, http://historymatters.gmu.edu/d/5838.

9 Taylor, *American Colonies*, 131–5.

10 As cited in James C. Giesen and Bryant Simon, eds., *Food and Eating in America: A Documentary Reader* (Malden, MA: Wiley-Blackwell, 2018), 18.

11 Taylor, *American Colonies*, 198, 110.

12 Grandjean, "New World Tempests," 92.

13 As cited in Giesen and Simon, *Food and Eating in America*, 26.

14 James E. McWilliams, *A Revolution in Eating: How the Quest for Food Shaped America* (New York: Columbia University Press, 2005), 82.

15 Giesen and Simon, *Food and Eating in America*, 25.

16 As cited in Joy Porter, *Land and Spirit in Native America* (Westport, CT: ABC-CLIO, 2012), 62.

17 Taylor, *American Colonies*, 129.

18 As cited in Jennifer Jensen Wallach and Lindsey R. Swindall, eds., *American Appetites: A Documentary Reader* (Fayetteville, AR: University of Arkansas Press, 2014), 28.

19 Taylor, *American Colonies*, 225.

20 As cited in Anya Zilberstein, "Bastard Breadfruit and Other Cheap Provisions: Early Food Science for the Welfare of the Lower Orders," *Early Science and Medicine* 21, no. 5 (2016): 507.

21 McWilliams, *A Revolution in Eating*, 114.

22 Giesen and Simon, *Food and Eating in America*, 52.

23 McWilliams, *A Revolution in Eating*, 10.

24 Wallach and Swindall, *American Appetites*, 37.

25 Taylor, *American Colonies*, 390.

Chapter 3

1 Harold C. Syrett, *"The Papers of Alexander Hamilton, Vol. 17, August 1794–December 1794"* (New York: Columbia University Press, 1972), 148–50.

2 Andrew F. Smith, *Drinking History: Fifteen Turning Points in the Making of American Beverages* (New York, NY: New York University, 2012), 18.

3 Robert Beverley, "Edibles, Potables, and Fuel in Virginia," in *The History and Present State of Virginia*, ed. Louis Booker Wright (Chapel Hill: University of North Carolina Press, 1947), 293 as cited in Smith, *Drinking History*, 12.

4 James E. McWilliams, *A Revolution in Eating: How the Quest for Food Shaped America* (New York: Columbia University Press, 2005), 263.

5 McWilliams, *A Revolution in Eating*, 14.

6 Mark Edward Lender and James Kirby Martin, *Drinking in America: A History* (New York: Free Press, 1987), 49.

7 Smith, *Drinking History*, 26.

8 Steven Stoll, *Ramp Hollow: The Ordeal of Appalachia* (New York: Hill and Wang, 2017), 110.

9 Lender and Martin, *Drinking in America*, 48.

10 Benjamin Rush, *An Inquiry into the Effects of Ardent Spirits upon the Human Body and Mind*, 6th edition (New York: Cornelius Davis, 1811), 24.

11 "From Benjamin Rush, 31 October 1777," *Papers of John Adams, Volume 5*, Adams Papers Digital Edition – Massachusetts Historical Society, http://www.masshist.org/publications/adams-papers/view?id=ADMS-06-05-02-0191

12 "From John Adams to William Willis, 21 February 1819," *Founders Online*, National Archives, https://founders.archives.gov/documents/Adams/99-02-02-7083.

13 McWilliams, *A Revolution in Eating*, 294–6.

14 Smith, *Drinking History*, 32.

15 McWilliams, *A Revolution in Eating*, 286–9.

16 Lender and Martin, *Drinking in America*, 31–2.

17 "From George Washington to Brigadier General John Armstrong, 5 March 1777," *Founders Online*, National Archives, https://founders.archives.gov/documents/Washington/03-08-02-0542.

18 "Ten Facts about the Distillery," George Washington's Mount Vernon, accessed February 21, 2021, http://www.mountvernon.org/the-estate-gardens/distillery/ten-facts-about-the-distillery/.

19 McWilliams, *A Revolution in Eating*, 283.

20 J. Hector St. John de Crevecoeur, "Letter II - on the Situation, Feelings, and Pleasures, of an American Farmer," in *Letters from an American Farmer* (London: T. Davies, 1782), https://avalon.law.yale.edu/18th_century/letter_02.asp.

21 Terry Bouton, *Taming Democracy: "The People," the Founders, and the Troubled Ending of the American Revolution* (New York: Oxford University Press, 2009), 218.

22 "Cabinet Battle #1 Lyrics – Hamilton Soundtrack," *ST Lyrics*, accessed February 24, 2021, https://www.stlyrics.com/lyrics/hamiltonthemovie/cabinetbattle1.htm.

23 Harrison Clark, *All Cloudless Glory: The Life of George Washington: Making a Nation* (Washington, DC: Regnery Publishing, 1996), 231.

24 Bouton, *Taming Democracy*, 232.

25 Stoll, *Ramp Hollow*, 122.

26 William Hogeland, "Whiskey, Rebellion, and the Religious Left," *Tikkun* 22, no. 4 (July 1, 2007): 48.

27 Stoll, *Ramp Hollow*, 119.

28 Smith, *Drinking History*, 72.

Chapter 4

1 Sylvester Graham, *A Treatise on Bread and Bread-Making* (Boston: Light & Stearns, 1837), 70.

2 Graham, *Treatise*, 34, 92–3.

3 Adam Shprintzen, "Abstention to Consumption: The Development of American Vegetarianism, 1817–1917," *Dissertations*, January 1, 2011, 327–30, https://ecommons.luc.edu/luc_diss/75.

4 Stephen Nissenbaum, *Sex, Diet, and Debility in Jacksonian America: Sylvester Graham and Health Reform* (Westport, CT: Greenwood Press, 1980), 9–15; Adam D. Shprintzen, *The Vegetarian Crusade: The Rise of an American Reform Movement, 1817–1921* (Chapel Hill, NC: University of North Carolina Press, 2015).

5 Richard H. Shryock, "Sylvester Graham and the Popular Health Movement, 1830–1870," *The Mississippi Valley Historical Review* 18, no. 2 (1931): 173.

6 Graham, *Treatise*, 9.

7 Tracy Frisch, "A Short History of Wheat," *The Valley Table*, 2008, https://www.valleytable.com/vt-article/short-history-wheat.

8 Graham, *Treatise*, 40.

9 As cited in Nissenbaum, *Sex, Diet*, 98.

10 Graham, *Treatise*, 45.

11 Sarah Josepha Buell Hale, *The Good Housekeeper* (Boston: Weeks, Jordan and Company, 1839), 17.

12 Shryock, "Graham," 175.

13 Aaron Bobrow-Strain, *White Bread: A Social History of the Store-Bought Loaf* (Boston: Beacon Press, 2012), 91; Shprintzen, *Vegetarian Crusade*, 25.

14 Nissenbaum argues that the rioters were commercial butchers and bakers who feared that his dietary advice would impact their business (*Sex, Diet*, 14), while historian April Haynes argues they were "self-appointed representatives of a masculine rake culture confronting a new doctrine of sexual restraint." April R. Haynes, *Riotous Flesh: Women, Physiology, and the Solitary Vice in Nineteenth-Century America*, *Riotous Flesh* (Chicago: University of Chicago Press, 2015), 47.

15 H. W. Brands, *Andrew Jackson: His Life and Times* (New York: Knopf Doubleday, 2006).

16 Angela G. Ray, *The Lyceum and Public Culture in the Nineteenth-Century United States* (East Lansing: Michigan State University Press, 2005).

17 Shprintzen, *Vegetarian Crusade*, 34.

18 As cited in James C. Giesen and Bryant Simon, eds., *Food and Eating in America: A Documentary Reader* (Malden, MA: Wiley-Blackwell, 2018), 38.

19 As cited in Jennifer Jensen Wallach and Lindsey R. Swindall, eds., *American Appetites: A Documentary Reader* (Fayetteville, AR: University of Arkansas Press, 2014), 64.

20 Graham, *Treatise*, 42.

21 Andrew F. Smith, *Eating History: Thirty Turning Points in the Making of American Cuisine* (New York, NY: Columbia University Press, 2009), 9–10.

22 Graham, *Treatise*, 43.

23 Nissenbaum, *Sex, Diet*, 8.

24 Eric Foner, *Give Me Liberty!: An American History*, Seagull 6th edition (New York: W. W. Norton & Company, 2020), 339.

25 Foner, *Give Me Liberty!*, 339.

26 Shprintzen, *Vegetarian Crusade*, 28.

27 April Haynes, "Radical Hospitality and Political Intimacy in Grahamite Boardinghouses, 1830–1850," *Journal of the Early Republic* 39, no. 3 (Fall 2019): 397–436.

28 Nissenbaum, *Sex, Diet*, 128.

29 Bobrow-Strain, *White Bread*, 92.

30 Amy H. Sturgis, *The Trail of Tears and Indian Removal* (Westport, CT: Greenwood Publishing Group, 2007).

31 Foner, *Give Me Liberty!*, 338.

32 As cited in Nissenbaum, *Sex, Diet*, 87.

33 "Vegetarian Festival," *New York Daily Times*, September 5, 1853, 1. https://documents.alexanderstreet.com/d/1004734264.

Chapter 5

1   Frederick Douglass, *My Bondage and My Freedom* (New York: Miller, Orton, & Mulligan, 1855), 252–3, https://docsouth.unc.edu/neh/douglass55/douglass55.html.

2   Herbert C. Covey and Dwight Eisnach, *What the Slaves Ate: Recollections of African American Foods and Foodways from the Slave Narratives* (Santa Barbara, CA: Greenwood Press/ABC-CLIO, 2009), 78.

3   Covey and Eisnach, *What the Slaves Ate.*

4   Michael W. Twitty, "Pot Likker," in *World of a Slave: Encyclopedia of the Material Life of Slaves in the United States*, ed. Martha B. Katz-Hyman and Kym S. Rice (Santa Barbara, CA: ABC-CLIO, 2011), 374.

5   Frederick Opie, *Hog and Hominy: Soul Food from Africa to America* (New York: Columbia University Press, 2010), 30.

6   John Egerton, *Southern Food: At Home, on the Road, in History* (New York: Knopf, 1987), 15.

7   Ira Berlin, *Many Thousands Gone: The First Two Centuries of Slavery in North America* (Cambridge: Harvard University Press, 1998).

8   Sven Beckert, *Empire of Cotton: A Global History* (New York: Alfred A. Knopf, 2014).

9   Jessica B. Harris, *High on the Hog: A Culinary Journey from Africa to America* (New York: Bloomsbury USA, 2012), 30.

10 Covey and Eisnach, *What the Slaves Ate*, 2.

11 As cited in Jennifer Jensen Wallach and Lindsey R. Swindall, eds., *American Appetites: A Documentary Reader* (Fayetteville, AR: University of Arkansas Press, 2014), 30.

12 Robert L. Hall, "Food Crops and the Slave Trade," in *African American Foodways: Explorations of History and Culture*, ed. Anne L. Bower (Champaign: University of Illinois Press, 2009), 25.

13 As cited in Twitty, "Pot Likker," 2011, 374.

14 Covey and Eisnach, *What the Slaves Ate*, 99.

15 Opie, *Hog and Hominy.*

16 Wallach and Swindall, *American Appetites*; Marcie Cohen Ferris, *The Edible South: The Power of Food and the Making of an American Region* (Chapel Hill: The University of North Carolina Press, 2014), 86–8.

17 Douglass, *My Bondage*, 107.

18 Covey and Eisnach, *What the Slaves Ate*, 148.

19 As cited in Wallach and Swindall, *American Appetites*, 89–90.

20 Covey and Eisnach, *What the Slaves Ate*, 99.

21 Michael W. Twitty, *The Cooking Gene: A Journey through African American Culinary History in the Old South* (New York: Amistad, 2017), 199.

22 Ferris, *Edible South*, 26.

23 As cited in Ferris, *Edible South*, 37.

24 Covey and Eisnach, *What the Slaves Ate*, 68.

25 Frederick Douglass, *Narrative of the Life of Frederick Douglass: An American Slave* (Boston: The Anti-Slavery Office, 1845), 16, 75.

26 Edward H. Davis and John T. Morgan, *Collards: A Southern Tradition from Seed to Table* (Tuscaloosa: University Alabama Press, 2015), 159.

27 As cited in Covey and Eisnach, *What the Slaves Ate*, 92.

28 Michael W. Twitty, "Pigs and Pork," in *World of a Slave: Encyclopedia of the Material Life of Slaves in the United States*, ed. Martha B. Katz-Hyman and Kym S. Rice (Santa Barbara, CA: ABC-CLIO, 2011), 373.

29 As cited in James C. Giesen and Bryant Simon, eds., *Food and Eating in America: A Documentary Reader* (Malden, MA: Wiley-Blackwell, 2018), 60–1.

30 Mart A. Stewart, "Slavery and the Origins and of African American Environmentalism," in *To Love the Wind and the Rain: African Americans and Environmental History*, ed. Dianne D. Glave and Mark Stoll (Pittsburgh, PA: University of Pittsburgh Press, 2005), 10.

31 Opie, *Hog and Hominy*, 29.

32 Kelley Fanto Deetz, *Bound to the Fire: How Virginia's Enslaved Cooks Helped Invent American Cuisine* (Lexington: University Press of Kentucky, 2017), 95.

33 Solomon Northup, *Twelve Years a Slave* (Auburn: Derby and Miller, 1853), 200.

34 As cited in Sam Bowers Hilliard, *Hog Meat and Hoecake; Food Supply in the Old South, 1840–1860* (Carbondale: Southern Illinois University Press, 1972), 148.

35 Harris, *High on the Hog*, 85.

36 As cited in Davis and Morgan, *Collards*, 7–8.

37 As cited in Hall, "Food Crops," 18.

38 Twitty, *Cooking Gene*, xii.

39 William C. Whit, "Soul Food as Cultural Creation," in *African American Foodways: Explorations of History and Culture*, ed. Anne L. Bower (Champaign: University of Illinois Press, 2009), 51.

40 Annette Gordon-Reed, *The Hemingses of Monticello: An American Family* (New York: W. W. Norton & Company, 2008).

41 Twitty, *Cooking Gene*, 107.

42 Rick McDaniel, *Irresistible History of Southern Food: Four Centuries of Black-Eyed Peas, Collard Greens & Whole Hog Barbecue* (Charleston, SC: The History Press, 2011), 38–9.

43 Ferris, *Edible South*, 21.

44 Eric Foner, *Gateway to Freedom: The Hidden History of the Underground Railroad* (New York: W. W. Norton & Company, 2015).

45 As cited in Beamish et al., "The Cotton Revolution."

46 "The Declaration of Causes of Seceding States," American Battlefield Trust, accessed April 19, 2021, https://www.battlefields.org/learn/primary-sources/declaration-causes-seceding-states.

Chapter 6

1   Jessie Bradford Bond, "Peanuts," *The Peanut Promoter* 2 (1918): 38.

2   R.O. Stutsman, "The R. O. Stutsman Company," *The Midwestern* 3 (1908): 70.

3   Etta Morse Hudders, "The Rise of the Peanut," *Table Talk* 18 (1903): 113.

4   Edward Mott Wooley, "Tom Rowland–Peanuts," *McClure's Magazine* 42 (1913): 184, 186.

5   Shane Mitchell, "Hot Wet Goobers," *The Bitter Southerner*, 2018, https://bittersoutherner.com/hot-wet-goobers-peanuts; Andrew F. Smith, *Peanuts: The Illustrious History of the Goober Pea* (Urbana: University of Illinois Press, 2002).

6   Theodore Steinberg, *Down to Earth: Nature's Role in American History* (New York: Oxford University Press, 2002), 89.

7   Andrew F. Smith, *Starving the South: How the North Won the Civil War* (New York: St. Martin's Press, 2011), 11–12.

8   As cited in Marcie Cohen Ferris, *The Edible South: The Power of Food and the Making of an American Region* (Chapel Hill, NC: The University of North Carolina Press, 2014), 51.

9   Rick McDaniel, *Irresistible History of Southern Food: Four Centuries of Black-Eyed Peas, Collard Greens & Whole Hog Barbecue* (Charleston, SC: The History Press, 2011), 26.

10 As cited in Ferris, *The Edible South*, 55.

11 Otho Clifford Ault, *The Peanut as an Agricultural Crop* (Madison: University of Wisconsin, 1919), 6.

12 As cited in John U. Rees, "Historical Overview: The Civil War and Reconstruction," in *Oxford Encyclopedia of Food and Drink in America*, ed. Andrew F. Smith, 2nd edition, vol. 3 (New York: Oxford University Press, 2013), 209.

13 As cited in Dorothy Denneen Volo and James M. Volo, *Daily Life in Civil War America* (Westport: Greenwood Press, 1998), 120.

14 Smith, *Peanuts*, 21.

15 As cited in Smith, *Starving the South*, 37.

16 Steinberg, *Down to Earth*, 95.

17 Steinberg, *Down to Earth*, 92, 97.

18 McDaniel, *Irresistible History*, 26.

19 As cited in Mitchell, "Hot Wet Goobers."

20 Steinberg, *Down to Earth*, 89.

21 Biographical information from Mark D. Hersey, *My Work Is That of Conservation: An Environmental Biography of George Washington Carver* (Athens: University of Georgia Press, 2011).

22 "Committee of Freedmen on Edisto Island, South Carolina, to the President," Freedmen and Southern Society Project, October 28, 1865, http://www.freedmen.umd.edu/Edisto%20petitions.htm.

23 As cited in Eric Foner, *Reconstruction: America's Unfinished Revolution, 1863–1877* (New York: Harper & Row, 1988), 143.

24 As cited in James D. Anderson, *Education of Blacks in the South, 1860–1935* (Chapel Hill: University of North Carolina Press, 1988), 5.

25 Eric Foner, *Give Me Liberty!: An American History*, Seagull 6th edition (New York: W. W. Norton & Company, 2020), 592, 661.

26 As cited in Hersey, *My Work Is That of Conservation*, 25.

27 Smith, *Peanuts*, 28; Wooley, "Tom Rowland–Peanuts," 197.

28 Christopher Farrish, "Food in the Antebellum South and the Confederacy," in *Food in the Civil War Era: The South*, ed. Helen Zoe Veit (East Lansing, MI: Michigan State University Press, 2015), 18.

29 As cited in Smith, *Peanuts*, 24.

30 B.W. Jones, *The Peanut Plant: Its Cultivation and Uses* (New York: Orange Judd Company, 1885), 67.

31 Jones, *Peanut Plant*, 27.

32 Wooley, "Tom Rowland–Peanuts," 198.

33 As cited in Smith, *Peanuts*, 112.

34 Adam Shprintzen, "Ella Eaton Kellogg's Protose: Fake Meat and the Gender Politics That Made American Vegetarianism Modern," in *Acquired Tastes: Stories about the Origins of Modern Food*, ed. Benjamin R. Cohen, Michael S. Kideckel, and Anna Zeide (Cambridge: MIT Press, 2021), 219–33; Almeda Lambert, *Guide for Nut Cookery* (Battle Creek, MI: J. Lambert & Co., 1899); Almeda Lambert, *Guide for Nut Cookery* (Battle Creek, MI: J. Lambert & Co., 1899).

35 Wooley, "Tom Rowland–Peanuts," 197.

36 Brent Staples, "How Italians Became 'White,'" *The New York Times*, October 12, 2019, sec. Opinion, https://www.nytimes.com/interactive/2019/10/12/opinion/columbus-day-italian-american-racism.html.

37 W. R. Beattie, *The Peanut* (Washington: Government Printing Office, 1911), 23.

38 Jones, *Peanut Plant*, 30.

39 Beattie, *The Peanut*, 24.

40 William Nathaniel Roper, *The Peanut and Its Culture* (Petersburg, VA: American Nut Journal, 1905), 46.

41 Foner, *Give Me Liberty!*, 659.

42 As cited in Jessica B. Harris, *High on the Hog: A Culinary Journey from Africa to America* (New York: Bloomsbury USA, 2012), 53.

43 Foner, *Give Me Liberty!*, 662.

44 Equal Justice Initiative, *Lynching in America Confronting the Legacy of Racial Terror*, 3rd edition, 2017, https://eji.org/reports/lynching-in-america/.

45 Ida B. Wells-Barnett, "How Enfranchisement Stops Lynchings," *Original Rights Magazine*, June 1910, 45.

46 Monica White, *Freedom Farmers: Agricultural Resistance and the Black Freedom Movement* (Durham, NC: University of North Carolina Press, 2018), 229.

47 Paul S. Sutter, foreword to Hersey, *My Work Is That of Conservation*, 9.

48 Virginia-Carolina Peanut Picker Co., Inc., v. Benthall Mach. Co., Inc, No. 1440–241 Fed. 89 (Circuit Court of Appeals, Fourth Circuit November 23, 1916).

49 "Social Rise of the Peanut," *Good Housekeeping*, 1902, 468.

Chapter 7

1 "What Shall We Have for Dessert?," *Ladies Home Journal Advertisement* (June 1902): 31.

2 *Desserts of the World* (LeRoy, NY: Genesee Pure Food Company, 1909), 3, as cited in Bria, "Jell-O," 28.

3 *Jell-O: Of What and How Made* (LeRoy, NY: Genesee Pure Food Company, n.d.), as cited in Carolyn Wyman, *Jell-O: A Biography* (San Diego: Harcourt, 2001), 77.

4 Mary Foote Henderson, *Practical Cooking and Dinner Giving* (New York: Harper, 1881), 293.

5 Wendy Wall, "Shakespearean Jell-O: Mortality and Malleability in the Kitchen," *Gastronomica* 6, no. 1 (2006): 41–50.

6 Joshua Specht, *Red Meat Republic: A Hoof-to-Table History of How Beef Changed America* (Princeton, NJ: Princeton University Press, 2019), 66.

7 George Catlin, *Letters and Notes on the Manners, Customs, and Condition of the North American Indians*, 4th edition (New York: Wiley and Putnam, 1842), 249.

8 Dodge, Richard Irving, *The Plains of the Great West and Their Inhabitants*, 1877. Reprint (New York: Archer House, 1959), as cited in William Cronon, *Nature's Metropolis: Chicago and the Great West* (New York: W. W. Norton, 1991), 217.

9 Specht, *Red Meat Republic*, 18.

10 Cronon, *Nature's Metropolis*, 219.

11 "The Metropolis of the Prairies," *Harper's New Monthly Magazine*, 1880, as cited in Cronon, *Nature's Metropolis*, 208.

12 Upton Sinclair, *The Jungle* (New York: Doubleday, Page & Company, 1906), 112.

13 "Wide Variety of Packinghouse Byproducts," *The National Provisioner* 54, no. 18 (April 29, 1916): 17.

14 "Wide Variety," 17, 35.

15 "Jell-O," *Modern Packaging*, December 1950, 34, as cited in Bria, "Jell-O," 127.

16 Shapiro, *Perfection Salad*, 201.

17   *Jell-O and the Kewpies* (LeRoy, NY: Genesee Pure Food Company, 1915), as cited in Bria, "Jell-O," 117.

18   *Jell-O America's Most Famous Dessert* (LeRoy, NY: Genesee Pure Food Company, 1916), as cited in Bria, "Jell-O," 192.

19   Eric Foner, *Give Me Liberty!: An American History*, Seagull 6th edition (New York: W. W. Norton & Company, 2020), 612.

20   Henry George, *Progress and Poverty* (London: John W. Lovell Company, 1884), 304.

21   Genesee Pure Food Co. Public Affairs, "Getting Your Just Desserts," Press release, June 11, 1923, as cited in Bria, "Jell-O," 30.

22   *Jell-O: At Home Everywhere* (LeRoy, NY: Genesee Pure Food Company, 1922).

23   *Jell-O Recipe Book* (LeRoy, NY: Genesee Pure Food Company, 1905), http://archive.org/details/jello-recipe-book.

24   Sinclair, *Jungle*, 117.

25   "Upton Sinclair Hits His Readers in the Stomach," *History Matters*, accessed June 23, 2021, http://historymatters.gmu.edu/d/5727/.

26   Wall, "Shakespearean Jell-O," 42.

27   Wyman, *Jell-O*, 15–16, 22.

28   Helen Zoe Veit, "Eating Cotton: Cottonseed, Crisco, and Consumer Ignorance," *The Journal of the Gilded Age and Progressive Era* 18, no. 4 (2019): 397.

29   Harvey A. Levenstein, *Revolution at the Table: The Transformation of the American Diet* (New York: Oxford University Press, 1988), 25.

30   *Jell-O Recipe Book.*

31   "Merely Child's Play," *Ladies Home Journal* Advertisement (May 1904): 27, as cited in Bria, "Jell-O," 102. 1911 ad cited in Wyman, *Jell-O*, 20.

32   *Jell-O Recipe Book.*

33   *All Doors Open to Jell-O, America's Most Famous Dessert* (LeRoy, NY: Genesee Pure Food Company, 1917), 11, as cited in Bria, "Jell-O," 33.

34   Wyman, *Jell-O*, 79.

35   *What Six Famous Cooks Say of America's Most Famous Dessert* (LeRoy, NY: Genesee Pure Food Company, 1913), 3, as cited in Wyman, *Jell-O*, 23.

36   Genesee Pure Food Co. Public Affairs, "Just Desserts," as cited in Bria, "Jell-O," 138.

Chapter 8

1   Maria Gentile, *The Italian Cook Book: The Art of Eating Well* (New York: Italian Book Co., 1919), 3, https://www.gutenberg.org/ebooks/24407.

2   Eric Foner, *Give Me Liberty!: An American History*, Seagull 6th edition (New York: W. W. Norton & Company, 2020), 696.

3   Helen Zoe Veit, *Modern Food, Moral Food: Self-Control, Science, and the Rise of Modern American Eating in the Early Twentieth Century* (Chapel Hill: University of North Carolina Press, 2015), 131.

4   Harvey Levenstein, "The American Response to Italian Food, 1880–1930," in *Food in the USA: A Reader*, ed. Carole M. Counihan (New York: Routledge, 2002), 79.

5   Veit, *Modern Food, Moral Food*, 45–6.

6   Tim Carman and Shelly Tan, "Made in America," *Washington Post*, October 11, 2019, https://www.washingtonpost.com/graphics/2019/voraciously/what-are-american-foods/.

7   Hasia R. Diner, *Hungering for America: Italian, Irish, and Jewish Foodways in the Age of Migration* (Cambridge: Harvard University Press, 2001), 40.

8   Diner, *Hungering for America*, 57.

9   As cited Diner, *Hungering for America*, 45–6.

10 Diner, *Hungering for America*, 63.

11 Diner, *Hungering for America*, 55.

12 Simone Cinotto, *The Italian American Table: Food, Family, and Community in New York City* (Urbana: University of Illinois Press, 2013), 149.

13 *The Story of a Pantry Shelf* (New York: Butterick Publishing Company, 1925), 108.

14 Levenstein, "American Response," 76.

15 John Hoenig, *Garden Variety: The American Tomato from Corporate to Heirloom* (New York: Columbia University Press, 2017), 97.

16 Cinotto, *Italian American Table*, 16.

17 Van Camp's, "A Secret We Shall Never Tell," *Good Housekeeping*, April 1920.

18 John Adams Lee, *How to Buy and Sell Canned Foods* (Baltimore: Canning Trade, 1914), 202.

19 Gentile, *Italian Cook Book*, 13.

20 Veit, *Modern Food, Moral Food*, 76.

21 Veit, *Modern Food, Moral Food*, 113.

22 As cited in Levenstein, "American Response," 84.

23 As cited in Harvey A. Levenstein, *Revolution at the Table: The Transformation of the American Diet* (New York: Oxford University Press, 1988), 143.

24 As cited in Levenstein, "American Response," 80.

25 Veit, *Modern Food, Moral Food*, 31.

26 Robert S. Lynd and Helen Merrell Lynd, *Middletown: A Study in Contemporary American Culture* (New York: Harcourt, Brace and Company, 1929), 88.

27 Laura Shapiro, *Perfection Salad: Women and Cooking at the Turn of the Century* (New York: Holt, 1987), 221–2.

28 Betty Fussell, "Hail to the Garlic Revolution!," *Sally's Place* (blog), accessed July 21, 2021, https://www.sallybernstein.com/food/columns/fussell/garlic.htm.

29 Cinotto, *Italian American Table*, 204.

30 Levenstein, *Revolution at the Table*, 158.

31 "Congressional Debate on Immigration Restriction," December 10, 1920, https://history.hanover.edu/courses/excerpts/227immigration.html.

32 Elizabeth Frazer, "The Secret Partner," *Saturday Evening Post*, March 25, 1922, 24.

33 "Sentencing Statements of Sacco and Vanzetti," *Famous American Trials*, April 9, 1927, http://law2.umkc.edu/faculty/projects/ftrials/SaccoV/courtspeech.html.

34 Livia Gershon, "Garlic and Social Class," *JSTOR Daily*, November 2, 2020, https://daily.jstor.org/garlic-and-social-class/.

35 As cited in Foner, *Give Me Liberty!*, 811.

Chapter 9

1 John Steinbeck, *The Grapes of Wrath* (New York: Viking Press, 1939; New York: Penguin, 1976), 449.

2 Eric Foner, *Give Me Liberty!: An American History*, Seagull 6th edition (New York: W. W. Norton & Company, 2020), 812.

3 Donald Worster, *Dust Bowl: The Southern Plains in the 1930s* (New York: Oxford University Press, 1979); David M. Kennedy, *Freedom from Fear: The American People in Depression and War, 1929-1945* (New York: Oxford University Press, 2004); T. H Watkins, *The Great Depression: America in the 1930s* (Boston, MA; London: Back Bay, 2010).

4 Studs Terkel, *Hard Times: An Oral History of the Great Depression* (New York: Pantheon Books, 1970), 50.

5 T. H Watkins, *The Hungry Years: A Narrative History of the Great Depression in America* (New York, NY: Henry Holt & Co., 2003).

6 Douglas Cazaux Sackman, *Orange Empire: California and the Fruits of Eden* (Berkeley: University of California Press, 2005), 140.

7 As cited in Paul S. Taylor, "Foundations of California Rural Society," *California Historical Society Quarterly* XXIV (September 1945): 206.

8 U. S. Senate, Subcommittee of Committee on Education and Labor (the La Follette Committee), 77th Cong., 2d Sess., Investigating Violations of Free Speech and Rights of Labor, Vol. 47 (Washington, 1939), 1944, as cited in Jones, Lamar B., "Labor and Management in California Agriculture, 1864–1964," *Labor History* 11, no. 1 (1970): 35.

9 *The Pacific Rural Press*, December 10, 1881, 336 as cited in Jones, 25.

10 National Defense Migration, Fourth Interim Report of the Select Committee Investigating National Defense Migration, House of Representatives, 77:2, H. Res. 113 Washington, 1942), 68, as cited in Jones 32.

11 "Fruit of Men," *Fresno Morning Republic,* 14 February 1910, as cited in Sackman 130–1.

12 Charles Collins Teague, *Fifty Years a Rancher* (Los Angeles: Ward Ritchie Press, 1944), 141.

13 Jones, 36.

14 James N. Gregory, *American Exodus: The Dust Bowl Migration and Okie Culture in California* (New York, NY: Oxford University Press, 1989), 20.

15 Steinbeck, *The Grapes of Wrath*, 118.

16 Worster, *Dust Bowl*, 4.

17 Worster, *Dust Bowl*, 14.

18 Charles L. Todd, "The Okies Search for a; Lost Frontier," *The New York Times*, August 27, 1939, SM6.

19 Todd, SM6.

20 Francisco E. Balderrama and Raymond Rodriguez, *Decade of Betrayal: Mexican Repatriation in the 1930s* (Albuquerque, NM: University of New Mexico Press, 1995), 53.

21 Sackman, *Orange Empire*, 181–2.

22 Panunzio, Constantine, *Self-Help Cooperatives in Los Angeles* (Berkeley: University of California Press, 1939).

23 "The Twelve Principles of EPIC," as cited in Brian L. Fife, *Winning the War on Poverty Applying the Lessons of History to the Present* (Santa Barbara, CA: Praeger, 2018).

24 Ira Katznelson, *Fear Itself: The New Deal and the Origins of Our Time* (New York, NY: W. W. Norton & Company, 2013).

25 Sackman, *Orange Empire*, 153, 221.

26 Sackman, *Orange Empire*, 218.

27 Greg Mitchell, *The Campaign of the Century: Upton Sinclair's Race for Governor of California and the Birth of Media Politics* (New York: Townsend Books, 2011).

28 Sackman, *Orange Empire*, 218–21.

29 Sackman, *Orange Empire*; Todd, "Okies Search."

30 Todd, "Okies Search."

31 Terkel, *Hard Times*, 47.

32 Sims, Damon, "Fruits of the Great Depression: Christmas Memories," *The Cleveland Plain Dealer*, December 14, 2008, http://blog.cleveland.com/metro/2008/12/fruits_of_the_great_depression.html.

33 Alan M. Kraut, *Goldberger's War: The Life and Work of a Public Health Crusader*, 1st ed (New York: Hill and Wang, 2003).

34 Pierre Laszlo, *Citrus: A History* (Chicago: University of Chicago Press, 2007), 86–9.

35 Sackman, *Orange Empire*, 87.

36 Rima D. Apple, *Vitamania: Vitamins in American Culture* (New Brunswick, NJ: Rutgers University Press, 1996), 76.

37 Andrew F. Smith, *Drinking History: Fifteen Turning Points in the Making of American Beverages* (New York, NY: New York University Press, 2012), 147.

38   Richard J. Hooker, *A History of Food and Drink in America* (Indianapolis, IN: Bobbs-Merrill, 1981), 317.

39   Smith, *Drinking History*, 147–9.

40   Anna Zeide, *Canned: The Rise and Fall of Consumer Confidence in the American Food Industry* (Oakland: University of California Press, 2018).

41   Tracey Deutsch, *Building a Housewife's Paradise: Gender, Politics, and American Grocery Stores in the Twentieth Century* (Chapel Hill, NC: University of North Carolina Press, 2010).

42   Steinbeck, *The Grapes of Wrath*, 107.

Chapter 10

1   Mark F. Quigley, "Spam," *Yank: The Army Weekly*, August 20, 1943.

2   Carolyn Wyman, *Spam: A Biography* (San Diego, CA: Harvest Books, 1999), 17.

3   Sidney Wilfred Mintz, *Tasting Food, Tasting Freedom: Excursions into Eating, Culture, and the Past* (Boston: Beacon Press, 1996), 25.

4   Kellen Backer, "When Meals Became Weapons," in *Nature at War: American Environments and World War II*, ed. Thomas Robertson et al. (Cambridge: Cambridge University Press, 2020), 176–96.

5   Frances Levison, "Hormel: The Spam Man," *Life*, March 11, 1946.

6   "Hormel Advertisement," *Life*, November 6, 1939, 58.

7   Wyman, *Spam*, 8.

8   Craig Santos Perez, "SPAM's Carbon Footprint," *Academy of American Poets*, 2010, https://poets.org/poem/spams-carbon-footprint.

9   Levison, "Hormel," 65.

10   Both prior quotes from Levison, 65.

11   Ann Vileisis, *Kitchen Literacy: How We Lost Knowledge of Where Food Comes from and Why We Need to Get It Back* (Washington, DC: Island Press, 2010), 186.

12   "Hormel Advertisement."

13   Levison, "Hormel."

14   Levison, "Hormel," 67.

15   "History with U.S. Military," *Hormel Foods*, accessed September 1, 2021, https://www.hormelfoods.com/careers/military-recruitment/history-u-s-military/.

16   Howard Yoon, "Spam: More Than Junk Mail or Junk Meat," *NPR*, July 4, 2007, https://www.npr.org/templates/story/story.php?storyId=11714236.

17   Wyman, *Spam*, 25.

18   Edward Crankshaw, *Khrushchev Remembers* (New York: Bantam Books, 1970), 226.

19 Elizabeth M. Collingham, *The Taste of War: World War II and the Battle for Food* (New York: Penguin Books, 2013), 1.

20 Linda Civitello, *Cuisine and Culture: A History of Food and People*, 3rd edition (Hoboken, NJ: Wiley, 2011), 675.

21 Primo Levi, *Survival in Auschwitz* (New York: Simon and Schuster, 1996), 74.

22 George H. Lewis, "From Minnesota Fat to Seoul Food: Spam in America and the Pacific Rim," *Journal of Popular Culture* 34, no. 2 (2000): 83–105.

23 Amy Bentley, *Eating for Victory: Food Rationing and the Politics of Domesticity* (Urbana: University of Illinois Press, 1998), 94.

24 Harvey A. Levenstein, *Paradox of Plenty: A Social History of Eating in Modern America* (New York; Oxford: Oxford University Press, 1993), 94.

25 Kellen Backer, "Constructing Borderless Foods: The Quartermaster Corps and World War II Army Subsistence," in *Food across Borders*, ed. Matt Garcia, E. Melanie DuPuis, and Don Mitchell (New Brunswick: Rutgers University Press, 2017), 134.

26 *The Army Air Forces in World War II: The Pacific, Guadalcanal to Saipan, August 1942 to July 1944* (Office of Air Force History, 1948), 270.

27 Wyman, *Spam*, 17–18.

28 Levison, "Hormel," 63.

29 *Army Air Forces in WWII*, 271.

30 Prior three quotes from Wyman, *Spam*, 21–9.

31 "Eisenhower Letter about Spam," *U.S. National Archives: Pieces of History* (blog), May 2013, https://prologue.blogs.archives.gov/eisenhower-letter-about-spam/.

32 Backer, "Constructing Borderless Foods"; Levenstein, *Paradox of Plenty*, 91.

33 Collingham, *Taste of War*, 75.

34 Clive McCay, "Eat Well to Work Well: The Lunch Box Should Carry a Hearty Meal," *War Emergency Bulletin*, no. 38, 1942.

35 Dan Armstrong and Dustin Black, *The Book of Spam* (New York: Atria Books, 2008), 79.

36 Bentley, *Eating for Victory*.

37 Bentley, *Eating for Victory*, 114.

38 "Letter from M. K. Gandhi to President Franklin D. Roosevelt and Reply," *DocsTeach*, July 1, 1942, https://www.docsteach.org/documents/document/letter-from-m-k-gandhi-to-president-franklin-d-roosevelt-and-reply.

39 Roy Wilkins, "The Negro Wants Full Equality," in *What the Negro Wants*, ed. Rayford Logan (Chapel Hill: University of North Carolina Press, 1944), 130.

40 Collingham, *Taste of War*, 80.

41 Catherine Toth Fox, "The History of Five Local Grinds," *Hawaii Magazine*, June 24, 2015, https://www.hawaiimagazine.com/the-history-of-five-local-grinds/.

42 Madhur Jaffrey, *Climbing the Mango Trees: A Memoir of a Childhood in India* (New York: Knopf Doubleday, 2008), 194.

43 Vileisis, *Kitchen Literacy*, 186.

44 As cited in Anastacia Marx de Salcedo, *Combat-Ready Kitchen: How the U.S. Military Shapes the Way You Eat* (New York: Penguin Press, 2015), 80.

45 As cited in Backer, "When Meals Became Weapons," 195.

Chapter 11

1 Brigit Katz, "The Woman Who Invented the Green Bean Casserole," *Smithsonian Magazine*, October 26, 2018, https://www.smithsonianmag.com/smart-news/remembering-dorcas-reilly-inventor-green-bean-casserole-180970635/.

2 Timothy Bella, "Dorcas Reilly, Inventor of the Green Bean Casserole, a Thanksgiving Favorite, Has Died at 92," *Washington Post*, October 24, 2018, https://www.washingtonpost.com/nation/2018/10/24/dorcas-reilly-inventor-green-bean-casserole-thanksgiving-favorite-has-died/.

3 Shane Hamilton, *Supermarket USA: Food and Power in the Cold War Farms Race* (New Haven, CT: Yale University Press, 2018).

4 As cited in Laura Shapiro, *Something from the Oven: Reinventing Dinner in 1950s America* (New York: Viking, 2004), 139.

5 "'Communists in Government Service,' McCarthy Says," U.S. Senate, February 9, 1950, https://www.senate.gov/about/powers-procedures/investigations/mccarthy-hearings/communists-in-government-service.htm.

6 "Little Rock, 1959. Rally at State Capitol," image, Library of Congress, August 20, 1959, https://www.loc.gov/resource/ppmsca.19754/.

7 "When Home Fallout Shelters Were All the Rage," *CBS News*, October 7, 2010, https://www.cbsnews.com/pictures/when-home-fallout-shelters-were-all-the-rage/.

8 As cited in Shane Hamilton and Sarah T. Phillips, *The Kitchen Debate and Cold War Consumer Politics: A Brief History with Documents* (Boston: Bedford/St. Martin's, 2014), 137.

9 As cited in Hamilton and Phillips, *Kitchen Debate*, 40.

10 As cited in Hamilton and Phillips, *Kitchen Debate*, 2, 48, 65.

11 As cited in Hamilton and Phillips, *Kitchen Debate*, 10.

12 Harvey A. Levenstein, *Paradox of Plenty: A Social History of Eating in Modern America* (New York; Oxford: Oxford University Press, 1993), 117.

13 Levenstein, *Paradox of Plenty*, 102.

14 Hamilton and Phillips, *Kitchen Debate*, 22.

15 Theodore Steinberg, *Down to Earth: Nature's Role in American History* (New York: Oxford University Press, 2002), 217.

16 As cited in Lizabeth Cohen, *A Consumer's Republic: The Politics of Mass Consumption in Postwar America* (New York: Vintage Books, 2004), 125.

17 Mark V. Siegler, *An Economic History of the United States: Connecting the Present with the Past* (London: Palgrave Macmillian, 2016), 165.

18 As cited in Sarah Archer, *The Midcentury Kitchen: America's Favorite Room, from Workspace to Dreamscape, 1940s–1970s* (New York, NY: Countryman Press, 2019), 122.

19 Archer, *The Midcentury Kitchen*, 44.

20 Danielle Dreilinger, *The Secret History of Home Economics: How Trailblazing Women Harnessed the Power of Home and Changed the Way We Live* (New York: W.W. Norton, 2021), 131.

21 Dreilinger, *Secret History of Home Economics*, 132.

22 Hamilton and Phillips, *Kitchen Debate*, 18.

23 As cited in Hamilton and Phillips, *Kitchen Debate*, 19.

24 As cited in Shapiro, *Something from the Oven*, 49.

25 Jane Snow, "Dorcas Reilly, Whose Test Kitchen Created Green Bean Casserole, Dies at 92; Read Our 2002 Interview," *Akron Beacon Journal*, November 27, 2002, https://www.beaconjournal.com/entertainmentlife/20181024/dorcas-reilly-whose-test-kitchen-created-green-bean-casserole-dies-at-92-read-our-2002-interview.

26 Bella, "Reilly."

27 Dreilinger, *Secret History of Home Economics*.

28 Dreilinger, *Secret History of Home Economics*, 178.

29 Douglas Collins, *America's Favorite Food: The Story of Campbell Soup Company* (New York, NY: Harry N. Abrams Inc, 1994), 138.

30 "The History of One of America's Most Fabled Foods: Hot Dish," *Yahoo Entertainment*, January 15, 2016, https://www.yahoo.com/lifestyle/the-history-of-hot-dish-141025667.html; Lucy Long, "Green Bean Casserole and Midwestern Identity: A Regional Foodways Aesthetic and Ethos," *Midwestern Folklore* 33, no. 1 (Spring 2007): 29–44.

31 Karen Zraick, "Dorcas Reilly, Creator of the Classic American Green-Bean Casserole, Dies at 92," *The New York Times*, October 24, 2018, https://www.nytimes.com/2018/10/24/obituaries/dorcas-reilly-dead-green-bean-casserole.html.

32 Anna Zeide, *Canned: The Rise and Fall of Consumer Confidence in the American Food Industry* (Oakland: University of California Press, 2018).

33 As cited in Collins, *America's Favorite Food*, 157.

34 Shapiro, *Something from the Oven*, 11.

35 As cited in Shapiro, *Something from the Oven*, 3; Levenstein, *Paradox of Plenty*, 130.

36 Collins, *America's Favorite Food*, 137, 151.

37 Shapiro, *Something from the Oven*, 62, 10.

38 Shapiro, *Something from the Oven*, 63–77, 185.

39 As cited in Hamilton and Phillips, *Kitchen Debate*, 110, 112.

Chapter 12

1   Katzen, Mollie, *The Enchanted Broccoli Forest: And Other Timeless Delicacies* (Berkeley, CA: Ten Speed Press, 1982), 188.

2   William Shurtleff and Akiko Aoyagi, *The Book of Tofu: Food for Mankind* (Berkeley, CA: Autumn Press, 1975).

3   As cited in Charles M. Payne, *I've Got the Light of Freedom: The Organizing Tradition and the Mississippi Freedom Struggle* (Berkeley: University of California Press, 1996), 250.

4   Frederick Douglass Opie, *Southern Food and Civil Rights: Feeding the Revolution* (Charleston, SC: The History Press, 2017).

5   Martin Luther King Jr., "The Negro Is Your Brother," *The Atlantic Monthly*, August 1963.

6   As cited in Opie, *Southern Food and Civil Rights*, 126–7.

7   As cited Theodore Sorensen, *Kennedy* (London: Hodder and Stoughton, 1965), 199.

8   As cited in Harvey A. Levenstein, *Paradox of Plenty: A Social History of Eating in Modern America* (New York; Oxford: Oxford University Press, 1993), 144.

9   As cited in Monica White, *Freedom Farmers: Agricultural Resistance and the Black Freedom Movement* (Chapel Hill: University of North Carolina Press, 2018), 70, 65.

10 As cited in James C. Giesen and Bryant Simon, eds., *Food and Eating in America: A Documentary Reader* (Malden, MA: Wiley-Blackwell, 2018), 224.

11 Elijah Muhammad, *How to Eat to Live, Book II* (Chicago: Elijah Muhammad Propagation Society, 1972), 91.

12 Muhammad, *How to Eat to Live, Book II*, 65.

13 Mary Potorti, "'Feeding the Revolution': The Black Panther Party, Hunger, and Community Survival," *Journal of African American Studies* 21, no. 1 (2017): 85.

14 "Distinguished Contributors to 20th Century Food Processing," *Canner/Packer* 139, no. 6 (June 1970): 31.

15 As cited in Matthew Roth, *Magic Bean: The Rise of Soy in America* (Lawrence, KS: University Press of Kansas, 2018), 191.

16 Levenstein, *Paradox of Plenty*, 184.

17 Foner, *Give Me Liberty!*, 1019.

18 Eliseo Medina, "Why a Grape Boycott?" (circa 1969), as cited in Giesen and Simon, *Food and Eating in America*, 227.

19 Rachel Carson, *Silent Spring*, 40th Anniversary edition (New York: Houghton Mifflin Harcourt, 2002), 178.

20 Warren J. Belasco, *Appetite for Change: How the Counterculture Took on the Food Industry* (New York: Pantheon Books, 1989), 23.

21 Sandra Blakeslee, "Challenge to Food Tests; Criticism Grows Over Tests to Determine Which Food Additives Are Safe," *The New York Times*, November 10, 1969.

22 Levenstein, *Paradox of Plenty*, 162.

23 Maria McGrath, *Food for Dissent: Natural Foods and the Consumer Counterculture since the 1960s* (Amherst: University of Massachusetts Press, 2019), 59.

24 Belasco, *Appetite for Change*, 48.

25 Ward Sinclair, "Championing the 'Diet for a Small Planet,'" *Washington Post*, August 17, 1981.

26 Jonathan Kauffman, *Hippie Food: How Back-to-the-Landers, Longhairs, and Revolutionaries Changed the Way We Eat* (New York, NY: HarperCollins, 2018), 183.

27 As cited in Kauffman, *Hippie Food*, 184–5.

28 As cited in Roth, *Magic Bean*, 204.

29 Roth, *Magic Bean*, 218.

30 Kauffman, *Hippie Food*, 161.

31 Kauffman, *Hippie Food*, 164.

32 McGrath, *Food for Dissent*, xi.

Chapter 13

1 N. R. Kleinfield, "America Goes Chicken Crazy," *The New York Times*, December 9, 1984, https://www.nytimes.com/1984/12/09/business/america-goes-chicken-crazy.html.

2 Roger Horowitz, *Putting Meat on the American Table: Taste, Technology, Transformation* (Baltimore: Johns Hopkins University Press, 2006).

3 Steve Striffler, *Chicken: The Dangerous Transformation of America's Favorite Food* (New Haven: Yale University Press, 2005), 49.

4 William Boyd, "Making Meat: Science, Technology, and American Poultry Production," *Technology and Culture* 42 (October 2001): 638.

5 As cited in Marvin Schwartz, *Tyson: From Farm to Market* (Fayetteville: University of Arkansas Press, 1991), 13.

6 Striffler, *Chicken*, 24.

7 Bryant Simon, *The Hamlet Fire: A Tragic Story of Cheap Food, Cheap Government, and Cheap Lives* (Chapel Hill: University of North Carolina Press, 2017), 144.

8 Michael Pollan, *The Omnivore's Dilemma: A Natural History of Four Meals* (New York: Penguin, 2007), 117.

9 Schwartz, *Tyson*, 35, 25.

10 Kleinfield, "America Goes Chicken Crazy"; Maryn McKenna, *Big Chicken: The Incredible Story of How Antibiotics Created Modern Agriculture and Changed the Way the World Eats* (Washington, DC: National Geographic Books, 2017), 71.

11 McKenna, *Big Chicken*.

12 Jimmy Carter, "Houston, Texas Remarks at a Democratic National Committee Fundraising Luncheon," *The American Presidency Project*, September 15, 1980, https://www.presidency.ucsb.edu/documents/houston-texas-remarks-democratic-national-committee-fundraising-luncheon.

13 Simon, *Hamlet Fire*, 233.

14 Warren J. Belasco, *Appetite for Change: How the Counterculture Took on the Food Industry* (New York: Pantheon Books, 1989), 175.

15 Harvey A. Levenstein, *Paradox of Plenty: A Social History of Eating in Modern America* (New York; Oxford: Oxford University Press, 1993), 209.

16 Michael Pollan, *In Defense of Food: An Eater's Manifesto* (New York: Penguin Press, 2008).

17 As cited in Horowitz, *Putting Meat on the American Table*, 120.

18 Ronald Reagan, "Inaugural Address," Reagan Foundation, January 20, 1981, https://www.reaganfoundation.org/media/128614/inaguration.pdf.

19 Richard L. McKee, "How Much Regulation Is Enough?," *Canner Packer* 142, no. 5 (May 1973): 6.

20 Simon, *Hamlet Fire*, 237.

21 Amy Bentley, "Ketchup as a Vegetable: Condiments and the Politics of School Lunch in Reagan's America," *Gastronomica* 21, no. 1 (February 1, 2021): 23.

22 Eric Schlosser, *Fast Food Nation: The Dark Side of the All-American Meal* (Boston: Houghton Mifflin, 2001), 139.

23 Emmie Martin, "How Billionaire Ray Dalio Helped Launch McDonald's Chicken McNugget," *CNBC*, May 3, 2018, https://www.cnbc.com/2018/05/03/how-ray-dalio-helped-launch-mcdonalds-chicken-mcnugget.html.

24 Striffler, *Chicken*, 18.

25 Simon, *Hamlet Fire*, 94; Margaret Visser, "A Meditation on the Microwave," *Psychology Today*, 1989, 213.

26 Levenstein, *Paradox of Plenty*, 225.

27 As cited in Simon, *Hamlet Fire*, 95.

28 Striffler, *Chicken*, 71.

Chapter 14

1 George Cohon and David Macfarlane, *To Russia with Fries* (Toronto: McClelland & Stewart, 1999).

2 Bill Keller, "Of Famous Arches, Beeg Meks and Rubles," *The New York Times*, January 28, 1990, https://www.nytimes.com/1990/01/28/world/of-famous-arches-beeg-meks-and-rubles.html.

3 Eric Schlosser, *Fast Food Nation: The Dark Side of the All-American Meal* (Boston: Houghton Mifflin, 2001), 229.

4 Martin Plimmer, "This Demi-Paradise: Martin Plimmer Finds Food in the Fast Lane Is Not to His Taste," *Independent (London)*, January 3, 1998.

5 James L. Watson, "China's Big Mac Attack," *Foreign Affairs* 79, no. 3 (2000): 128.

6 Josh Ozersky, *The Hamburger: A History, Icons of America* (New Haven: Yale University Press, 2008), 127.

7 Marc Fisher, "German McDonald's up against the Wall," *Washington Post*, July 31, 1990, https://www.washingtonpost.com/archive/lifestyle/1990/07/31/german-mcdonalds-up-against-the-wall/2b123015-3952-4d88-adc2-20b9ceab0458/.

8 George Ritzer, *The McDonaldization of Society: An Investigation into the Changing Character of Contemporary Social Life* (Newbury Park, CA: Pine Forge Press, 1993).

9 Watson, "China's Big Mac Attack," 124.

10 As cited in Schlosser, *Fast Food Nation*, 231.

11 Watson, "China's Big Mac Attack," 132.

12 Nicholas D. Kristof, "Big Macs to Go," *New York Times*, March 22, 1998, https://archive.nytimes.com/www.nytimes.com/books/98/03/22/reviews/980322.22kristot.html.

13 Suzanne Leclere-Madlala, "Big Mac Comes to South Africa," *Anthropology News* 37, no. 4 (1996): 5.

14 Watson, "China's Big Mac Attack," 127–8.

15 Watson, "China's Big Mac Attack," 127.

16 Schlosser, *Fast Food Nation*, 243.

17 Judit Bodnár, "Roquefort vs Big Mac: Globalization and Its Others," *European Journal of Sociology* 44, no. 1 (2003): 133.

18 Schlosser, *Fast Food Nation*, 246–9.

19 Marion Nestle, *Food Politics: How the Food Industry Influences Nutrition and Health* (Berkeley: University of California Press, 2002), 164.

20 Andrew F. Smith, *Eating History: 30 Turning Points in the Making of American Cuisine* (New York: Columbia University Press, 2011), 292.

21 Ronald Steel, "When Worlds Collide," *The New York Times*, July 21, 1996, sec. Opinion, https://www.nytimes.com/1996/07/21/opinion/when-worlds-collide.html.

22 Rob Walker, "When a Brand Becomes a Stand-In for a Nation," *The New York Times*, March 30, 2003, https://www.nytimes.com/2003/03/30/weekinreview/the-world-when-a-brand-becomes-a-stand-in-for-a-nation.html.

23 Jeffrey M. Jones, "Latest Poll Shows High Point in Opposition to Iraq War," *Gallup*, July 11, 2007, https://news.gallup.com/poll/28099/Latest-Poll-Shows-High-Point-Opposition-Iraq-War.aspx.

24 Brian Naylor, "Greenspan Admits Free Market Ideology Flawed," *NPR*, October 24, 2008, https://www.npr.org/templates/story/story.php?storyId=96070766.

25 Daniel Gross, "Who Won the Recession?," *Slate*, August 11, 2009, https://slate.com/business/2009/08/how-mcdonald-s-won-the-recession.html.

Chapter 15

1   "Barack Obama's Speech on Race," *The New York Times*, March 18, 2008, https://www.nytimes.com/2008/03/18/us/politics/18text-obama.html.

2   Andrew Romano, "Thanks to Twitter, America's First Viral Eatery," *Newsweek,* February 27, 2009, https://www.newsweek.com/thanks-twitter-americas-first-viral-eatery-82325.

3   John T. Edge, "The Tortilla Takes a Road Trip to Korea," *The New York Times*, July 27, 2010, https://www.nytimes.com/2010/07/28/dining/28united.html.

4   Jessica Gelt, "A Street Sensation Is Born," *Los Angeles Times*, February 11, 2009, https://www.latimes.com/archives/la-xpm-2009-feb-11-fo-kogi11-story.html.

5   Oliver S. Wang, "Learning from Los Kogi Angeles: A Taco Truck and Its City," in *Eating Asian America: A Food Studies Reader*, ed. Robert Ji-Song Ku, Martin F. Manalansan, and Anita Mannur (New York: NYU Press, 2013), 78–97.

6   Gelt, "A Street Sensation Is Born."

7   Robert Lemon, *The Taco Truck: How Mexican Street Food Is Transforming the American City* (Champaign: University of Illinois Press, 2019), 137.

8   Anthony Bourdain, "TIME 100: Roy Choi," *Time*, April 21, 2016, https://time.com/collection-post/4301775/roy-choi-2016-time-100/.

9   Jeffrey M. Pilcher, *Planet Taco: A Global History of Mexican Food* (New York: Oxford University Press, 2017), 222.

10   Lemon, *The Taco Truck*, 156.

11   Michael Pollan, "Farmer in Chief," *The New York Times*, October 9, 2008, https://www.nytimes.com/2008/10/12/magazine/12policy-t.html.

12   Michael Pollan, "Why Did the Obamas Fail to Take on Corporate Agriculture?," *The New York Times*, October 5, 2016, https://www.nytimes.com/interactive/2016/10/09/magazine/obama-administration-big-food-policy.html.

13   Kerry Close, "The 1% Pocketed 85% of Post-Recession Income Growth," *Money*, June 16, 2016, https://money.com/income-inequality-recession/.

14   Alexander Abad-Santos, "Instead of Raises, McDonald's Tells Workers to Sign Up for Food Stamps," *The Atlantic*, October 24, 2013, https://www.theatlantic.com/business/archive/2013/10/instead-living-wage-mcdonalds-tells-workers-sign-food-stamps/309625/.

15   Jill Lepore, *These Truths: A History of the United States* (New York: W. W. Norton & Company, 2018), 727.

16   Jacob Poushter, "Smartphone Ownership and Internet Usage Continues to Climb in Emerging Economies" (Pew Research Center, February 22, 2016), https://www.pewresearch.org/global/2016/02/22/smartphone-ownership-and-internet-usage-continues-to-climb-in-emerging-economies/.

17   Pollan, "Why Did the Obamas Fail to Take on Corporate Agriculture?"

18 "More Than 12M 'Me Too' Facebook Posts, Comments, Reactions in 24
    Hours," *CBS News*, October 17, 2017, https://www.cbsnews.com/news/
    metoo-more-than-12-million-facebook-posts-comments-reactions-24-hours/.

19 Hunter Walker, "Donald Trump Just Released an Epic Statement Raging
    against Mexican Immigrants and 'Disease,'" *Business Insider*, July 6,
    2015, https://www.businessinsider.com/donald-trumps-epic-statement-on-
    mexico-2015-7.

20 The Institute of Politics at the Harvard Kennedy School, *Campaign for
    President: The Managers Look at 2016* (Lanham: Rowman & Littlefield,
    2017), 29.

21 Lepore, *These Truths*, 779–80.

22 Sam Sanders, "#MemeOfTheWeek: Donald Trump's Taco Bowl," *NPR*, May 7,
    2016, https://www.npr.org/2016/05/07/477023446/-memeoftheweek-donald-
    trumps-taco-bowl.

23 Suzanne Gamboa, "Latino Business Group Starts 'Guac The Vote' Effort,"
    NBC News, September 6, 2016, https://www.nbcnews.com/news/latino/
    latino-business-group-starts-guac-vote-effort-n643551.

24 Lepore, *These Truths*, 770–1.

25 Jonathan Haidt and Tobias Rose-Stockwell, "The Dark Psychology of Social
    Networks," *The Atlantic*, November 12, 2019, https://www.theatlantic.com/
    magazine/archive/2019/12/social-media-democracy/600763/.

26 Glenn Kessler, Salvador Rizzo, and Meg Kelly, "Trump's False or Misleading
    Claims Total 30,573 over 4 Years," *Washington Post*, January 24, 2021,
    https://www.washingtonpost.com/politics/2021/01/24/trumps-false-or-
    misleading-claims-total-30573-over-four-years/.

27 Carolyn Crist, "U.S. COVID-19 Deaths in 2021 Surpass 2020 Total," *WebMD*,
    November 22, 2021, https://www.webmd.com/lung/news/20211122/us-
    covid-deaths-2021-surpass-2020-total; "The True Death Toll of COVID-19,"
    World Health Organization, accessed January 20, 2022, https://www.who.
    int/data/stories/the-true-death-toll-of-covid-19-estimating-global-excess-
    mortality.

Epilogue

1 Sigal Samuel, "How to Help People during the Pandemic, One Google
   Spreadsheet at a Time," *Vox*, March 24, 2020, https://www.vox.com/future-
   perfect/2020/3/24/21188779/mutual-aid-coronavirus-covid-19-volunteering;
   Saria Lofton et al., "Mutual Aid Organisations and Their Role in Reducing
   Food Insecurity in Chicago's Urban Communities during COVID-19,"
   Public Health Nutrition 25, no. 1 (n.d.): 119–22, https://doi.org/10.1017/
   S1368980021003736.

2 Claudia Kolker, "How a Houston Restaurant Became the Source for Afghan
   Refugees' First Meals in America," *Texas Monthly*, January 13, 2022, https://
   www.texasmonthly.com/food/houston-afghan-village-refugee-meals/; Ivey

DeJesus, "Afghan Refugees Struggle with American Foods; New Donation Drive Looks for Basmati Rice, Lentils, Beans," *PennLive*, October 19, 2021, https://www.pennlive.com/news/2021/10/afghan-refugees-struggle-with-american-foods-new-donation-drive-looks-for-basmati-rice-lentils-beans.html; Brett Anderson, "They Fled Afghanistan for America. Now They Feed the Newest Arrivals." *The New York Times*, April 18, 2022, https://www.nytimes.com/2022/04/18/dining/afghan-restaurants-refugees-taliban.html.

3   Joe Hernandez, "Chef José Andrés and His Team Are Feeding Ukrainians on the Front Lines of the War," *NPR*, March 13, 2022, sec. Food, https://www.npr.org/2022/03/12/1086309022/ukraine-jose-andres-interview-world-central-kitchen.

4   Food justice activists and scholars have introduced the term "food apartheid," which more accurately reflects the *intentional* creation of spaces of food inequality than the older term "food desert," which suggests that this is a naturally occurring phenomenon. Jeremy Stahl, "What We Get Wrong about Food Insecurity in Buffalo's East Side," *Slate*, May 19, 2022, https://slate.com/news-and-politics/2022/05/how-to-help-feed-buffalo-east-side-tops-shooting.html.

5   Many food advocates have grown skeptical about these plant-based meats, but strong arguments can be made for their value as one plank alongside broader food system reform. See, for example, Jan Dutkiewicz and Garrett Broad, "Op-Ed: Getting Real about Fake Meat," *Food Tank* (blog), May 20, 2022, https://foodtank.com/news/2022/05/opinion-editorial-getting-real-about-fake-meat/.

Discussion Questions

Chapter 1

1 What does the chapter title's reference to the "not-so-new world" indicate? Why does this kind of terminology matter in discussions of European colonization of the Americas?

2 What is pemmican, and what does it teach us about the broad themes of foodways among American peoples before colonization?

3 Based on this chapter's narrative, develop a simple timeline to characterize the major changes in climate, migration, food acquisition practices, colonization, and bison distribution.

4 What are the major regional groups that scholars divide Native American peoples into and what are they based on? What are the benefits and limitations of these categorizations?

Chapter 2

1 What was it about corn that made it so important in the early Americas? Describe at least three key features, drawing from different parts of the chapter.

2 What was the "Columbian Exchange" and what role did corn play in it? What effects did it have on different parts of the globe and human populations?

3 How was corn an important crop in British-Native American relations and power dynamics in both the Virginia and New England colonies? Compare and contrast the two locations.

4 Describe the relationship between corn and enslavement in the North American colonies. Was corn a new crop for enslaved Africans? What role did it play in their diets once in the colonies?

Chapter 3

1 Why was alcohol, and especially rum, so important in the colonies and early America? Describe at least three reasons.

2 Explain the role of whiskey in American independence from Britain. What did it represent, both before and after the American Revolution?

3 What are the two sides of the debate as described in the Tully letters? What do they each want and what do these desires represent?

4 Do you think the "whiskey rebellion" is the appropriate term for what was going on in the new nation at the end of the eighteenth century? Why or why not? What do other scholars say about this?

Chapter 4

1 Why was Sylvester Graham nostalgic about an earlier era and an earlier way of making bread, looking back "30 or 40 years" from 1837? What dimensions of this past period did he celebrate, and why?

2 What was the "Jacksonian era" and how was Graham bread a product of this time?

3 How did Graham's teachings spread? What does this tell us about how people encountered new ideas in the 1830s and 1840s?

4 Why is it significant that Graham got his start in the temperance movement? How were the different reform movements of this period intertwined?

Chapter 5

1 What is potlikker, and what does it teach us about the broad themes of foodways among enslaved peoples in the antebellum period?

2 Describe three ways that enslaved peoples used food, or the refusal of food, to try to reclaim power.

3 What does potlikker's status as a "waste product" tell us about relationships between enslavers and their enslaved workers, and about the relationship of enslaved people to the physical environment?

4 How did enslaved people shape Southern food, and American food more broadly? What evidence do we have of this?

Chapter 6

1 How did the social status of the peanut shift from the Civil War era to around 1918? What associations did the legume have before and after?

2 What role did food abundance and scarcity play in the Civil War? Describe the circumstances in both the North and South.

3 Why do scholars refer to Reconstruction as an "unfinished revolution"? Describe three attempts at or ideas for progress that were not fully realized, and the reasons why.

4 How does the story of the peanut fit into the "Lost Cause" narrative? What is one example of how the Black labor that helped the peanut become popular was made invisible?

Chapter 7

1 How was Jell-O like the Gilded Age in which it originated? What did they each conceal and reveal?

2 What was the transcontinental railroad and why was it important? What role did it play in the rise of meatpacking?

3 What was the domestic science movement, and how was it tied into issues of gender, Progressivism, and the growing food industry?

4 How was Jell-O a pioneer in advertising? What was it about this product that made it especially primed for persuasive advertising pitches?

Chapter 8

1 What did the Progressive dietary reformers want to do and why did they make little headway with Italian immigrants in particular?

2 Who ate at Italian restaurants over the early twentieth century, and what was the appeal for different groups at different times?

3 What role did food play in the US government's response to the First World War?

4 Why do you think the years of the First World War and after were such a time of repression? Describe three ways that this repressiveness took shape.

Chapter 9

1   In your own words, what does John Steinbeck's title "grapes of wrath" mean, in the historical context of Depression-era California?

2   Describe how immigration was critical to the California orange industry, and how different attitudes and policies shaped the racial make-up of agricultural labor in the late nineteenth and early twentieth centuries.

3   What are the underlying reasons that people moved from the Plains to the American West in search of farm work in the 1930s?

4   Describe three different groups who pushed back against the oppressive agricultural system in the 1930s. Were their efforts successful?

Chapter 10

1   Why is unwanted email called "spam" today? What does the Second World War context teach us about this origin story?

2   How were hunger and power over food wielded as a weapon during the Second World War?

3   How did scientific standardization for military purposes shape the production of industrialized food, both during and after the war? What long-term effects did this have?

4   How did government efforts link food and consumption to patriotism? How did this play out in the mandatory rationing?

Chapter 11

1   Describe three on-the-ground conflicts that were part of the Cold War in which food and agriculture played a significant role.

2   How did green bean casserole push against American fears of communism? What did it represent in this ideological battle?

3   What was the "Kitchen Debate" and what role did processed foods and kitchen technologies play in it? Why was it significant in its historical context?

4 What was the location and context in which Dorcas Reilly invented green bean casserole? What does this teach us about the power and methods of the food industry by the 1950s?

Chapter 12

1 Describe three examples of how food and food issues were at the heart of the civil rights movement in the 1960s.

2 Describe three examples of how food and food issues were at the heart of *other* rights movements (besides civil rights) in the 1960s and 1970s.

3 Although tofu itself wasn't central to the civil rights movement, how did that movement's politicization of food pave the way for tofu's rise?

4 Why did soybeans and tofu come to be so important to the counterculture and back-to-the-land movement? What issues did they represent or address?

Chapter 13

1 What was "chicken fatigue," why was it a problem for the industry, and how did the industry respond? To what effect? Describe both the "value-added" and "further-processed" phases.

2 What did USDA Director Earl Butz do with the 1973 Farm Bill? What were the far-reaching consequences of this move?

3 How did chicken nuggets express "the values of Reagan-era America"? Be sure to put this in your own words and draw from sections beyond the introduction.

4 Describe the state of American nutrition and nutrition science in the 1970s and 1980s. How did chicken nuggets fit into this context?

Chapter 14

1 What was the context that allowed journalist Nicholas Kristof's son to consider McDonald's a "Japanese food," alongside rice balls? How did this come to be, and what does this say about American fast food's global reach?

2 What was the 1999 "Battle in Seattle" and why was French McDonald's-protester José Bové there? What did the WTO protests and the anti-McDonald's protests have in common?

3 Why did McDonald's shift away from Styrofoam hamburger containers in the 1990s? Was this a significant environmental solution, relative to the company's broader environmental impact? Why or why not?

4 Describe two different critiques of McDonald's in the early 2000s. What did each represent?

Chapter 15

1 How were Korean tacos an embodiment of the Obama era? What did the food and the president's public image and/or campaign have in common?

2 Compare and contrast the new gourmet food trucks that Kogi laid the groundwork for with the traditional *loncheras*.

3 What were the main food system problems that Michael Pollan laid out in his 2008 letter to the future president? How did Obama deal with these problems once in office and what held back solutions?

4 Describe the role of social media throughout the early twenty-first century in both promoting and harming democracy. Give at least one example of its benefits and its drawbacks in this regard.

Selected Bibliography

The following is a selection of sources that I found especially helpful in writing this book, and to which you might turn for further reading. Many other sources not included here, both primary and secondary, informed the research and writing process.

Alkon, Alison Hope, and Julian Agyeman, eds. *Cultivating Food Justice: Race, Class, and Sustainability*. Cambridge: MIT Press, 2011.

Anderson, James D. *Education of Blacks in the South, 1860–1935*. Chapel Hill: University of North Carolina Press, 1988.

Apple, Rima D. *Vitamania: Vitamins in American Culture*. New Brunswick, NJ: Rutgers University Press, 1996.

Arellano, Gustavo. *Taco USA: How Mexican Food Conquered America*. New York: Simon and Schuster, 2012.

Backer, Kellen. "Constructing Borderless Foods: The Quartermaster Corps and World War II Army Subsistence." In *Food across Borders*, edited by Matt Garcia, E. Melanie DuPuis, and Don Mitchell, 121–39. New Brunswick: Rutgers University Press, 2017.

Backer, Kellen. "When Meals Became Weapons." In *Nature at War: American Environments and World War II*, edited by Thomas Robertson, Richard P. Tucker, Nicholas B. Breyfogle, and Peter Mansoor, 176–96. Cambridge: Cambridge University Press, 2020.

Beckert, Sven. *Empire of Cotton: A Global History*. New York: Alfred A. Knopf, 2014.

Belasco, Warren J. *Appetite for Change: How the Counterculture Took on the Food Industry*. New York: Pantheon Books, 1989.

Belasco, Warren. *Food: The Key Concepts*. Oxford: Berg, 2008.

Bentley, Amy. *Eating for Victory: Food Rationing and the Politics of Domesticity*. Urbana: University of Illinois Press, 1998.

Berlin, Ira. *Many Thousands Gone: The First Two Centuries of Slavery in North America*. Cambridge: Harvard University Press, 1998.

Berzok, Linda Murray. *American Indian Food*. 1st edition. Westport, CT: Greenwood, 2005.

Biltekoff, Charlotte. *Eating Fight in America: The Cultural Politics of Food and Health*. Durham: Duke University Press, 2013.

Bittman, Mark. *Animal, Vegetable, Junk: A History of Food, from Sustainable to Suicidal*. Boston: Harvest, 2021.

Bobrow-Strain, Aaron. *White Bread: A Social History of the Store-Bought Loaf*. Boston: Beacon Press, 2012.

Bouton, Terry. *Taming Democracy: "The People," the Founders, and the Troubled Ending of the American Revolution*. New York: Oxford University Press, 2009.

Bowen, Sarah, Joslyn Brenton, and Sinikka Elliott. *Pressure Cooker: Why Home Cooking Won't Solve Our Problems and What We Can Do about It*. New York: Oxford University Press, 2019.

Bower, Anne L., ed. *African American Foodways Explorations of History and Culture*. Champaign: University of Illinois Press, 2009.

Bria, Rosemarie Dorothy. "*How Jell-O Molds Society and How Society Molds Jell-O: A Case Study of an American Food Industry Creation*." Dissertation. Columbia University, 1991.

Calloway, Colin G. *One Vast Winter Count: The Native American West before Lewis and Clark*. Lincoln: University of Nebraska Press, 2003.

Carroll, Abigail. *Three Squares: The Invention of the American Meal*. New York: Basic Books, 2013.

Carson, Rachel. *Silent Spring*. 40th Anniversary edition. New York: Houghton Mifflin Harcourt, 2002.

Case, Andrew N. *The Organic Profit: Rodale and the Making of Marketplace Environmentalism*. Seattle: University of Washington Press, 2018.

Choi, Roy, Tien Nguyen, and Natasha Phan. *L.A. Son: My Life, My City, My Food*. New York, NY: Anthony Bourdain/Ecco, 2013.

Cinotto, Simone. *The Italian American Table: Food, Family, and Community in New York City*. Urbana: University of Illinois Press, 2013.

Civitello, Linda. *Cuisine and Culture: A History of Food and People*. 3rd edition. Hoboken, NJ: Wiley, 2011.

Cohen, Benjamin R. *Pure Adulteration: Cheating on Nature in the Age of Manufactured Food*. Chicago, IL: University of Chicago Press, 2022.

Cohen, Lizabeth. *A Consumer's Republic: The Politics of Mass Consumption in Postwar America*. New York: Vintage Books, 2004.

Collingham, E. M. *The Taste of War: World War II and the Battle for Food*. New York: Penguin Books, 2013.

Colpitts, George. *Pemmican Empire: Food, Trade, and the Last Bison Hunts in the North American Plains, 1780–1882*. Cambridge; New York: Cambridge University Press, 2014.

Counihan, Carole, ed. *Food in the USA: A Reader*. New York: Routledge, 2002.

Covey, Herbert C., and Dwight Eisnach. *What the Slaves Ate: Recollections of African American Foods and Foodways from the Slave Narratives*. Santa Barbara, CA: Greenwood Press/ABC-CLIO, 2009.

Cowie, Jefferson. *Stayin' Alive: The 1970s and the Last Days of the Working Class*. New York: The New Press, 2010.

Cronon, William. *Changes in the Land: Indians, Colonists, and the Ecology of New England*. New York: Hill and Wang, 1983.

Cronon, William. *Nature's Metropolis: Chicago and the Great West*. New York: W. W. Norton, 1991.

Crosby, Alfred W. *The Columbian Exchange: Biological and Cultural Consequences of 1492*. Westport, CT: Greenwood Pub. Co., 1972.

Curtis, Kimberly, et al. *The Immigrant-Food Nexus: Borders, Labor, and Identity in North America*. Cambridge: MIT Press, 2020.

Davis, Edward H., and John T. Morgan. *Collards: A Southern Tradition from Seed to Table*. Tuscaloosa: University Alabama Press, 2015.

Deetz, Kelley Fanto. *Bound to the Fire: How Virginia's Enslaved Cooks Helped Invent American Cuisine*. Lexington: University Press of Kentucky, 2017.

Deutsch, Tracey. *Building a Housewife's Paradise: Gender, Politics, and American Grocery Stores in the Twentieth Century*. Chapel Hill, NC: University of North Carolina Press, 2010.

Diamond, Jared. "The Worst Mistake in the History of the Human Race." *Discover Magazine*, May 1, 1999. https://www.discovermagazine.com/planet-earth/the-worst-mistake-in-the-history-of-the-human-race.

Diner, Hasia R. *Hungering for America: Italian, Irish, and Jewish Foodways in the Age of Migration*. Cambridge: Harvard University Press, 2001.

Douglass, Frederick. *Narrative of the Life of Frederick Douglass: An American Slave*. Boston: The Anti-Slavery Office, 1845.

Dreilinger, Danielle. *The Secret History of Home Economics: How Trailblazing Women Harnessed the Power of Home and Changed the Way We Live*. New York: W.W. Norton, 2021.

Edge, John T. "The Tortilla Takes a Road Trip to Korea." *The New York Times*, July 27, 2010. https://www.nytimes.com/2010/07/28/dining/28united.html.

Egerton, John. *Southern Food: At Home, on the Road, in History*. New York: Knopf, 1987.

Ferris, Marcie Cohen. *The Edible South: The Power of Food and the Making of an American Region*. Chapel Hill: The University of North Carolina Press, 2014.

Foner, Eric. *Give Me Liberty!: An American History*. Seagull 6th edition. New York: W. W. Norton & Company, 2020.

Freedman, Paul. *Why Food Matters*. New Haven: Yale University Press, 2021.

Gabaccia, Donna R. *We Are What We Eat: Ethnic Food and the Making of Americans*. Cambridge: Harvard University Press, 1998.

Gálvez, Alyshia. *Eating NAFTA: Trade, Food Policies, and the Destruction of Mexico*. Oakland: University of California Press, 2018.

Gelt, Jessica. "A Street Sensation Is Born." *Los Angeles Times*, February 11, 2009. https://www.latimes.com/archives/la-xpm-2009-feb-11-fo-kogi11-story.html.

Giesen, James C., and Bryant Simon, eds. *Food and Eating in America: A Documentary Reader*. Malden, MA: Wiley-Blackwell, 2018.

Glave, Dianne D., and Mark Stoll, eds. *To Love the Wind and the Rain: African Americans and Environmental History*. Pittsburgh, PA: University of Pittsburgh Press, 2005.

Gordon-Reed, Annette. *The Hemingses of Monticello: An American Family*. New York: W. W. Norton & Company, 2008.

Grandjean, Katherine A. "New World Tempests: Environment, Scarcity, and the Coming of the Pequot War." *The William and Mary Quarterly* 68, no. 1 (2011): 75–100.

Gregory, James N. *American Exodus: The Dust Bowl Migration and Okie Culture in California*. New York, NY: Oxford University Press, 1989.

Guptill, Amy E, et al. *Food & Society: Principles and Paradoxes,* 2nd edition. Cambridge, MA: Polity Press, 2017.

Hall, Robert L. "Food Crops and the Slave Trade." In *African American Foodways: Explorations of History and Culture*, edited by Anne L. Bower, 17–44. Champaign: University of Illinois Press, 2009.

Hamilton, Shane. *Supermarket USA: Food and Power in the Cold War Farms Race*. New Haven, CT: Yale University Press, 2018.

Hamilton, Shane, and Sarah T. Phillips. *The Kitchen Debate and Cold War Consumer Politics: A Brief History with Documents*. Boston: Bedford/St. Martin's, 2014.

Harris, Jessica B. *High on the Hog: A Culinary Journey from Africa to America*. New York: Bloomsbury USA, 2012.

Hersey, Mark D. *My Work Is That of Conservation: An Environmental Biography of George Washington Carver*. Athens: University of Georgia Press, 2011.

Hilliard, Sam Bowers. *Hog Meat and Hoecake; Food Supply in the Old South, 1840–1860*. Carbondale: Southern Illinois University Press, 1972.

Hisano, Ai. *Visualizing Taste: How Business Changed the Look of What You Eat*. Cambridge: Harvard University Press, 2019.

Hoenig, John. *Garden Variety: The American Tomato from Corporate to Heirloom*. New York: Columbia University Press, 2017.

Hogeland, William. "Whiskey, Rebellion, and the Religious Left." *Tikkun* 22, no. 4 (July 1, 2007): 48–51.

Holmes, Seth. *Fresh Fruit, Broken Bodies: Migrant Farmworkers in the United States*. Berkeley: University of California Press, 2013.

Horowitz, Roger. *Putting Meat on the American Table: Taste, Technology, Transformation*. Baltimore: Johns Hopkins University Press, 2006.

Hurtado, Albert, and Peter Iverson, eds. *Major Problems in American Indian History: Documents and Essays*. 2nd edition. Boston: Cengage Learning, 2000.

Isenberg, Andrew C. *The Destruction of the Bison: An Environmental History, 1750–1920*. Cambridge: Cambridge University Press, 2000.

Jacobson, Matthew Frye. *Whiteness of a Different Color: European Immigrants and the Alchemy of Race*. Cambridge: Harvard University Press, 1999.

Katznelson, Ira. *Fear Itself: The New Deal and the Origins of Our Time*. New York, NY: W. W. Norton & Company, 2013.

Kauffman, Jonathan. *Hippie Food: How Back-to-the-Landers, Longhairs, and Revolutionaries Changed the Way We Eat*. New York, NY: HarperCollins, 2018.

Kennedy, David M. *Freedom from Fear: The American People in Depression and War, 1929–1945*. New York: Oxford University Press, 2004.

Kleinfield, N. R. "America Goes Chicken Crazy." *The New York Times*, December 9, 1984. https://www.nytimes.com/1984/12/09/business/america-goes-chicken-crazy.html.

Lemon, Robert. *The Taco Truck: How Mexican Street Food Is Transforming the American City*. Champaign: University of Illinois Press, 2019.

Lender, Mark Edward, and James Kirby Martin. *Drinking in America: A History*. New York: Free Press, 1987.

Lepore, Jill. *These Truths: A History of the United States*. New York: W. W. Norton & Company, 2018.

Levenstein, Harvey A. *Paradox of Plenty: A Social History of Eating in Modern America*. New York; Oxford: Oxford University Press, 1993.

Levenstein, Harvey A. *Revolution at the Table: The Transformation of the American Diet*. New York: Oxford University Press, 1988.

Lewis, George H. "From Minnesota Fat to Seoul Food: Spam in America and the Pacific Rim." *Journal of Popular Culture* 34, no. 2 (2000): 83–105.

Locke, Joseph L., and Ben Wright, eds. *The American Yawp: A Massively Collaborative Open U.S. History Textbook*, Vol. 2: Since 1877. Stanford: Stanford University Press, 2019. www.americanyawp.org.

Long, Lucy. "Green Bean Casserole and Midwestern Identity: A Regional Foodways Aesthetic and Ethos." *Midwestern Folklore* 33, no. 1 (2007): 29–44.

Ludington, Charles C. and Matthew Morse Booker. *Food Fights: How History Matters to Contemporary Food Debates*. Chapel Hill: University of North Carolina Press, 2019.

Mann, Charles C. *1491: New Revelations of the Americas before Columbus*. 1st edition. New York: Vintage, 2006.

Marx de Salcedo, Anastacia. *Combat-Ready Kitchen: How the U.S. Military Shapes the Way You Eat*. New York: Penguin, 2015.

McDaniel, Rick. *Irresistible History of Southern Food: Four Centuries of Black-Eyed Peas, Collard Greens & Whole Hog Barbecue*. Charleston, SC: The History Press, 2011.

McGrath, Maria. *Food for Dissent: Natural Foods and the Consumer Counterculture since the 1960s*. Amherst: University of Massachusetts Press, 2019.

McKenna, Maryn. *Big Chicken: The Incredible Story of How Antibiotics Created Modern Agriculture and Changed the Way the World Eats*. Washington, DC: National Geographic Books, 2017.

McMillan, Tracie. *The American Way of Eating: Undercover at Walmart, Applebee's, Farm Fields and the Dinner Table*. New York: Scribner, 2012.

McWilliams, James E. *A Revolution in Eating: How the Quest for Food Shaped America*. New York: Columbia University Press, 2005.

Mintz, Sidney. *Sweetness and Power: The Place of Sugar in Modern History*. New York: Penguin Books, 1986.

Montoya, Maria, et al. *Global Americans: A History of the United States*. 1st edition. Boston, MA: Cengage Learning, 2017.

Nestle, Marion. *Food Politics: How the Food Industry Influences Nutrition and Health*. Berkeley: University of California Press, 2002.

Nestle, Marion. "Writing the Food Studies Movement." *Food, Culture, and Society* 13, no. 2 (2010): 159–79.

Nissenbaum, Stephen. *Sex, Diet, and Debility in Jacksonian America: Sylvester Graham and Health Reform*. Westport, CT: Greenwood Press, 1980.

Opie, Frederick. *Hog and Hominy: Soul Food from Africa to America*. New York: Columbia University Press, 2010.

Opie, Frederick. *Southern Food and Civil Rights: Feeding the Revolution*. Charleston, SC: The History Press, 2017.

Ozersky, Josh. *The Hamburger: A History*. New Haven: Yale University Press, 2008.

Petrick, Gabriella M. "*The Arbiters of Taste: Producers, Consumers and the Industrialization of Taste in America, 1900–1960.*" Dissertation, University of Delaware, 2007.

Phippen, J. Weston. "'Kill Every Buffalo You Can! Every Buffalo Dead Is an Indian Gone.'" *The Atlantic*, May 13, 2016.

Pilcher, Jeffrey M. *Food in World History*. London: Routledge, 2005.

Pilcher, Jeffrey M. *Planet Taco: A Global History of Mexican Food*. New York: Oxford University Press, 2017.

Pollan, Michael. *In Defense of Food: An Eater's Manifesto*. New York: Penguin Press, 2008.

Pollan, Michael. "Farmer in Chief." *The New York Times*, October 9, 2008. https://www.nytimes.com/2008/10/12/magazine/12policy-t.html.

Pollan, Michael. *The Omnivore's Dilemma: A Natural History of Four Meals*. New York: Penguin, 2007.

Potorti, Mary. "'Feeding the Revolution': The Black Panther Party, Hunger, and Community Survival." *Journal of African American Studies* 21, no. 1 (2017): 85–110.

Reese, Ashanté M. *Black Food Geographies: Race, Self-reliance, and Food Access in Washington*. Chapel Hill: University of North Carolina Press, 2019.

Ritzer, George. *The McDonaldization of Society: An Investigation into the Changing Character of Contemporary Social Life*. Newbury Park, Calif: Pine Forge Press, 1993.

Romano, Andrew. "Thanks to Twitter, America's First Viral Eatery." *Newsweek*, February 27, 2009. https://www.newsweek.com/thanks-twitter-americas-first-viral-eatery-82325.

Roth, Matthew. *Magic Bean: The Rise of Soy in America*. Lawrence, KS: University Press of Kansas, 2018.

Rozin, Paul. "Food Is Fundamental, Fun, Frightening, and Far-Reaching." *Social Research* 66, no. 1 (1999): 9–30.

Sackman, Douglas Cazaux. *Orange Empire: California and the Fruits of Eden*. Berkeley: University of California Press, 2005.

Schlosser, Eric. *Fast Food Nation: The Dark Side of the All-American Meal*. Boston: Houghton Mifflin, 2001.

Schwartz, Marvin. *Tyson: From Farm to Market*. Fayetteville: University of Arkansas Press, 1991.

Shapiro, Laura. *Perfection Salad: Women and Cooking at the Turn of the Century*. New York: Holt, 1987.

Shapiro, Laura. *Something from the Oven: Reinventing Dinner in 1950s America*. New York: Viking, 2004.

Shiva, Vandana. *Who Really Feeds the World?: The Failures of Agribusiness and the Promise of Agroecology*. Berkeley: North Atlantic Books, 2016.

Shprintzen, Adam D. *The Vegetarian Crusade: The Rise of an American Reform Movement, 1817–1921*. Chapel Hill, NC: University of North Carolina Press, 2015.

Shurtleff, William, and Akiko Aoyagi. *The Book of Tofu: Food for Mankind*. Autumn Press, 1975.

Simon, Bryant. *The Hamlet Fire: A Tragic Story of Cheap Food, Cheap Government, and Cheap Lives*. Chapel Hill: University of North Carolina Press, 2017.

Sinclair, Upton. *The Jungle*. New York: Doubleday, Page & Company, 1906.

Smith, Andrew F. *Drinking History: Fifteen Turning Points in the Making of American Beverages*. New York, NY: New York University, 2012.

Smith, Andrew F. *Eating History: Thirty Turning Points in the Making of American Cuisine*. New York, NY: Columbia University Press, 2009.

Smith, Andrew, ed. *The Oxford Encyclopedia of Food and Drink in America: 3-Volume Set*. 2nd edition. New York, NY: Oxford University Press, 2012.

Smith, Andrew F. *Peanuts: The Illustrious History of the Goober Pea*. Urbana: University of Illinois Press, 2002.

Smith, Andrew F. *Starving the South: How the North Won the Civil War*. New York: St. Martin's Press, 2011.

Specht, Joshua. *Red Meat Republic: A Hoof-to-Table History of How Beef Changed America*. Princeton, NJ: Princeton University Press, 2019.

Steinbeck, John. *The Grapes of Wrath*. New York, NY: Penguin Books, 1976.

Steinberg, Theodore. *Down to Earth: Nature's Role in American History*. New York: Oxford University Press, 2002.

Stoll, Steven. *Ramp Hollow: The Ordeal of Appalachia*. New York: Hill and Wang, 2017.

Strasser, Susan. *Satisfaction Guaranteed: The Making of the American Mass Market*. Washington, DC: Smithsonian Institution Press, 1995.

Striffler, Steve. *Chicken: The Dangerous Transformation of America's Favorite Food*. New Haven: Yale University Press, 2005.

Taylor, Alan. *American Colonies: The Settling of North America*. New York: Viking Press, 2001.

Terkel, Studs. *Hard Times: An Oral History of the Great Depression*. New York: Pantheon Books, 1970.

Tompkins, Kyla Wazana. "Sylvester Graham's Imperial Dietetics." *Gastronomica* 9, no. 1 (2009): 50–60.

Turner, Katherine Leonard. *How the Other Half Ate: A History of Working-Class Meals at the Turn of the Century*. Oakland: University of California Press, 2014.

Twitty, Michael W. *The Cooking Gene: A Journey through African American Culinary History in the Old South*. New York: Amistad, 2017.

Veit, Helen Zoe. "Eating Cotton: Cottonseed, Crisco, and Consumer Ignorance." *The Journal of the Gilded Age and Progressive Era* 18, no. 4 (2019): 397–421.

Veit, Helen Zoe. *Modern Food, Moral Food: Self-Control, Science, and the Rise of Modern American Eating in the Early Twentieth Century*. Chapel Hill: University of North Carolina Press, 2015.

Vileisis, Ann. *Kitchen Literacy: How We Lost Knowledge of Where Food Comes from and Why We Need to Get It Back*. Washington, DC: Island Press, 2010.

Volo, Dorothy Denneen, and James M. Volo. *Daily Life in Civil War America*. Westport: Greenwood Press, 1998.

Wallach, Jennifer Jensen, and Lindsey R. Swindall, eds. *American Appetites: A Documentary Reader*. Fayetteville, AR: University of Arkansas Press, 2014.

Wallach, Jennifer Jensen, and Michael D. Wise, eds. *The Routledge History of American Foodways*. New York: Routledge, Taylor & Francis Group, 2016.

Watkins, T. H. *The Great Depression: America in the 1930s*. Boston, MA; London: Back Bay, 2010.

Watson, James L. "China's Big Mac Attack." *Foreign Affairs* 79, no. 3 (2000): 120–34.

White, Monica. *Freedom Farmers: Agricultural Resistance and the Black Freedom Movement*. Durham, NC: University of North Carolina Press, 2018.

Worster, Donald. *Dust Bowl: The Southern Plains in the 1930s*. New York: Oxford University Press, 1979.

Wyman, Carolyn. *Jell-O: A Biography*. San Diego: Harcourt, 2001.

Wyman, Carolyn. *Spam: A Biography*. San Diego, CA: Harvest Books, 1999.

Zeide, Anna. *Canned: The Rise and Fall of Consumer Confidence in the American Food Industry*. Oakland: University of California Press, 2018.

Zhen, Willa. *Food Studies: A Hands-On Guide*. London: Bloomsbury Academic, 2019.

Index